DEMOCRATIC PARTICIPATION IN TANZANIA

The Voices of Workers Representatives

Samuel E. Chambua

DAR ES SALAAM UNIVERSITY PRESS

Published in Tanzania by:
Dar es Salaam University Press Ltd
University of Dar es Salaam
P.O. Box 35182
Dar es Salaam - TANZANIA

ISBN 9976 - 60 - 363 - 0

Copy Editing and Book Design: Bernhard J. Sanyagi

CONTENTS

1

EMERGENCY AND GROUNDS FOR WORKERS' PARTICIPATION

2

DEVELOPMENT OF TRADE UNIONS IN TANZANIA

3

THE HISTORY OF WORKERS' PARTICIPATION IN TANZANIA

4

WORK PLACE CONDITIONS

5

TRADE UNIONS AND PARTICIPATION OF WOMEN IN DECISION-MAKING BODIES

6

7

8

LIST OF TABLES

LIST OF BOXES

ABBREVIATIONS

ACEA	African Commercial Employees Association
APADEP	African Workers Participation Development Programme
ASP	Afro-Shiraz Party
CCM	Chama cha Mapinduzi
CHODAWU	Conservation, Hotels, Domestic and Allied Workers Union
COTWU	Communication and Transport Workers Union
DHS	Demographic and Health Survey
ERP	Economic Recovery Programme
ESAPs	Economic and Social Adjustment Programmes
FES	Friedrich Ebert Stifng
FICAWU	Fishing Crew and Allied Workers Union
FNV	Dutch Federation of Trade Unions
FRELIMO	Mozambique Liberation Front
FRTU	Federation of Revolutionary Trade Unions
HBS	Household Budget Survey
HIPIC	Highly Indebted Poor Countries
ICFTU	International Confederation of Free Trade Unions
ICPE	International Centre for Public Enterprises in Developing Countries
IDS	Institute of Development Studies
IGWUTA	Industrial and General Workers Union of Tanzania
ILO	International Labour Organisation
IMF	International Monetary Fund
JUWATA	Jumuiya ya Wafanyakazi wa Tanzania
LGPF	Local Government Provident Fund
MCM	Morogoro Canvas Mill
MWEMA	Mradi wa Wanawake Mashambani
NDC	National Development Corporation
NESP	National Economic and Survival Programme
NPES	National Poverty Eradication Strategy
NPF	National Provident Fund
NUTA	National Union of Tanganyika Workers
OATUU	Organization of African Trade Union Unity
OTTU	Organisation of Tanzania Trade Unions
PLT	Permanent Labour Tribunal
PPF	Parastatal Provident Fund
PRSP	Poverty Reduction Strategy Paper
PSRP	Parastatal Sector Reform Programme
RAAWU	Researchers, Academicians and Allied Workers Union

SAPs	Structural Adjacent Programmes
SCOPO	Standing Committee on Parastatal Organisations
SIDA	Sweden International Development Agency
SSA	Sub-Saharan Africa
TALGWU	Tanzania Local Government Workers Union
TAMICO	Tanzania Mines and Construction Workers Union
TANU	Tanganyika African National Union
TASIWU	Tanzania Social Industry Workers Union
TASU	Tanzania Seamen Union
TFL	Tanganyika Federation of Labour
TFTU	Tanzania Federation of Free Trade Unions
TLAI	Tanzania Leather Associated Industries
TPAWU	Tanzania Plantation and Agricultural Workers Union
TRAWU	Tanzania Railways Workers Union
TTU	Tanzania Teachers Union
TU	Trade Union
TUC	Trade Union Congress
TUCTA	Trade Union Congress of Tanzania
TUGHE	Tanzania Union of Government and Health Employees
TUICO	Tanzania Union of Industries and Commercial Workers
TUJ	Tanzania Union of Journalists
URT	United Republic of Tanzania
USHIRIKA	Co-operative Union of Tanzania
UWT	Union of Women in Tanzania
VIJANA	National Youth Association
WAZAZI	Tanzania Parents Association
WCEC	Workers' Council Executive Committee
ZPFL	Zanzibar and Pemba Federation of Labour

ACKNOWLEDGEMENTS

On behalf of IDS, I would like to extend my sincere gratitude to the Dutch Federation of Trade Unions (FNV) and the Dutch Ministry of Development Cooperation (DGIS) for funding the APADEP (education and research) activities in Tanzania. This funding enabled IDS to collect most of the information and data contained in this book. I wish also to extend my sincere gratitude to the Institute of Social Studies (ISS) for providing the initial technical support needed for the execution of APADEP in Tanzania.

Apart from institutions, special thanks go to individual persons within and outside the mentioned institutions who gave a helping hand at every stage of the programme. Here I would like to specifically mention Mr. P. Coret (FNV) and Dr. G. Kester (ISS) for both their dedication, moral and material support; and Ms. R. de Vries for her effort to transfer her computer/data analytical skills to the IDS research team.

I would also like to extend my sincere gratitude to all the members of the IDS APADEP Research Team (persons I did research with and whose input this book is based on): Dr. Godwin Naimani, Mr. J. Kiduwanga, Mr. H. Semkiwa, Ms. Joice Shaidi and Prof. Ibrahim Shao.

Last but not least, special thanks should go to the OTTU/TFTU APADEP education team mebers, especially Mr. H.S. Msolla and Ms. J. Kajula for their good cooperation in arranging for, and conducting, the APADEP workers' education seminars during which the questionare surveys were administered. They also took part in some of the research activities and provided valuable information about the trade union movement in Tanzania. Their contribution is highly appreciated. While all these friends and colleagues should share the credit for whatever value this work brings, I alone remain solely responsibile for any errors and ommissions that may have emerged on these printed pages.

PREFACE

This book is about democratic workers' participation in Tanzania. It is based on data and information gathered over a period of five years, between 1992 and 1997, through APADEP's education and research activities. The overall aim of the programme in Tanzania (and in Africa) was to strengthen the trade unions in their effort to respond to emerging structures of trade union and workers' participation. The unions were to acquire the necessary knowledge, experience and skills to achieve effective and meaningful participation. The major means for realising this aim was seen, and remains to be, education for trade union leaders, workers' education instructors and for enterprise level union and worker representatives. The education effort was directed towards grassroots representatives. Another specific aim of the programme was to develop research and other supporting activities relevant for the development of policy formulation, education and trade union action.

To this end, the main research objective was to investigate how the trade union movement in Tanzania, can achieve a more effective and meaningful representation of workers interests through democratic workers' participation. Three main methods were used in this inquiry: a questionnaire survey of trade union and workers' representatives, case studies and trend studies.

Questionnaire Surveys

The questionnaire survey was the main method of data collection and the surveys were linked with, and conducted during, the education seminars for worker and trade union representatives. This constituted a unique opportunity to obtain systematic information on the position and situation of these representatives: their problems, needs, and expectations through questionnaires. The seminars/ surveys were systematically spread over all parts of the country covering all regions of Tanzania Mainland, Zanzibar and Pemba Islands. The first questionnaire surveys were conducted in 1992 and from 1992 to 1996 1,116 workers and trade union representatives responded to the questionnaire as follows: 202 (1992), 221 (1993), 271 (1994), 249 (1995) and 173 (1996).

In the absence of a reliable and up to date sampling frame of all elected worker and trade union representatives in Tanzania, it was not possible to draw a pure random sample. However, the survey was close to a random sample in that it was systematically spread all over the country as mentioned above. Furthermore, in order to ensure a good number of female respondents, the participants in the seminars (who were at the same time the respondents to the questionnaire) were drawn in such a way that at least 25 percent of them were females. 99 percent of all the respondents were trade union members and 80 percent held trade union office. Other additional characteristics of the sample were as shown in Table 1.

Case Studies

Exploratory and descriptive case studies were conducted to supplement the data obtained through questionnaire surveys. They provided detailed information on the functioning of workers' participation, and the role of trade union in the development of participation.

Table 1: *Sample Characteristics of the Questionnaire Survey*

1. Number of respondents	Total	Male	Female
	1116	69%	31%
2. Age (Years)			
Below 30	11%		
30 to 39	50%		
40+	39%		
3. Level of Education			
Primary	37%		
Secondary	53%		
Higher Ed.	10%		
4. Job Type			
Manual	14%		
White Collar	70%		
Professional	16%		
5. Economic Sector			
Services	51%		
Industry	21%		
Others	28%		
6. Employer*			
Public	29%		
Parastatal	57%		
Private	13%		
7. Size of Workforce			
<25 persons	22%		
25 to 99	36%		
100+ persons	42%		

*Note: Some of the enterprises that by then were categorised as public (i.e. government owned) and some of the parastatals have now been privatised.

A total of 11 case studies on workers' participation were conducted, six at enterprise level and five at the national level. The case studies examined trade union and participation in relation to local, regional and national development and focused on the challenges of the representation of the interests of workers both unionised and non-unionised.

Trend Studies

Trend studies of the development of labour relations, trade unionism and workers' participation were also conducted in order to put the quantitative questionnaire and qualitative case study results in appropriate perspective: data were collected on the historic, economic, political, legal and socio-cultural context of the country. These studies commenced in December 1993 and continued up to the end of 2000.

Main Research Results

APADEP research in Tanzania shows that to some extent some of the officially stated objectives of workers' participation have been attained. Issues normally discussed in workers' councils include: production targets/plans; budget and investment plans; work problems (including enterprise and workers problems); incentives to employees and social welfare. In a nut shell, workers' participation has been meaningful but not very effective due to the following limitations: constrained mandate/powers of workers' council in that it had only advisory role and the representatives had no obligation to consult with their constituencies or report to them; although workers' councils were worker-dominated in terms of numbers they were dominated by management in terms of influence. There was/is lack of effective participation in the workers' council meetings by the elected worker representatives from departments or sections partly due to low level of education and understanding of participation; and workers' participation in Tanzania was/is not backed by law but by a Presidential directive which also further limits workers' participation to state/public enterprises/institutions .

New Wind of Change and Participation

In the mid 1980s, Tanzania like many African countries introduced economic reforms that shifted economic power away from the state, to the individual, to the private sector and to market forces. These were followed by political reforms that stressed on promoting democracy through multiparty politics. However, in all these economic and political reforms, participation is conspicuously absent. Indeed some people: individuals, government officials and employers, associate workers' participation and participation in general with the failed socialist or Marxist systems of Eastern Europe and of the Third World, including the Ujamaa policy of Tanzania. The implication of this is that there is no workers' participation in the advanced capitalist countries. Thus, chapter one of this book is devoted to a discussion on the emergency of workers' participation in capitalist countries, in socialist countries of Eastern Europe and in Africa. Arguments for workers' participation are also presented and we argue that democratic participation is not only necessary for the survival and promotion of democracy but it is also a necessary condition for sustainable development.

Organisation of the Book

This book is organised into eight chapters. Chapter One is on emergence and grounds for workers' participation. The chapter discusses different forms of participation, its emergence and development as well as the grounds for workers' participation. Although there are many people who closely associate workers' participation with socialism/communism (including one former Minister for labour in Tanzania, some leaders in government and employer associations), the concept and the initial experiences of workers' participation originated in the capitalist countries. Rather than erroneously associating participation with a particular political ideology, it is an ideology on its own right and if not manipulated by the powers that be, it could promote democracy and harmonious industrial relations.

Chapter Two describes the development of trade unions in Tanzania during and after the colonial era. The chapter describes how the unions were placed under the control of both the ruling political party and state soon after the attainment of political independence up to the early 1990s. The reasons behind such a control and the effects are also discussed. The process of forming trade unions that are free from direct political party/state control is also discussed including the new 1998 Trade Union Act, the trade union situation after this Act became operational on 1st July 2000 and the challenges ahead.

The history of workers' participation is discussed in chapter three. The focus is on both workers committees that existed even before the official adoption of workers' participation and works councils (in Tanzania referred to as workers' councils). The councils were introduced through a Presidential directive in 1970 that was only applicable to the public sector. The chapter also discusses the implementation of the directive generally and in one enterprise in particular, the Morogoro Canvas Mills. It is noted that workers' participation at this enterprise was meaningful but not effective.

An overview of the general socio-economic conditions that prevailed in Tanzania from the 1960s up to 1999 as well as the conditions that prevailed at workplaces during the 1990s are presented in Chapter Four (co-authored with Godwin Naimani). Other issues discussed in this chapter include adoption, implementation of the IMF/World Bank structural adjustment programmes (SAPs) and their effects especially on poverty reduction and employment; education and training offered or paid by employers, satisfaction with work conditions and with economic conditions. The effects of SAPs include growing unemployment, retrenchment of about 26,000 public employees, widening of income inequality and increasing levels of poverty to mention but a few. Partly because of this, there has been bitter discontent with both working and economic conditions. Wages and salaries have remained very low throughout the 1990s and workers have had to engage in other income supplementing/generating activities. In spite of this engagement, however, for the majority of the workers household income is not sufficient to meet basic needs expenses such as food and children's education. Thus, it is the workers and peasants who are paying dearly for the economic reforms.

The trade union structure in Tanzania and the conditions in which the unions operated in the 1990s is described in Chapter Five. Other issues discussed in this chapter include attitudes of trade union officials to SAP reforms, trade union activities and resources, workers education and training organised or paid by unions and participation of women in decision-making bodies.

Chapter Six is mainly preoccupied with workers' participation values and attitudes as well as workers' participation structures. Here, achievements, obstacles and support needed to workers' participation are discussed.

Information on developmental and workers problems were/are considered by respondents as priority issues; their suggestions on how to solve them and the desired trade union policy are thus discussed in Chapter Seven. The respondents were aware of the developmental problems facing their respective districts as well as of problems facing workers, and were eager to participate in finding solutions to those problems. Moreover, they had a lot of faith in participation and education in solving problems.

Finally, the main preoccupation in chapter eight is with how to make democratic participation in Tanzania more meaningful and effective to workers.

1

EMERGENCE AND RATIONALE FOR WORKERS' PARTICIPATION

INTRODUCTION

In the current approach to socio-economic and political development (neo-liberalism, privatisation, and structural adjacent programmes (SAPs) including the economic and social adjustment programmes - ESAPs), workers' participation is being closely associated with socialism/communism. As such it might appear ridiculous and unfashionable to discuss the issue of workers' participation at a time when almost all socialist/communist regimes or systems have collapsed. But the issue of workers' participation is even more justified to discuss now because of several reasons.

One, the initial ideas as well as experiences of workers' participation originated in capitalist (mainly European) countries, and not in socialist/communist ones. Two, the European Community's new Social Charter specifically raises the question of worker representation in all Boards of Directors of large enterprises Bayat, 1991: 1). Furthermore, the 1991 African Charter of Popular Participation in Development and Transformation explicitly regards participation as a basic human right. Thirdly, participation greatly suffered under socialist/communist regimes (due to empty slogans, rhetoric, bureaucracy, corruption and manipulation), so much so that with the collapse of socialist/communist regimes in these countries, participation had become a dirty word in political debate.

Fourth, Japan's impressive economic growth has invariably been attributed to its peculiar management style which combines workers' participation and paternalism (Bayat, 1991: 1). Actually, American attempts to close the gap with Japanese competition during the 1980s involved the introduction of workers' participation similar to that in many Japanese firms (Anstey, 1997: 29-33).

The point to be stressed here is that far from being a product of East European or Chinese bureaucratic and authoritarian socialism, workers' participation is now seriously being considered as an alternative to it (Shanin, 1989; Kagarlitsky, 1990). Indeed, Lawler (1985 as quoted by Anstey, 1997: 55) observes that:

> Participative management suits the current workforce, technologies, and societal conditions better than any other alternative... there is reason to believe that it can produce improvements in areas which are badly needed, such as product quality and labour costs ... it offers the possibility of further gains in organisational effectiveness and employee well-being.

Furthermore, in view of the renewed democratic attempts in Tanzania and other countries of the Third World, workers' participation needs to be seen as a key factor in the struggle for democracy. Actually, in daily life, and particularly at the workplace, participation is a necessary condition for the sustainability and deepening of political democracy and the development of a democratic culture (Kester and Sidibe, 1997).

This chapter discusses the various forms of workers' participation as well as its emergence and development. The grounds for, or arguments in favour of, participation are also discussed.

DIFFERENT FORMS OF WORKERS' PARTICIPATION

The term "workers' participation" as used in this book refers to the process of involving workers in decision-making within enterprises in which they work. It is a process recognising the needs and rights of workers to participate with management in organisational decision-making areas beyond those usually associated with collective bargaining.

Workers all over the world and under different socio-economic arrangements have always struggled for influencing decisions on issues that affect their living and working conditions. Forming trade unions and taking industrial action are some of the ways in which workers have struggled for the right to be heard. Sometimes, this struggle involved revolutionary upheavals leading to the occupation and/or control of factories by workers. But in the course of this struggle, more and more firms realised that it was in their best interest to introduce some forms of participatory management to motivate workers to increase productivity. As a result, in capitalist countries there occurred a change of terminology from workers' control to workers' participation (Mapolu, 1976: 187).

Conceptually, the idea of workers' participation is based on the widely held notion that people affected by decisions made by others (people or institutions) should be involved in making those decisions. This involvement can be viewed in two directions: the participation of people in political life (political democracy) and the participation of workers in decision-making at their workplace (industrial/ work place democracy). Our concern is with the latter, the participation of workers in enterprise's decision-making in general and in Tanzania in particular. The extent, degree and effectiveness of this involvement, that is, the actual influence and degree of control over enterprise decisions that ordinary workers are able to exert is, by and large, dependent on the form/type of participation adopted.

Currently, there are many different forms and types of participation. It is however, possible to categorise them according to several different characteristics such as the channel for participation involved: direct or indirect; the extent to which they involve real influence in enterprise decisions; and the issues or areas in which workers' are involved in decision-making. If the workers themselves take decisions, this is referred to as direct participation, while indirect participation entails some form of representation or consultation of the workers. According to Pinaud (1996: 12), there are two main types of direct participation: one, organisational participation or "participative management" and two, financial participation. The former refers to a situation whereby workers either directly or indirectly become involved in the operational management (production process) of an enterprise mainly by means of various forms of shop-floor participation such as quality circles or semi-autonomous groups in which they are encouraged to assume greater responsibility for their work. The latter is a procedure by which employees share in the profits (profit-sharing) and the capital (employee share-ownership systems) of a company. Kester and Schiphorst (1987) discuss seven (direct and indirect) forms of workers' participation: the suggestion box; shop/office-floor participation; works councils; workers' councils; workers on the Board of Directors; profit sharing and participation in ownership; and workers' self management. Below is a brief discussion of each of these main forms of participation.

Suggestion Box.

This is an indirect form of participation in which workers merely provide written suggestions or opinions on all aspects of the enterprise or workplace on a piece of paper and then put it into suggestion box. The management can ignore or act on these suggestions. This form can be valuable to the workers only if management is systematic about the box and there are other forms of participation to discuss and follow-up the suggestions or complaints of the workers.

Shop or Office-floor Participation

This form of participation involves workers who work together as one work team, say in an office, machine room, ministry or a small workplace. Here work teams are given the freedom to execute their work the way they think best provided they meet certain production targets laid down by management, each working day. An important aim of this form of participation is to increase both work motivation and satisfaction. Thus, management gives away some decision-making powers (but none of its power to run the enterprise as a whole) to workers who, in turn, take more responsibility for the benefit of both parties.

Quality Circles

These are a specific form of shop-floor participation. They usually consist of small voluntary groups of workers from the same work area who meet together on a regular basis to identify and solve problems related to quality, maintenance, work flow, productivity, cost reduction, safety and employee welfare (Anstey, 1997: 27; Levine and Tyson, 1990: 189). However, this form of participation is actually a suggestion scheme in that while workers (quality circle members) are allowed to give their opinions/suggestions final decisions are still made by management.

In Japan, quality circles started in the 1950s and since then they have expanded dramatically to become a way of life in Japanese enterprises. Today, the annual average number of suggestions per employee in Japan is about 19 compared to about five in the 1950s (Anstey, 1997: 29).

Works Councils or Committees

These are committees made up of worker and management representatives. Members of a works council representing the management are usually appointed by the enterprise's top management while worker representatives are either elected by all the workers of the enterprise/department/section or they may be appointed by the trade union branch. Sometimes, both methods may be employed to get them. The ideal situation is, however, for the workers themselves to elect their representatives.

During works council meetings, many issues can be discussed which are important to both workers and management. In some countries, however, there are specific regulations (laws or statutes) that specify what matters may be discussed or must be discussed in the works council. Apart from involving workers in decision-making, works councils provide a forum for workers to voice their grievances, problems and views.

Workers' Councils

Workers' councils are composed of only worker representatives. Sometimes some members of the management may be invited to attend workers council meetings. During workers' council meetings, many issues important both to workers and the enterprise are discussed. The suggestions and/or opinions expressed therein are then passed, through written reports, to the management for final decision-making. If the representatives feel that the final decisions made by the management have not taken into account workers' interests they may ask for an explanation, and if they are not satisfied, the matter may be taken up by their trade union. In some European countries, workers' councils are supported by law (Kester and Schiphorst, 1987: 33). Thus, the decisions of such councils may be imposed on management through legal appeal.

Workers on the Board of Directors and Co-determination

In many countries today, worker representatives are appointed or elected to serve on the Board of Directors (hereinafter called the Board) where they enjoy the same voting rights as other members of the Board. Worker representatives on the Board are expected to influence and/or modify the policy of the enterprise in the light of workers' specific interests. In most cases however, the worker representatives on the Board are relatively few compared to other Board members. Thus, they normally lose on votes. Even so, this form of participation has two main advantages to workers: it gives them the opportunity to get more information on the situation of the enterprise (which can be very valuable in collective bargaining); and Board decisions on social and labour matters are only taken after hearing workers' views or opinions.

Co-determination is a specific democratic institution in which workers wield influence by means of specific procedures and in which the workers enjoy decision-making power through their representatives. The best, if not the only, example of co-determination is the German Mitbestimmung system that grants staff and trade union representatives the right to sit on company Supervisory Board. This Board usually consists of 11 members. Five are appointed at the shareholders' meeting and five are appointed to represent the workers as follows: the Works Council appoints two (one a factory worker and the other an office worker) the remaining three are appointed by the trade union from within or outside the enterprise concerned (Kester & Schiphost, 1987: 37).

These ten members of the Supervisory Board together appoint an independent chairperson acceptable to both sides. All members of this Board receive all company information and records, they make company policy and they appoint all the top management and the Management Board. Furthermore, one of the members of the Management Board is a labour director, appointed by the Supervisory Board, who is in charge of all the enterprises personnel decisions and he/she also takes part in all other managerial decisions. Thus, co-determination gives worker representatives considerable power in many issues and it links two forms of participation: workers on the Board of Directors; and the Works Council (Kester and Schiphost, 1987: 38).

Profit Sharing and Participation in Ownership

Profit-sharing is a form of participation in which workers get a share of the profit made by an enterprise. This may be effected directly, i.e. workers are paid in cash or indirectly whereby they are given equity shares and thus become owners. When profit-sharing is effected by giving shares to workers, we refer to this as participation in ownership. This said, there is need to point out that share-holding and profit-sharing by workers need not involve participation in managerial decision-making or control of the enterprise.

Workers' Self-management

In this form of participation the workers fully control the enterprise in which they work. They make policy for running the enterprise, supervise its implementation and they also decide how profits are distributed. Although workers' self-management has been practised in different socio-economic conditions, it is generally associated with socialist/communist systems. Now given the wide collapse of socialist/communist regimes, forms of worker ownership are currently being neglected.

THREE BROAD TYPES OF PARTICIPATION

The above seven forms of participation can be grouped into the following three broad types of participatory arrangements (Levine and Tyson, 1990: 189-190): consultative, substantive and representative.

Consultative participation refers to participatory arrangements in which workers are allowed to give their opinions but final decisions are still made by management. The focus of such arrangements is usually on work organisation and other shop-floor and personnel issues important to workers. The suggestion box and quality circles fit in this category. In the United States, quality circles are the most common forms of consultative participation. "Typically about 25 percent of a firm's workers participate in voluntary quality circles" (Levine and Tyson, 1990: 189).

Substantive participation includes formal direct participation schemes such as workers' self-management and shop or office floor forms of participation as described above. Even if we exclude workers' self-management, the degree of workers influence over decisions is higher in this type of participation as compared to consultative participation.

Representative participation includes works councils, workers councils and representation of workers on enterprise Boards. In terms of workers influence in decision-making, representative arrangements are usually similar to consultative ones (with the exception of co-determination) especially because many serve purely as advisory or information channels. The major difference is that they encompass a wider range of issues including investment policy and technology. Even in the case of workers representation on Boards with worker-directors having the same voting rights as other directors, their influence, as already pointed out, is still minimal due to the small number of worker-directors compared to other directors and limited knowledge and understanding. This said, there is need to emphasise that when we talk of workers' participation, its emergence etc. what we usually have in mind is this type of participation, especially through the institutions of works and workers councils. Thus, although collective bargaining (discussed below) can be seen as belonging to this type of participation, when we talk of workers' participation we usually exclude it.

WORKERS' PARTICIPATION AND COLLECTIVE BARGAINING

Workers' participation in Western European countries was preceded by collective bargaining. It is vital to make a distinction between them. The term "collective bargaining," in its most usual form, refers to discussions between parties representing employers' and workers' interests whose aim is to agree on wages and working conditions. It can take place at various levels: at the enterprise level; the level of industry or sector; and at the national level. At any level, the partner on the workers' side is a trade union or several trade unions. The party representing employers may be a single employer (when bargaining takes place at enterprise level) or an employers' organisation/s when bargaining takes place at higher levels. Thus, collective bargaining is essentially a procedure by which workers wages and conditions of employment are agreed upon between trade union representatives and employers.

The principles of freedom of association and collective bargaining are widely recognised as basic rights essential for the normal exercise and promotion of sound labour relations. There are several ILO conventions which back up these principles: the Freedom of Association and Protection of the Right to Organise Convention, No. 87 of 1948; and the Right to Organise and Collective Bargaining Convention, No. 98 of 1949.

There has been a tendency of viewing collective bargaining and participation as contradictory. The fact is, however, that in most industrialised market economy countries, the two institutions (collective bargaining and workers' participation) have and continue to exist side by side. "It is true that two different orientations underlie both. Collective bargaining emphasises the worker as the wage labourer and focuses trade union action on the conditions of the employment contract, whilst participation emphasises the worker as a partner in production who can claim, on the basis of his or her work input, a respected place in the production process" (Kester, 1996: 44). The principal differences between the two institutions are threefold. One, participation is a more co-operative process while collective bargaining is a more conflictual one. Two, collective bargaining takes place periodically (at fixed intervals: once a year, or once every two years, or once every three years) while participation takes place on a permanent basis and deals with relatively more subject-matters or issues.

Three, workers' participation is essentially practised at enterprise level whereas collective bargaining can take place at various levels as pointed above (ILO, 1994: 35). Even so, both are institutions for problem solving and joint decision-making. This being the case, the two are not contradictory, they are actually complementary means of solving labour relations issues. Our major concern in this article is, however, with workers' participation to which we now return.

EMERGENCY AND DEVELOPMENT OF WORKERS' PARTICIPATION

The idea of involving workers in decisions that affect the operation of the enterprise in which they work, and thus their lives, is not new. It has evolved parallel with the industrialisation process and has been a component part of the history of the workers movement. Indeed, the initial idea as well as the first experiences of workers' control, originated in the capitalist countries in Europe during the nineteenth century. The idea emerged as an intellectual reaction to the social disorder and economic exploitation inherent in the capitalist system (Vanek, 1975: 16-17). As a matter of fact, most struggles for workers control have occurred in the capitalist countries although such struggles have also been waged in other socio-economic systems that have authoritarian work relations such as in the former socialist/communist systems of Eastern Europe. A discussion on the emergence of workers' participation in capitalist countries of Europe, former socialist countries of Eastern Europe and in Africa follows, albeit briefly. Our major interest is with representative participation especially through the institution of works/workers councils.

Workers' Participation in European Capitalist Countries

As already pointed out earlier, it was in the European capitalist countries of the 19th century that the first ideas of workers' participation and control emerged. It was there and in other parts of the world since then that they have been experimented with. It is possible to identify three historical phases within which widespread struggles for workers' control took place in these capitalist countries of Europe: the earliest phase in the 19th century, the end of the first world war, and the late 1960s (Bayat, 1991: 14-23).

The Early Phase in the 19th Century

The earliest ideas of workers' control and self-managed workers' associations were formulated by utopian socialists of the time. The utopian socialists sought, inter alia, to regulate the property rights of the capitalists in order to minimise the social disorder and economic exploitation inherent in the capitalist system. They believed that the control of social affairs should be exercised by the producers in society through the establishment of autonomous communities to be organised by the working people for their own good. These forms of administration, both in industry and agriculture, were to be subordinated to the general management of the whole community. But by the term 'producers' they also included capitalist employers. In other words, they presupposed the capitalist system and sought merely to reduce some of its glaring miseries. Indeed, in the words of one of the leading utopian socialists, Robert Owen of England, they were seeking to humanise capitalist enterprise and not to destroy it (see Mapolu, 1976: 186). The ideas of utopian socialists were expressed later by other socialists as well as by some anarchists. One wing of anarchists emphasised education as opposed to revolutionary violence as the means of dismantling not only capitalism but also the state. The other wing of the anarchist movement advocated for revolutionary violence to achieve similar goals (Abendroth, 1972).

After the utopian socialists came the syndicalists who envisaged a society in which each industry would be managed by its own workers. They were of the view that in a conglomeration of such units, society would function better both for the individual members as well as for society as a whole. Following syndicalism, guild socialism was centred on the idea that the guilds, consisting of all the workers, would ultimately control industry but with due regard for the interests of other sections of the community.

Guild socialism was a mixture of syndicalism and collectivism; it assumed that the means of production should be owned by the state but that the control of production should lie with guilds. The guilds would be democratically organised and would negotiate on equal terms with the state. Furthermore, different guilds would be able to merge into a single union, after which it would be possible to transform capitalism by industrial unionism (Cole, 1975; Bayat, 1991: 18).

The above ideas on workers' control began to receive both widespread expression and concrete experimentation after the end of the First World War. Even so, towards the end of the 19th century (as a reaction to the growth of the labour movement) some employers voluntarily introduced some rudimentary forms of workers' participation. The aim was twofold: to keep trade unions out of the establishment, and to provide better legitimisation to employer policies at plant level. In the case of Germany, for example, Anstey (1997: 104) observes that two strands developed in the early labour movement: a powerful socialist wing that pursued a political agenda of radical transformation, and a liberal wing that supported a free market. Capital and state pursued a policy of destroying the socialist trade unions with: (a) the government banning them in 1878 and (b) employers dividing workers through the introduction of in-house participation bodies that met strong opposition from the socialist trade unions. In 1890, the government lifted the ban on trade unions and in 1891, the Trade Act recognised both independent trade unions and in-house participation bodies. But:

These first laws, introduced in 1891 to govern workplace participation, were met with strong trade union and Social Democratic Party resistance. However, the conflict was deflected by the First World War which saw a national drive uniting socialist unions behind the government" (Anstey, 1997: 104).

Second Phase: Post WW I

The idea of workers' participation in decision-making in enterprise took broad practical shape with the emergence of joint committees and workers' councils in Bulgaria, Germany, Hungary, Italy, and Poland at the end of the First World War. This was the period when revolutionary movements had sprang-up throughout Europe while at the same time the bourgeois states had been severely undermined because of the war. With the growing contradictions within the capitalist countries there was a greater need to regulate industrial conflicts. In addition to this, towards the end of the war in October 1917 the world witnessed the birth of the first socialist state. Now, with the first socialist state onto the scene, there was need to challenge the socialist central thesis that the interests of capitalists were completely hostile if not antagonistic to those of workers. The best way to challenge this was by demonstrating that in capitalist societies there exists a democracy that permeates not only the political arena but also the economic field, i.e. industrial democracy. Perhaps the term 'workers control' was not palatable enough for capitalists to swallow, thus there was a shift from workers' control to workers' participation. Participation of workers in management decision-making was seen as a tool not only for maintaining good industrial relations but also for foreseeing and even forestalling critical periods.

Austria and Germany were the first countries to adopt laws on works councils in 1919 and 1920 respectively. In the following decades, works councils spread to other industrialised capitalist countries, "particularly in Western Europe, and were complemented in some of them by a system of workers' representation on the management bodies of enterprises" (ILO, 1994: 34-35).

At this juncture there is need to point out that organs for workers control were set up in capitalist countries of Europe as a result of the concrete socio-economic conditions in individual countries. In Germany, for example, the idea of workers' councils, and the practice evolved during the war. Three factors were responsible for this: "the economic effects of the war; the suppression of every free movement of the working class through the administration of the state of siege; and the complete refusal of the trade unions and political parties to act" (Muller, 1975: 211). The trade unions in Germany complied with the state-of-siege policies while the working-class parties were divided into two with the stronger faction supporting the state. Thus, the politically conscious section of the working class decided to act independently against the economic and political restrictions imposed by the state-of-siege policies. This took the form of establishing workers councils in large factories (Bayat, 1991: 17). These councils organised the great political general strike of January and February 1918 in which over half a million workers took part. And as already pointed out earlier, the first laws on works councils in Germany were adopted in 1920. But this first Works Council Law still reflected the thinking of conservative rather than trade union elements that insisted that the councils be worker-controlled. The unions, therefore, were against their establishment. Thus, the law was enacted in spite of the trade unions and not because of them (see Anstey, 1997: 104).

The Late 1960s

During the period from the late 1960s to early 1970s, capitalist countries in Europe experienced increased social uprising and economic militancy by the working class. The capitalist boom that was experienced after the Second World War was over. Capitalists resorted to laying-off workers in order to reduce costs of production. Partly because of this, trade unions used the weapon of strikes while the working class resorted to the radical strategy of mass occupation of factories in their struggle against redundancies. As a result of this, the number of strikes as well as factory occupations increased sharply especially in Britain, France and Italy. These direct actions by workers succeeded in forcing employers to abandon plans to lay off workers (Bayat, 1991: 21).

Three things deserve special emphasis here. First, is the fact that workers resorted to the occupation of factories and other protests in order to secure jobs, better conditions of work and life. Second, the social movements that fought against bad working conditions also fought against Taylorism, the so called "scientific organisation of work." These movements were therefore a decisive factor in provoking increased union demands for improvements in the quality of the work environment as well as the development and expansion of various direct and indirect forms of workers' participation during the late 1960s and 1970s in Europe. Third, although the initial main thrust towards participation came from the workers and their trade unions, governments have, in cooperation with or instigation of trade unions, also played an important role in the development of these direct and indirect forms of workers' participation by offering them a legal basis through constitutional means and legislation.

> This has been achieved constitutionally, as in Italy, or by legislation passed by Labour, Socialist or Social Democratic governments in Malta, the Netherlands, France, Germany and other countries. These governments have also offered financial support and facilitated participation schemes in the public sector and nationalised companies. Funding for education, training and academic research into worker participation has considerably helped spread and legitimate worker participation (Kester and Pinaud, 1996: 2).

In the 1980s, many Western European countries experienced socio-economic problems resulting into rising unemployment. Consequently, unemployment, working hours, wages and deregulation became the immediate worries of many workers. Trade unions were compelled to return to their traditional strategies:

collective bargaining and industrial action. In so far as workers' participation is concerned, this was the period of stagnation. Even so, during those same years some existing forms of participation were enshrined in legal form while education and advice services were introduced. The decade also witnessed a rapid rise in management and employer-initiated forms of participation, mainly participation in profits and ownership. These forms of participation "have tended to reduce the influence of workers in decision-making" (Kester and Pinaud, 1996: 2). Thus, workers' participation is becoming an expression of capital, "a thirst for gold rather than a thirst for democracy" (Kester and Pinaud, 1996: 3).

Workers' Participation in Eastern Europe

Towards the end of the First World War, the Russian Revolution of October 1917 occurred that led to the formation of the first socialist country in the world. February of that year, it can be recalled, witnessed the collapse of the Tsarist regime following a massive demonstration of women. Immediately after the collapse, grassroots organisations emerged among the workers, soldiers and peasants. Of these three, workers "organisations were by far the strongest" (Bayat, 1991: 63). The main organs for workers control that were set up by Russian workers were factory committees and councils (the Soviets).

Factory committees were shop-floor organisations aimed at asserting control over both the process and administration of production at the workplace level. The councils were composed of representatives of workers, soldiers and sometimes even peasants and were essentially political entities. Three factors have been identified as being responsible for the emergence of factory committees (Bayat, 1991: 67; Smith, 1983: 258). These were: (a) the desire of the workers to save jobs and maintain production under conditions of mass lay off; (b) the informal job control practised by skilled workers, whose jobs at that time were in danger from rationalisation and deskilling; and (c) the traditional election of village headmen in the rural areas (from which the workers originated) was adapted and transformed in the urban industrial settings as follows: first, into the election of workers representatives at the factory level and, second, into the organisation of factory committees during the revolution. Thus, the struggle for workers' control in Russia initially revolved around wages and other conditions of work but later in the process, especially the period between the February and the October revolutions, workers developed an ideological commitment to workers' control. Even so, the experience was short lived. After the October revolution, there was an ideological division between advocates (the Left Communists) and opponents (Lenin) of workers' control within the communists. "With Lenin's victory, workers' control became stigmatised as an anarcho-syndicalist hearsay.... During Stalin's regime, workers' control was virtually abandoned and authoritarian managerialism prevailed both in industry and agriculture" (Bayat, 1991: 79).

The end of World War Two witnessed the emergence of socialist countries in Eastern Europe (Czechoslovakia, Hungary, Poland, Rumania, Yugoslavia, etc.) with the support of USSR under Stalin. These socialist states, with the exception of Yugoslavia, adopted the Stalinist version of socialist construction in which not the labouring masses (the grassroots) from below but the single ruling party from above determined socio-economic policies. The implication of this is that even the conceived role of the workers changed dramatically from 'control' to 'association' with management. In such a system all working class organisations such as trade unions were incorporated into the apparatus of the ruling party. Ironically, these countries were ruled under the name of the dictatorship of proletariat but it was not the workers who dictated matters. Under such a situation, periodic crises were inevitable and actually became the norm in these socialist countries. The workers struggled for the autonomy of their organisation from the political party and the state. Thus, the crises saw the emergence of an independent movement of the working people especially during the 1950s.

Workers' councils, soldiers' councils and an autonomous labour movement, for instance, emerged in Hungary and Poland in 1956. But the Hungarian councils were crushed by the invasion of the USSR's army while the independent Polish movement was gradually institutionalised and deformed by the ruling party (Bayat, 1991:18).

In Czechoslovakia, the demand for economic reforms and self-management was raised from below by the working people towards the end of the 1960s when the Stalinist elements lost power in the communist party. Trade unions supported the initiative and actually worked to prepare the future workers' councils. Within a period of one year, workers' councils were set up in about 50 per cent of the country's industrial enterprises. In every enterprise, the workers' council had the powers to appoint and recall the chief executive of the enterprise as well as the right to make decisions on the reallocation of the gross revenue, and give opinions about wages and other conditions of work. Even so the experience did not last long. With the backing of the conservative elements within the Communist Party, workers' councils were dismantled by the occupying forces of Warsaw Pact. The councils were accused of being anti-socialist pressure groups (Pelican, 1973: 12-16).

The struggle by the Polish workers for the democratisation of both the economy and polity and for workers control during the crises episodes of 1970s and culminated in 1980 with the birth of the Solidarity movement. This movement demanded self-management not only at the enterprise level but also at the level of the economy. After long negotiations, the Polish government responded by passing a law on self-management in public enterprises in 1981 (Bayat, 1991: 18).

As mentioned earlier, Yugoslavia was the only country in socialist Europe that did not adopt the USSR version or Stalinist line of socialism. Instead of concentrating power within the state, the Communist Party there in 1952 introduced a self-management system in which powers of decision-making regarding the enterprise were vested on the enterprises. That is, enterprise level decisions were made by the workers' assemblies and councils.

Workers' Participation in Africa

The initiative or call for workers' participation and control in the Third World in general and Africa in particular has not come as a result of conflict between capital and labour as was the case in the industrialised countries of Europe. Rather, workers' participation and in some cases, self-management were launched as a development strategy in a number of countries in the early years of political independence. In this section we present a brief overview of workers' participation in Africa.

Different forms of workers participation in enterprise decision-making are/ have been practised in African countries after attainment of political independence. The way independence was attained and the political ideology adopted by the post-colonial states are some of the major factors that explain the emergence of participation. Two examples are in order at this point: Mozambique and Zambia.

Mozambique attained independence following a war of liberation led by the Mozambique Liberation Front (FRELIMO) whose leadership advocated for democratic workers' control. During the last period of the armed struggle the Portuguese colonial settlers left the country in large numbers while many enterprises were abandoned due to sabotage and closures by their owners. This led to serious socio-economic problems as the proper functioning of the production process was greatly undermined. To resolve the crisis the FRELIMO government resorted to setting up Dynamising groups to carry out the work of both mobilising and organising workers to better carry out the work in the enterprise. In 1976 President Samora Machel directed the establishment of a new organisation of workers: the Production Councils which performed the function of workers' participation at workplace alongside state-appointed managers and administrators (Bayat, 1991: 100; Hansen, 1997: 256-57). These state-appointed managers and their administrators tried to reduce the Production Councils to organs wit' a policing role against indiscipline, lateness and absenteeism on the part of th workers. As a result, conflict developed between the production councils and the workers. This conflict was resolved through the formation of party cells i enterprises. These cells replaced the Dynamising groups and they encouraged workers' activities against authoritarian management. Another change occurred in 1984 when the Productions Councils were converted into trade unions. Thus, in the Mozambican case trade unions were a direct creation of the ruling party FRELIMO (Hansen, 1997: 253) and the initiative for workers' participation came from above, being advocated by FRELIMO - the ruling party.

Zambia did not resort to armed struggle to attain political independence that was attained in 1964. However, several years after political independence it adopted the philosophy/ideology of Humanism. This was followed by economic reforms in 1968 that led to nationalisation and state ownership of major means of production. One year later, in December 1969 President Kaunda called for workers' participation in management decision-making through 'works councils' and workers representation at Board level. Workers' participation also received ideological substantiation in the official philosophy of Humanism. Participation was conceived as a strategy for effecting social change and economic development. In other words, it was viewed as an instrument for the transformation of the Zambian society from capitalism to humanism through socialism (Kalombo, et. al, 1985). Thus, the initiative came from the top.

The regulations governing the formation and operation of works councils in Zambia were later embodied in the country's Industrial Relations Act of 1971 (it became operational in 1974). But works councils came into being in 1976 when President Kaunda announced their establishment in all enterprises (public and private) employing 100 or more employees (p. 370).

In other African countries also, workers' participation was launched as a development strategy and or within the political or ideological context then prevailing in each individual country such as: Harambee in Kenya, Ujamaa in Tanzania, and Islamic Socialism in Libya. In addition to this, many African countries subscribed to the notion of responsible participation of all groups of the population (especially of labour and management) in the socio-economic development process. "Thus, at the national level, employers' and workers' organisations have been called upon to take part in a variety of consultative organs designed to advise the government on the preparation of economic development plans, the determination of wage policy, the elaboration of labour law and such issues as job classification, safety and health at workplace and vocational training. Many of these bodies have actually ceased to function after a few years but in a number of cases they have played a useful part in the making of decisions in the fields concerned, particularly in the development of labour legislation" (ILO, 1994: 35-36).

However, with passage of time, participation that originally had been a source of economic as well as social liberation fell prey to manipulation and exploitation. Responsible participation actually was used to co-opt civil society, in particular working people organisations, with the view of securing their support for objectives already determined by the sole ruling party or the military regime. Then came the economic difficulties from the mid 1970s which became more severe in the early 1980s and with them the structural adjustment programmes (SAPs) under the sponsorship of the International Monetary Fund (IMF) and the World Bank. In the name of economic recovery, many African governments now no longer support the kind of participation they themselves or previous governments introduced; these governments also pass new labour laws to attract both local and foreign investors, thereby "guaranteeing them 'carte blanche' in running their enterprises. Trade unionism is also seen as a form of harassment, and participation as an error for which previous governments are to blame" (Kester and Sidibe, 1997:9).

Economic difficulties led to both economic and political reforms. People all over Africa demanded more democracy: end of one party and military regimes, freedom of expression and association (including independence or autonomy of working peoples' organisations such as trade unions), more transparency on the part of government and the leadership in general, rule of law and an independent press and other mass media - to mention but a few. The wind of change is clearly blowing across Africa. In short old ideologies and socio-economic systems are being rejected. But as the old order is being discarded, participation is not jettisoned together with it. Actually, people are demanding their involvement in decision-making on social, economic and political matters. It is as if they are telling their leaders that development goes hand in hand with democracy and the latter cannot be separated from participation that should be democratic as opposed to responsible participation. A brief discussion of the grounds for participation is in order.

GROUNDS FOR WORKERS' PARTICIPATION

There are three main grounds or arguments for which workers' participation has been advocated: increasing labour productivity and efficiency (the productivity argument), extending democracy (the socio-political argument), and fundamental human right (the philosophical argument).

The Productivity Argument

In neo-classical theory, the decision-making powers/rights of an enterprise are vested in the owner(s), the supplier of capital or the means of production. An owner may be one individual, a small group, a large group of shareholders or the state. Unless the enterprise is very small, owners usually delegate some of their rights to agents or managers to act in their behalf. In big enterprises employing hundreds of people, owners usually employ directors to ensure the proper functioning of the enterprise. The main functions of directors are threefold: to give general guidelines on how to run the enterprise; to decide on the appointment of top and middle level managers; and to formulate guidelines for workers' salaries and other working conditions. In such a situation the managers are not directly responsible to owners but to directors who are, in turn, responsible to the owners. Thus, in any enterprise the directors and or managers are representatives of capital, the owners.

The delegation of at least some decision making rights by managers to workers, some scholars argue, is likely to have negative effects on enterprise performance. The main postulate here is that as the number of decision makers or agents increases, the cost of monitoring increases. This postulate has led scholars working in the agency framework to conclude that "participatory arrangements are inevitably inefficient" (Levine and Tyson, 1990: 185). But even working within this framework, one can identify circumstances in which participatory arrangements can improve enterprise efficiency and profitability. For instance, if workers have knowledge and or information that managers lack about the workplace and the behaviour of fellow workers, then participatory arrangements that motivate workers to use such information on their jobs or to communicate it to the managers can increase the firms performance (Levine and Tyson, 1990: 186).

Actually, the main economic argument for workers participation is that it has a positive impact on productivity and efficiency because it increases the sense of job satisfaction which in turn leads to increased productivity and greater efficiency; secondly it allows for tapping and using the initiative and expertise of many workers who are deeply involved and are familiar with the problems/technicalities of production and administration; thirdly, it tends to create an atmosphere of collectivity and communality which makes workers to be more responsible by inculcating a feeling of belonging to the enterprise; and fourth, it minimises the alienation effects inherent in authoritarian labour relations such as high labour turn-over and absenteeism, wastage and product rejects, and sabotage. In short, it promotes humane labour relations, industrial harmony and stability (Cooley, 1987; Bayat, 1991; Friedman, 1977; Levine and Tyson, 1990; Palloix, 1976).

There is considerable literature and empirical evidence supporting the above arguments (see Blinder, 1990). Blumberg (1968) claims that there is hardly any study in the entire literature of participation (especially through the institution of works councils) that fails to demonstrate that work satisfaction is enhanced or that generally acknowledged positive effects accrue from a genuine increase in decision making power on the part of workers. For him it is almost a matter of common sense why democratic workers' participation works: workers take greater pride and pleasure in their work when they are allowed to participate in shaping the policies and decisions which affect their work.

The Socio-political Argument

This argument advocates for workers' participation on the grounds of (extending) democracy that many governments identify with. The main idea here is that no country is fully democratic if its political democracy does not go hand in hand with industrial democracy. In other words, the work place is equated to a country. This is so because work relations are not only technical but also social and are characterised by relations of domination and subordination. Seen in this light, the work site becomes a political site as well. In this framework, just as the citizens of any country have the right to elect their representatives in a government to manage the country, workers in an enterprise must have the right to elect their representatives in the management (Jones and Seabrook, 1969; Street, 1983). To Adu-Amankwah and Kester (1999), participation is democracy.

> Democracy is not just about control of a country's administration, transparency and good governance at national level. These factors are equally necessary both in the workplace and for the economy, . . . If democracy is to be deepened, given the resources to survive and made a permanent feature, the workplace is the battlefield par excellence (Adu-Amankwah and Kester, 1999: 85, 86).

It is also important to resist the notion/idea that democracy, both in society and in enterprises, is a luxury at a time of social and economic difficulties or crisis such as rising unemployment and widening gap between rich and poor. "At a time such as this, democracy is indispensable if we are to succeed in finding any lasting solutions to these problems.... It is true that we all live by bread but not by bread alone. The means and the ends are linked and democratic participation will make it possible for workers to earn their bread and win democracy" (Pinaud, 1996: 24).

The Philosophical Argument

This argument treats workers' participation as a fundamental basic human right and desire. "The Universal Declaration of Human Rights as well as the European Charter of Fundamental Rights" [and also the 1991 African Charter of Popular Participation in Development and Transformation] " both implicitly or explicitly regard participation as a basic right" (Kester, 1996: 35). This is based on the belief that if there is one single characteristic that might be considered to be uniquely human, then, it is perhaps the desire for freedom and the struggle against domination by others. Thus as long as the work site is characterised by relations of domination and subordination, workers will continue to struggle against such relations. Therefore, workers' participation is justified because that is what workers as human eings deserve (Bayat, 1991: 26). In other words, democratic participation has to be defended on ethical-moral grounds irrespective of its effects or contribution to efficiency, productivity or democracy.

Although participation may be considered a universal human right, it does not necessarily follow that every one would like to exercise this right. Just like the right to vote, to exercise participation remains a matter of free choice of every individual employee. Lack of interest in exercising it among some individuals or categories of workers does not affect this fundamental human right. Thus, it must be defended for those who wish to exercise it. You do not do away with 'the right to vote' simply because in elections not all eligible voters exercise this right.

The three major arguments or grounds for democratic workers' participation, in our opinion, are all valid, sound and thence, complementary. Problems only arise if any one of the following takes place.

One, when participation falls prey to manipulation and exploitation (c.f., responsible participation in Africa). In such situations one is actually not talking of democratic participation.

Two, when the nature or form of involvement of workers in decision-making becomes more consultative than participatory and management rarely implement the suggestions given by the workers.

Three, when workers' participation involves only one form, and this form has been initiated by management, such as financial participation. Here there is need to point out that this form of participation (i.e., share-holding and profit-sharing by workers) is of a different kind and does not necessarily involve workers' participation in managerial decision-making or control of the enterprise. Even so, "financial participation in the form of profit-sharing has been successful in private-sector companies in several countries of Western Europe. But different forms of participation in capital (internal employee share-ownership plans encouraged by company buy-ups by employees, etc.) have not been successful in Western Europe" (Pinaud, 1996: 14, 15).

Four, when participation or some forms of it are used to replace collective bargaining as opposed to complement it, and as such trade unions will be against it.

Five, when participation is badly planned or is confined only to insignificant forms, what one might call 'token participation,' such as tea, toilet and towels democracy.

CONCLUSION

In summing up this chapter we need to emphasise that although the initial ideas as well as experiences of workers' participation originated in the capitalist countries of Western Europe, the concept of participation has been closely associated with or included into leftist and or progressive political ideologies. This is not surprising since main stream intellectuals researching this field of participation tended to enclose themselves in leftist territory and formulated various theories which assumed that Socialism was a necessary prerequisite for effective/meaningful participation (see Horvat, 1982). Workers' participation, therefore, became a battle cry for Socialism and workers' self management a show-piece for some Socialist/Marxist oriented countries, although other Marxist ideologies and systems rejected both workers' participation and self-management (Kester, 1996: 37). But the fact still remains that workers' participation is not the exclusive preserve of any one political ideology. This implies that it is an ideology on its own right and the challenge to day is to place it fairly and squarely in all political systems, not associating it only with the socialist/communist regimes that did a lot of damage to it.

Democratic workers' participation can be defended on the grounds that it is a fundamental human right, it contributes to productivity and it promotes democracy. Indeed, democracy can only survive if it is participative, and that participation is a necessary condition for development. Participation and collective bargaining are not contradictory but complementary, both should be seen as basic rights and the choice is not between one of them but rather both need to be promoted and exist side by side.

2

THE DEVELOPMENT OF TRADE UNIONS IN TANZANIA: A HISTORICAL PERSPECTIVE

DEVELOPMENT OF TRADE UNIONS IN COLONIAL TANZANIA

Labour movements in Tanzania originated from the poor social and working conditions maintained by the colonial regime. These included: very low wages paid to African workers in different sectors of the economy; poor housing and living conditions; and horrible sanitary conditions. In general workers were dissatisfied with these conditions and initially resorted to passive resistance (go slow), followed by industrial action and finally formation of trade unions.

Trade union elements in the country can be traced way back to 1931 when various workers and tribes reacted differently to wage employment and the evils it brought about including detaching African workers from their traditional cultural practices and their associated social economic and political activities. This unrest compelled the colonial government to enact the 1932 Trade Union Ordinance that legalised the formation of workers' organisations. At this time, however, workers lacked organisational abilities and together with attitudes of the colonial government to control labour, prevented the emergence of effective trade unions. Even so, as the cost of living increased to unbearable levels, the workers at various work places started putting up spontaneous resistance through strikes, picketing and work stoppage. For instance, 250 dock workers at Tanga port stopped working in 1937 in protest against low wages and poor working conditions. Also, in 1939 casual workers at the Dar es Salaam dockyard staged a two-day strike in protest against piece rates as well as low wages. These two strikes marked the beginning of industrial instability in Tanganyika, now Mainland Tanzania. Indeed, dock workers in Dar es Salaam, Lindi and Mwanza went on strike in 1943 protesting against the same things: low wages and poor living conditions (Mihyo, 1983: 14).

The general dissatisfaction of workers in Tanganyika was expressed in the general strike of 1947, which actually laid down the basis for proper trade unions in the country. The strike was initiated by Dar es Salaam dock workers in September of that year and spread like bush fire throughout most towns upcountry, lasting for a week and was supported by many segments of the African population. It was the biggest and the most widespread strike in colonial Tanganyika. It was out of this strike that the Labour Office advised the strikers to form a legal trade union which should be registered. At the end of 1947, five trade unions had registered themselves (p. 15). These were:

+ The Stevedores and Dockworkers' Union;
+ The African Cooks, Washermen and House Servants Association;
+ The African Tailors' Association;
+ The Morogoro Personal Servants' Association; and
+ The Dar es Salaam African Motor Drivers Association.

More associations were formed between 1952 and 1955. Even so, the colonial government was not enthusiastic about the formation of trade unions. Thus, it rushed to ensure that the unions were organised on accepted lines of compromise with the colonial government and lack of hostility on the part of union leaders. For instance, in 1951 the African Commercial Employees Association (ACEA) was formed in Dar es Salaam but the authorities hesitated to register it. ACEA was officially registered as a trade union in 1953 after many initial hurdles in the registration process. The hurdles were mainly created by employers and the colonial government who feared the formation of resistance groups to the colonial administration. In addition to this, it was the intention of the colonial government not to form national unions but to have trade unions from various districts or craft unions. This intention was meant to limit the influence of the various trade unions to local locations only. One of the intentions of the ACEA leaders was to form national/industrial trade unions instead of the craft unions.

Although the immediate effect of the 1947 general strike was the organisation of workers into trade unions, it also sent a clear message to the colonial government that there was a limit beyond which African workers could not endure. That is, strikes and work stoppages were bound to continue if the colonial government could not listen to the demands of African workers and take appropriate action. As a matter of fact, strikes went on throughout 1948 and 1950. Consequently, the colonial authorities had no choice but to try to resolve the problem of labour unrest.

However, it was not until 1951 that a committee (the Manpower Committee) was appointed to inquire into the conditions of labour and to make recommendations on how best to improve them so as to avoid labour dissatisfaction.

In response to the Manpower Committee's recommendations, the colonial government took measures aimed at striking a balance between the needs of the African workers and those of employers so as to encourage good industrial relations. These included issuing a circular to legalise obligation to establish workers' committees at workplace and enacting the Employment Ordinance- it was first drafted in 1953 and completed in 1955 but came into operation in 1957 (Mihyo, 1983: 19). In 1956, a new Trade Union Ordinance (No. 48 of 1956) was enacted and the 1932 Ordinance was repealed. This new ordinance provided for the procedures for forming and registering trade unions and their participation in collective bargaining. The Ordinance, therefore, established a Registrar of Trade Unions with the principle that unions had no rights, immunities or privileges until they were registered. The Ordinance however, placed the trade unions under the control of the state.

The forging of closer ties between various trade unions in the country took place in 1955 as a result of a three-day visit of Mr. Tom Mboya, by then the leader of Kenya Federation of Labour. It was out of this visit that in October of that year (1955) various trade unions united to form a federation of trade unions, the Tanganyika Federation of Labour (TFL). TFL was registered with an initial number of 17 trade unions. This was a federation mainly incorporating 'crafts unions' and its first Secretary General was Mr. R.M. Kawawa. Other leaders were as follows: President (Mr. J.B. Changa); Senior Vice President (Mr. F. B. Jumbe); Junior Vice President (Mr. J.E. Shaba); Assistant Secretary General (Mr. M.M. Mpangala); General Treasurer (Mr. M. Kamaliza); and Assistant General Treasurer (Mr. A. Andoro). One of the first tasks of TFL was to create, out of the numerous craft unions, a small number of national industrial organisations. By 1960, most of the unions affiliated to TFL were industrial unions.

Furthermore, from 1956 to 1960 TFL efforts were also directed towards labour unrest that eventually culminated in strikes. The number of strikes increased annually during this period as follows: 1956 (54 strikes); 1957 (114); 1958 (153); 1959 (205); and 1960 (203 strikes) (Chambua and Naimani, 1996a: 5; Jackson, 1979: 220). Most of the strikes were started after consultation with TFL officials. The main cause of the strikes was inequality in the remuneration and treatment of African and non-African workers. Non-African workers were mostly favoured by employers and this brought misunderstandings between these two categories of workers on one hand and between employers and the underprivileged African workers on the other.

During the struggle for political independence, a strong alliance between by then the sole anti-colonial political movement/party, Tanganyika African National Union (TANU), and TFL developed. TANU was formed in 1954 and waged anti-colonial struggles seeking recognition of workers and trade unions rights. The alliance was so strong that one can actually regard TFL as constituting, by then, an industrial wing of TANU.

On the other side of the union (Zanzibar) a federation of trade unions called Zanzibar and Pemba Federation of Labour (ZPFL) was formed in 1958. One characteristic common to both federations and the individual unions forming them was that they co-operated with political parties to fight for political independence.

At this juncture, there is need to stress that before independence the relationship between the main political parties (TANU in Tanganyika and ASP i.e. the Afro-Shiraz Party in Zanzibar) and the trade unions including TFL and ZPFL was one of solidarity in the struggle for independence to get rid of a common enemy, the colonial system. During that time, the unions and their federations in Tanganyika and Zanzibar were independent and autonomous of both political parties and the state. Actually, the constitutions of these federations did not allow them nor the unions affiliated to them to unite with or to come under any political party control. However, the political parties just before independence began to develop an interest of uniting with the federations. This interest did not receive support from all the members of the federations.

Consequently, in the case of Tanganyika, TFL split into two factions: one faction (led by the late Michael Kamaliza, who was then the leader of TFL) was ready to unite with TANU and the other (led by Kassanga Tumbo by then the General Secretary of Tanganyika Railways African Workers Union) wanted TFL to maintain its autonomy. After a lot of friction, discussions and debate, the Tumbo faction won. In other words, it was decided that TFL should not unite with TANU but continue to operate as an autonomous federation of trade unions. Thus, the first attempt by TANU, just before independence, to control and/or subordinate trade unions failed.

POST-INDEPENDENCE TRADE UNIONS

Tanganyika attained political independence on the 9th of December 1961. Friction and/or misunderstandings between TANU and TFL continued to grow and intensified even after independence in 1961. TANU and its new government wanted to put working class organisations under its control and subordination while TFL maintained its stand of asserting the autonomy of the trade union movement. At the same time it disagreed with TANU and its government on a number of issues, including the following:

+ The demands for the break-up of the East African High Commission for its disregard and insensitivity on trade union's demands; and
+ Rapid Africanisation while the government appeared some what slow to act.

But some of the TFL leaders were already in the Government. For example, TFL's first Secretary General and later its President, Mr. R. M. Kawawa was appointed to be the Minister for Local Governments and Housing in September 1960 (during the internal self-government) while retaining TFL's presidency. As a result of this situation, the split in the trade union leadership into two factions became more glaring. The first supported TANU and its government while the second did not. The trade union leadership was faced with another but related crisis at the end of 1961 when Mr. Kawawa was again appointed Minister (without portfolio) in the newly formed nationalist post-colonial government and he had to resign from TFL's presidency. With his resignation, the anti-TANU elements within the trade union movement led by Mr. K. Tumbo contested strongly for the presidency of TFL. In spite of their campaign Mr. Tumbo lost to Mr. M. Kamaliza who was by then TFL's Secretary General and also an ardent member of TANU and in agreement with its policies and those of the Government (Mihyo, 1983: 51).

The immediate reaction of the Tumbo group after TFL's presidential elections was to demand the resignation of Kamaliza because of, *inter alia*, his stand that TFL and TANU were so much complementary of each other that there was no need for any one of them to be independent of the other. When this failed, Tumbo called upon other affiliated trade unions to withdraw from TFL and form another federation under his leadership. This campaign also failed (Mihyo, 1983: 52).

The trade union leaders opposed to TANU policies (but in favour of maintaining trade union's autonomy) used the TFL to voice their opposition against government/TANU policies. They demanded immediate Africanisation and called upon TANU and its government to take immediate action or face a general strike. But, the President of TANU (J.K. Nyerere) and by then the Prime Minister was for gradual Africanisation. Perhaps because of this, Nyerere resigned as Prime Minister on 23 January 1962 and left R. M. Kawawa, the former President of TFL, in charge of government and thence to deal with trade union leaders opposed to TANU. However, Nyerere continued to be the President of TANU. In his capacity as party leader, he challenged trade union leaders opposed to TANU to form a political party and contest with TANU for the leadership of the country. Some trade union leaders tried but failed to form a political party because most the influential union leaders: M. Kamaliza, A. Tandau, and J. Rwegasira, to mention but a few, were in favour of the government and TANU's policies.

In an attempt to deal with the trade union movement, the new Prime Minister, Mr. Kawawa on 10 March 1962 appointed Mr. M. Kamaliza, TFL's President, Minister for Labour and the latter's chief opponent, Mr. Tumbo, was appointed the country's ambassador in London. The appointment of Kamaliza as Minister for Labour was followed by a wave of strikes organised by individual trade unions in the country and many had TFL's support. At issue was the demand for rapid Africanisation and higher wages. It was against such a background that the Government, through the Parliament, enacted laws not only to control and contain strikes but also to bring about state control of the trade union movement.

This was achieved through several pieces of legislation: the Trade Disputes (Settlement) Act No. 43 of 1962; Trade Union Ordinance (Amendment) Act No. 51 of 1962; the Civil Service (Negotiating Machinery) Act No. 52 of 1962; and the Preventive Detention Act No. 60 of 1962.

The Trade Disputes (Settlement) Act (1962) narrowed the scope for industrial action by restricting a legal trade dispute to a dispute between the employees and their own employer and requiring that such dispute should relate to the conditions of only those employees involved in the dispute. Consequently, secondary strikes/picketing and solidarity strikes were outlawed. The Act also virtually abolished strikes by setting up a complex procedure for compulsory arbitration.

The Trade Union Ordinance (Amendment) Act (1962) authorised the Minister for Labour to declare any federation a 'designated federation' to which all trade unions in the country had to affiliate. That is, any union that was not prepared to affiliate with or break away from it would be de-registered. The Minister for Labour was also given powers to regulate the manner in which the finances of the designated federation could be spent. In the midst of strong opposition, TFL was designated the sole federation to which every trade union had to affiliate and consult before taking any industrial action. TFL itself had to act in accordance with the directives of the Minister for Labour and of the Registrar of Trade Unions. This was the beginning of the process of removing the autonomy of trade unions in the country, a process spear-headed and (as we shall see later) completed by former trade union leaders who had become top government leaders.

The Civil Service (Negotiating Machinery) Act of 1962, among other things, excluded all civil servants earning more than £702 per month from becoming members of any trade union; and established a Joint Staff Council to negotiate issues related to terms and conditions of service of junior civil servants. One of its sections barred junior civil servants from taking part in strikes until the Act's procedure for negotiating disputes had been exhausted. Failure to comply with this provision was punishable by a fine and/or imprisonment.

The Preventive Detention Act is a particularly illiberal piece of legislation:

> Under it, the President can detain anyone whenever he is satisfied that the person to be detained is a danger to peace and good order or is acting in a manner prejudicial to the defence of the country or the security of the state. The President may also detain anyone if he is satisfied that this is necessary to prevent that person from becoming a danger to peace and good order, to the defence or to the security of Tanganyika.... The period of detention is unlimited rather than specified. There is no requirement that the names of

those detained should be made public. Judicial review of the exercise of detention is carefully excluded and there is no alternative appeal procedure... the regulations issued under the Act... also deny the detainee the right extended to other prisoners to be visited by ministers of religion and to be visited by relatives when ill" (Pratt, 1976: 185-86).

Although this Act is not directly related to trade union issues, it is significant to note that the first persons to be detained under it included a trade union leader and Member of Parliament (Mr. C. Tumbo) in 1963 (Pratt, 1976: 186) and the so called stubborn leaders of TFL, including its president (Kapinga, 1985: 90). The implication of this is that this piece of legislation was, *inter alia*, intended to contain government opposition by the trade union leadership.

The fatal blow to the autonomy of the trade union movement came in 1964. In February of that year, the soldiers staged a mutiny demanding wage increases and Africanisation of the Officer Corps - demands similar to those made earlier by TFL. After the mutiny had been suppressed by British troops, some 200 leading trade unionists were among the 500 people detained (Pratt, 1976: 189). While still in detention, the government through the National Union of Tanganyika Workers (NUTA) Act, No. 18 of 1964, banned all trade unions in the country, dissolved TFL and established in its place a single union, NUTA (Rutinwa, 1995: 6-7).

NUTA was compelled to affiliate with and promote the activities of the ruling party (TANU). Its top executives: the General Secretary and Deputy General Secretary became presidential appointees; in turn, the General Secretary (who was also the Minister for Labour) appointed all other key officers: nine Assistant Generals Secretaries of the industrial divisions; the Financial Secretary; and Directors of Organisation, Research and Economics. NUTA was denied the powers to dissolve itself. This power was reserved for the President of Tanzania who could, at any time, dissolve NUTA and establish another body that would be deemed to be a trade union.

NUTA was therefore a creature of and for the TANU government. Indeed, the objectives of establishing NUTA, according to its own constitution (JUWATA, 1990: 20 - 21) included the following:

+ To establish a strong workers union by having only one trade union for all the workers in the country
+ To bring about economic development by promoting discipline, hard-work and common sense among workers while discharging their duties
+ To take part in and spread the policies of TANU and to mobilise/encourage NUTA members to also become faithful members of TANU, and
+ To promote and protect good relations at workplace between employers and employees and between the workers.

The NUTA Act which completed the process of removing the autonomy of the trade union movement was enacted when Mr. M. Kamaliza, the former Secretary General of TFL and later its President, was the Minister for Labour. Actually, he was the architect of the incorporation bills. According to him, the above developments were a major guarantee of industrial peace and political stability necessary to attract foreign investments (Kamaliza, 1965: 204). But although strike prevention was somehow successful and by the 1970 strikes had virtually disappeared in Tanzania (see Jackson, 1979) that alone failed to attract much foreign investments, at least up to 1967, and the adoption of the policy of ujamaa/socialism and self-reliance early in February 1967 was partly due to the failure to attract foreign investment (Centre for Development Research, 1995: 9-10; Mlimuka and Kabudi, 1985: 68-69).

Having removed/destroyed trade union autonomy, the Government had to take measures aimed at rallying the support of the workers behind it. This was done through legislation and Presidential directives.

The Security of Employment Act No. 62 of 1964 (enacted after the establishment of NUTA) was, amongst other things, intended to improve industrial democracy. It required the establishment of Workers' Committees at every place of work with at least 10 union members employed. Union members themselves elected the members of the committee. But the Workers' Committees were independent of the trade union structure and were therefore different from the union branch committees.

The Workers' Committees had two main functions. Firstly, they were supposed to advise the employers on such matters as efficiency, safety and welfare arrangements for workers, work rules, redundancies, and the promotion of good relations between employees and workers. Secondly, the committees had to be consulted by the employers before they impose any punishment on the worker/s. These committees thus helped to administer the disciplinary code yet they were abolished in 1975 for being too militant. Actually, they were seen as the cause of the indiscipline in factories of the early 1970s. This was attributed to their grass-root character as well as to their relative autonomy from trade union structures. Thus, through an Act of Parliament (No. 1 of 1975) a new section (s.7A) was added to the Security of Employment Act that abolished Workers' Committees and their functions assigned to the trade union field branches.

In spite of the limitations of NUTA as a trade union, it registered certain important benefits to itself and the workers in general. Its major achievements included the following:

a) The establishment of the 'check-off' system, which is still operative, in collecting membership fees directly from employers. This solved to a large extent the financial problems within the union.

b) Security of employment started to be established through the Security of Employment Act of 1964 that abolished the system allowing employers to hire and fire/dismiss workers whenever they wanted without giving them the chance to defend themselves/challenge that decision. The Act set out a specific procedure to be followed before disciplinary measures beyond severe reprimand can be imposed.

c) The National Provident Fund (NPF) was also introduced under NUTA. Under the NPF Act (No. 34 of 1964), employers and employees are required to contribute each month 15 and 5 percent respectively of the employees' salary/wage to be accredited to the account of the employee. The money is paid to employees upon retirement, resignation or termination of employment or to relatives upon death. This Act has now been reoganised and new law passed, the National Social Security Fund Act, No. 28 of 1997.

In 1967 state tightened further its control over NUTA through yet another Act of Parliament, the Permanent Labour Tribunal Act (PLT Act) No. 41 of 1967. This Act repealed and replaced the Trade Dispute Settlement Act of 1962 but the Act did not change neither the compulsory arbitration procedure nor the definition of a trade dispute. PLT Act also established a permanent body known as the Permanent Labour Tribunal (PLT), a kind of industrial court, which was made the final arbitrator of all collective labour disputes and controller of wage increases.

The PLT Act was only a prelude to far more drastic changes involving the adoption and enforcement of a stringent income policy through the statutory PLT and Presidential Standing Committee on Parastatal Organisations (SCOPO), which was also set up in 1967 with, among other functions, to examine/determine the salaries and conditions of service of parastatal employees (Hazlewood, 1989: 40). The Government also adopted a strategy that limited increases of pay to a maximum of five percent per annum (Jackson, 1979: 231). These arrangements severely constrained/curtailed the freedom of collective bargaining. Indeed, as further noted by Jackson (1979: 232-33), in the event of a negotiated wage agreement, the Labour Commissioner had to submit a report to the Minister for Labour that set fourth the following particulars:

a) The rate of wages payable prior to the agreement;
b) The date of the last revision of wages;
c) The increase in labour costs if the agreement was enforced;
d) The expected rise in labour productivity in the trade/industry affected;
e) The possibility of ensuing redundancy in employment;
f) The effect on the price of the product concerned; and
g) Whether the agreement, if enforced, was likely to affect any planned expansion in the trade/industry concerned.

The Minister had to transmit the agreement, the above report and his/her own other comments, if any, to the PLT for its consideration. But the Tribunal was

30

CHAPTER TWO

required to take into consideration the Governments' income policy as well as directives from the President.

In the case of Zanzibar (which united with Tanganyika to form the United Republic of Tanzania on 26 April 1964), the ZPFL was replaced by the Federation of Revolutionary Trade Unions (FRTU) soon after the January 1964 revolution which brought ASP to power. FRTU was formed and controlled by ASP, which was the ruling political party in Zanzibar. FRT was dissolved in 1966 and its activities were taken over by the Workers Department of ASP, and from 1966 up to 1979 there were no trade unions in Zanzibar.

Although in 1965 Tanzania was officially declared a one political party state, there were two political parties TANU (for the Mainland/Tanganyika) and ASP for Zanzibar. Constitutional amendments of 1977 led to the merger of TANU and Afro-Shiraz to form one political party (Chama cha Mapinduzi - CCM) for the United Republic of Tanzania in 1977.

CCM came with the policy of Party Supremacy, meaning that the Party was above the Government and the latter had to receive orders/directives from the former. Thus, the Party became very powerful and nearly all leaders of public institutions (village governments, schools, hospitals, public enterprises, etc.) were/ had to be CCM members. As for the armed forces, all of its employees had to be members of TANU, now CCM as from 1964 following the army mutiny. In short, the Party and its government abhorred any organised opposition. Thus, in the same year (1977) the people's mass organisations were brought under CCM's control and leadership. That is they were made CCM's mass organisations and had no separate constitutions of their own except that of CCM. These included: NUTA, Union of Women in Tanzania (UWT), Co-operative Union of Tanzania (USHIRIKA), Tanzania Parents Association (WAZAZI) and VIJANA (National Youth Association).

The above political changes stirred the need for having a trade union that would cater for the entire republic. So in 1979, an Act of Parliament was passed to repeal the NUTA Act and replace it with the Jumuiya ya Wafanyakazi wa Tanzania (JUWATA) Act. The Act disestablished NUTA and established JUWATA as the sole trade union for the entire republic. JUWATA also became one of the CCM's mass organisations which dealt with workers. The objectives of JUWATA were similar to those of NUTA. The only differences were that JUWATA extended to cover Zanzibar, which was initially not covered by NUTA and NUTA had its own constitution while JUWATA operated under CCM's constitution. The General Secretary of JUWATA and his/her two Deputies (one for the Mainland and the second for Zanzibar) were appointees of the Party Chairperson (who was also the President of Tanzania) while all of its' chief regional and district executives had to be screened and appointed by the National Executive Committee of CCM. The tradition of appointing the Minister for Labour to be also the General Secretary of the trade union continued. Thus, the first General Secretary of JUWATA was also the Minister for Labour. Consequently, the so called workers union was actually a department of the ruling party (Chambua, 1997: 290). Going back to the issue of industrial conflicts, there is need to point out that after the establishment of PLT in 1967, the system for resolving labour disputes was divided into two phases. Phase one (conciliation by the trade union) was governed by the NUTA Act and later by the JUWATA Act while phase two operated under the PLT Act.

Conciliation by JUWATA

According to rule 53 of the JUWATA Act, any dispute between JUWATA members or between a JUWATA member and an employer has to be reported to the respective JUWATA field branch for conciliation. If it fails to do so it had to refer the dispute to the union's District Secretary (with a full report of the steps it took) for settlement. Failure to reach a settlement she/he was required to refer the matter to the JUWATA Regional Secretary for another attempt to settle the dispute. If at this stage the dispute remain unresolved, it is referred to the union's General Secretary who would also make yet another attempt to resolve the dispute, and upon failure report the dispute to the Labour Commissioner. The disputing workers were prohibited by rule 53(d) not only from undertaking a strike action or lock-out but also from threatening to do so until the above procedure has been exhausted and the Executive Committee of the Central Committee of the whole union has authorised such action. Ironically, the same rule also prohibited the Committee from authorising any strike or lockout in any dispute until the procedure established by the law (i.e. the PLT Act) has been fully exhausted, and the workers have through a secret ballot approved the strike. Since this procedure included reference of the dispute to the PLT, and as every award of the PLT was final and binding on both parties, it follows therefore that strikes and lockouts were, in effect, banned altogether.

Settlement Under the PLT Act

The PLT Act provided for two main procedures of dispute settlement found in sections 4 and 9. Under section 4(1), any trade dispute, if not otherwise settled could be reported to the Labour Commissioner by either the employer or a registered union representing its own members involved in the dispute. After going through the report, the Commissioner had to appoint a conciliator to resolve the dispute. However, if he/she was of the opinion that machinery for settlement exists in the trade/industry involved the Commissioner may remit it to the parties for negotiation and settlement (section 4(2)). Otherwise, the Commissioner had to inform the Minister for Labour who could establish a settlement procedure and refer the dispute to it (section 4(3).

   If the conciliator succeeded in settling the dispute, a negotiated agreement ensues. But such agreement still had to be referred to the PLT for registration as a binding award and those not registered by it had no legal effect. However, section 22(e) of the PLT Act, required PLT to first scrutinise and where necessary modify the contents of any such agreement or settlement before registering it to ensure that it conformed with the government's income policy or guidelines. The guidelines or principles guiding the PLT included:

* The need to maintain a high level of domestic capital accumulation and expand employment opportunities;
* Providing incentives for increasing labour productivity such as payment-by-result schemes;
* Preserving and promoting the competitive position of locally produced products in the domestic as well as in other markets;
* Maintaining reasonable differentials in rewards between different categories of skill and levels of responsibility;
* Maintaining a favourable balance of trade/payments for the United Republic of Tanzania; and
* The need to ensure the continued ability for the Government to finance both development and recurrent expenditure in the public sector (see also Rutinwa, 1975: 14; and Kapinga, 1985: 92).

In the case of the conciliator failing to reach a settlement, the Labour Commissioner had to transmit the dispute to the Minister for Labour. The Minister, in turn, had to refer the matter to the PLT for final and binding settlement. Every settlement/award, whether arrived at through a negotiated agreement or by the decision of PLT, was final. It was not subject to challenge, review or questioning in any court of law except for lack of jurisdiction (s.27(1)). Section 9A empowers the Labour Commissioner to inquire into the causes of any trade dispute, and with the approval of the Minister, refer it to the PLT. The PLT in its part simply inquired into the matter and recommended to the Minister terms of settlement. The Minister made the final decision and sent the terms of settlement to the PLT for registration, whereupon it became final.

From our discussion so far, it is obvious that the procedures were and still are complex, effectively controlled by the state, and they left no room for any industrial action (strikes or lock-outs) on the part of disputing employees/workers. The obligations imposed on workers and on the trade union by both the income policy and the PLT had significant socio-economic effects, which are discussed in the next section.

EFFECTS OF POST-INDEPENDENCE INDUSTRIAL RELATIONS

The main goals of the post-independence industrial relations system were to prevent strikes, to improve economic efficiency and address workers' rights and legitimate interests and achievement of rapid economic development. The strategies employed to achieve these goals included state/ruling political party control of the union, complex dispute settlement procedures that actually outlawed strikes and adoption of an income policy which undermined collective bargaining as the mechanism for fixing wages and other benefits to workers. The mechanisms for fixing wages and other benefits to workers were governed by SCOPO directives and the statutory PLT, which was also required to follow directives from the President. Various effects of this system emerged.

One, after the formation of NUTA in 1964 the number of strikes drooped significantly from 235 (in 1962 and 1963 inclusive) to only 24 in 1964 to 13 in 1965 and 16 in 1966. Again after the introduction of the PLT Act in 1967 there was a marked and progressive decline of strikes as shown by Jackson (1979: 220). These strikes were however unconstitutional as they were not only opposed by the state controlled trade union but also their execution did not follow the dispute settlement procedures as provided for by law.

Two, the legal prevention of strikes made workers in Tanzania to engage in other forms of protest such as indiscipline, destruction of property and negligence (Rutinwa, 1975: 20).

Three, the strategy of undermining collective bargaining created a situation whereby workers expected salary/wage increases to be announced by the government, usually during the President's May Day speeches, which he used to announce minimum wage increases. But, since the official government policy was against wage increases, the result was a drastic fall in real wages estimated at an annual rate of - 14.4% throughout the 1980s (p.20-21).

Four, the combination of one to three above resulted in a demoralized, unstable and unreliable labour force. This is definitely one of the factors behind poor economic performance in Tanzania from the mid 1970s.

Five, the absence of time-limits within which disputes had to be settled under the PLT Act led to many labour disputes taking many years before they were finally resolved. Because most of these disputes arose out of redundancies and dismissal, the costs were great regardless of the outcome of the case. The costs were even much higher in those instances where the disputing employees successfully challenged their redundancy or lay-off by their employers since they had to be reinstated and to be paid all their back wages and other benefits. Many such bills were presented to the ailing public corporations that were unable to pay them and, as a result, they had to be paid by the Treasury (p.26).

De-Registration of JUWATA

In the late 1980s and early 1990s Tanzania and most of the Sub-Saharan Africa (SSA) witnessed processes of democratisation and the implementation of Structural Adjustment Programmes (SAPs). There were forces from both within and without the country that demanded that a process of democratic transition be seen through. Hand in glove with the process of democratisation was the liberalisation movement in the economic, political and social sectors, although the latter movement came only a couple of years earlier.

As a result of these new political developments in Tanzania, in the early 1990s, when the multiparty political system was allowed, JUWATA was no longer relevant to such a system. In this respect a trade union that was neutral and independent, with respect to political parties, had to be established. Thus, in 1991 the Organisation of Tanzania Trade Unions (OTTU) was formed through an Act of Parliament, No. 20 of December 1991. The Act provided for de-registration of JUWATA, repeal of the JUWATA Act, and for the establishment of OTTU.

Section 4-(1) of the Act stated categorically that 'OTTU shall be the sole trade union body representative of all employees in the United Republic' while section 5-(2) provided that 'every person who is, immediately before the effective date, a member of JUWATA, be deemed to have become... a founder member of OTTU'. Section 5-(1) opened OTTU membership to other persons in accordance with OTTU's constitution. Section 8 allowed for the formation of other trade unions by OTTU or otherwise but any trade union so formed shall not only be affiliated to OTTU but shall also be known as an 'OTTU Union;' and deemed to have been registered as such along with OTTU. This said, there is need to point out the following:

a) That unlike JUWATA, OTTU was free of direct political party control and had its own constitution;
b) All other trade unions in Tanzania had to be affiliated to OTTU; and
c) The Act made OTTU both a trade union and a federation of trade unions.

It follows therefore that the OTTU Act contravened one of the basic human rights and freedoms, the Freedom of Association as well as the ILO Convention No. 87 on freedom of association.

OTTU, as a federation of trade unions, was supposed to be composed of different industrial unions. The sectors identified were: Industries and Trade/Commerce; Mining and Construction; Communication and Transport; Railways; Agriculture; Teachers; Central Government and Hospitals; Local Government; Hotels, Residential and Allied Workers; and Institutions of Higher Learning and Research. However, the formation of these other unions had to await the formation of OTTU first whose leadership would oversee the formation of industrial unions to be affiliated to it. The process of forming OTTU unions started in 1992 and was completed in 1995. The following 11 industrial unions were formed and became OTTU affiliates:

◆ Communication and Transport Workers Union (COTWU);
◆ Conservation, Hotels, Domestic and Allied Workers Union (CHODAWU);

- Researchers, Academicians and Allied Workers Union (RAAWU);
- Tanzania Local Government Workers Union (TALGWU);
- Tanzania Mines and Construction Workers Union (TAMICO);
- Tanzania Plantation and Agricultural Workers Union (TPAWU);
- Tanzania Railways Workers Union (TRAWU);
- Tanzania Seamen Union (TASU);
- Tanzania Teachers Union (TTU);
- Tanzania Union of Government and Health Employees (TUGHE); and
- Tanzania Union of Industries and Commercial Workers (TUICO).

Elections for OTTU leadership took place in August 1995 in Dodoma. In this meeting OTTU and its 11 affiliates decided to change the name of the umbrella organization from OTTU to TFTU (Tanzania Federation of Free Trade Unions).

The registration of TFTU was, however, doubtful unless the OTTU Act was repealed. Yet, the status of OTTU as a trade union was unclear, individual persons who constituted its membership had joined the industrial unions. Its status as a federation of trade unions was also open to question since the other unions had no separate registration and their affiliation to OTTU was not by choice but by law. OTTU leaders tried without success to have separate registration of the 11 industrial unions. As a result they waged a struggle to have the OTTU Act repealed and be replaced by another Act which will provide for the registration of TFTU as well as separate registration of its affiliates. Attempts by the industrial unions to have separate registration also failed because of the same reason.

Industrial Relations after 1990

Before the adoption of a multiparty political system in Tanzania in early 1990s, the government embarked on a legislative programme to accommodate the new political and economic system. This included the deregistration of JUWATA and the establishment of OTTU as discussed above; and the established of an Industrial Court through the PLT (Amendment) Act No. 3 of 1990. The Act elevated the PLT to an Industrial Court, with powers similar to those of the High Court to be presided over by a High Court judge. In 1993 the Industrial Court (Amendment) Act (No. 2 of 1993) was enacted. The Act introduced the Category of essential services and modified the procedure for conciliation and arbitration.

The essential services listed in the Act are: water, electricity, fire, and meteorological services; Air Traffic Control and Civil Aviation; telecommunications; and, transport services necessary to the operation of the essential services listed here. Employees in these services are prohibited from taking part in strikes and lock-outs. Furthermore, the Act did not modify the procedure for settlement of industrial disputes in respect of these services.

Regarding other trade disputes, the Act set time limits within which a dispute has to be dealt with at each stage. The new procedure is as follows:

a) Any trade dispute arising at any place of work, whether existing or apprehended, must first be reported by a trade union member to the union branch at place of work within seven days of its occurrence, and the union in turn must report it to the District Labour officer within 14 days. Where there is no union branch, then it has to be reported to the District Secretary of a registered union within 14 days. An employee who is not a trade union member is required to report the matter directly to the District Labour Officer.

b) After reporting the dispute to the District Labour Officer he/she or any labour officer appointed by the Labour Commissioner has to attempt to conciliate the dispute and effect a settlement within 21 days. The settlement has to be recorded in writing and after its endorsement by the Commissioner is referred to as a negotiated agreement. If the District Labour Officer or the Labour Officer appointed by the Commissioner fails to settle the dispute, he/she has to report in writing to the Commissioner within 21 days of receiving the dispute. The Commissioner or her/his appointee has, within 21 days, to transmit the matter (and any comments) to the Industrial Court which has to consider the dispute and make a binding arbitration on the parties as an award of the Court.

c) The Labour Commissioner also has to transmit every negotiated agreement, together with a report and any comments therein, to the Industrial Court for registration.

d) The Industrial Court also has to consider the entire case and examine whether the negotiated agreement is in compatible with the government's wage/income policy before it registers it. The agreement becomes operative only after being duly registered by the Court.

The Amendment Act also gives room for industrial action in the course of dispute settlement if certain conditions are fulfilled. That is, an employer may take part in a lock-out and an employee may take part in a strike if the prescribed time at any stage elapsed since the dispute is reported and (a) there has been no attempt to settle it, (b) it has not been reported/referred to the next stage and/or (c) the Industrial Court made an award but no step was taken, within 14 days, to comply with the Court's award and the Court has not taken action. Even so, for any industrial action to become lawful, a secret ballot under the supervision of the Labour officer must be held and at least two thirds of all the disputing employees must vote for it.

From our discussion so far, one may note that although the new legislation has modified the dispute settlement procedures, they are still complex and lengthy. The new trade union Act, to which we now turn, does not address or did not change the dispute handling procedures.

THE 1998 TRADE UNION ACT AND DE-REGISTRATION OF OTTU

In November 1998 the Parliament enacted the new Trade Unions Act No.10 of 1998. This Act, among other things, repealed the Trade Unions Ordinance Act as well as the OTTU Act (No.20 of 1991). Unlike the previous enactment, the 1998 Trade Unions Act did not establish any trade unions or a federation of trade unions. Instead, its provisions provide for freedom of association and both workers and employers are free to organise and establish trade unions of their own choice and draw their constitutions, rules and elect their leaders.

Highlights of the 1998 Trade Union Act

The new Trade Union Act No.10 of 1998 (which came into operation on 1st July 2000) contains provisions covering the establishment of the Registrar of Trade Unions including modalities of registration of trade unions and powers of the Registrar; provisions which provide for procedures for registering trade unions and appeal procedures by aggrieved parties; and for the formation of trade union federation/s and consultative bodies of trade unions, rights and liabilities, prohibitions and cancellation of registration.

The Act authorizes the Minister for labour matters to appoint a Registrar and Deputy Registrar of Trade Unions to be responsible for the due performance of the duties and functions assigned to them under the Act. The Minister is also authorized to appoint other officers who may, from time to time, be required for the purposes of the Act [Sec- 3-(1) and 3-(4)].

Every trade union established after the commencement of this Act should be registered with the Registrar in order to acquire legal status of identity within one month from the date in which it is so established [Sec. 7-(2)]. Also, every trade union registered or deemed to have been registered as a trade union before the coming into operation of this Act, shall either apply to be registered as a trade union or be dissolved within a period of three months from the commencement of the Act or the date of its formation, whichever is the later [Sec. 7-(1)]. However, the Registrar has powers to grant an extension of the periods specified in subsections 7-(1) and 7-(2) for any further period/s not exceeding six months in the aggregate.

Where several registered unions exist in a particular establishment, trade, occupation or industry as the case may be, the Registrar may, if s/he is satisfied that it is in the best interest of the employees concerned so to do, cancel the certificate of registration of the union/s other than the one which has the largest number of employees as its members [Sec. 15-(2)].

Two or more trade unions may form/create a federation of trade unions if: (a) the consent of members of each of the unions wishing to form a federation is obtained by a majority of votes taken at a general meeting or a meeting of delegates; and (b) prior to the meeting mentioned above [i.e. in (a)], a not less than three months notice of the proposed resolution to participate in the federation is served upon both the Registrar and all the members of the unions concerned [Sec. 22-(1)].

Furthermore, any registered union under the Act may affiliate with, or be a member of, any consultative bodies registered within or outside Tanzania. Also, according to this Act, unless context requires otherwise:

> 'Federation' means any combination or association of two or more trade unions which has a separate legal existence from the trade unions of which it is comprised; and 'Trade union' means any combination, either temporary or permanent of twenty or more employees or of four or more employers, the principal purposes of which are under its constitution the regulation of relations between employees and employers, or between employees and employees or between employers and employers whether that combination would not, if this Act had not been enacted be deemed enacted, and be deemed to have an unlawful combination by reason of some one or more of its purposes being restraint of trade and includes a federation [Trade Union Act, 1998: s. 2 (1)].

The Act also gives a lot of powers to the Registrar. These include the power to:

- Refuse to register any trade union and to cancel and/or to withdraw the certificate of registration of any union if s/he is satisfied that it has not complied with or conflicts with any provisions of the Act, or for other reasons elaborated under sections 14 and 15 of the Act.
- Order the suspension of a Trade Union branch, after consultation with the union concerned, if s/he is satisfied that it has contravened the provisions of the Act or the rules of the union [Sec. 20-(1)].
- Suspend, by order published in the Gazette, for a period not exceeding six months (after consultation with a trade union or federation), any union or any class or description of trade unions which in his/her opinion is, or is being, used for purposes prejudicial to or incompatible with the interests of the security of the United Republic of Tanzania or any part of URT [Sec. 21-91). Even so, Sec. 21-(2) empowers the Minister for Labour, if in his/her opinion the exigencies of the situation require, may bring any order made under Sec. 20-(1) into force immediately after its being made, after publishing it in any manner s/he thinks fit, even before its publication in the Gazette.
- Control the funds/finance of trade unions [Sections 65 - 73] as well as, by order in writing, s/he may suspend from office either indefinitely or for a specified period of time the officers of the union or federation or any of them named in the order if s/he is satisfied that: the funds of a union or federation have been or are being expended in an unlawful manner or on an unlawful object or on an object not authorized by the Act; or the accounts of a trade union or federation are not being kept in accordance with the provisions of the Act [Sec. 72-(1)].

It is obvious from our discussion that although the new 1998 trade union law provides for both employers and workers to organize and establish trade unions of their own choice, the Government through the Registrar of Trade Unions and the Minister for Labour still has a lot of control over the unions to be formed and registered after 1st July 2000. In addition to this, the Act does not cover Zanzibar since labour issues are not union matters. Thus, Zanzibar is currently working towards enactment of its own new trade union Act.

The coming into effect of the new trade union Act on the 1st of July 2000 made the trade union situation unclear. What is certain is that OTTU and thence TFTU have been dissolved by this Act. Even so, by December 2000, 12 trade unions had been registered under the new Trade Union Act. These are the 11 industrial unions that existed before the coming into effect of the new Act (with their former names) and one completely new union, the Fishing Crew and Allied Workers Union (FICAWU) which was formed after the split of TASU into two unions: TASU and FICAWU.

Three new unions applied for registration but were yet to be registered because they have not yet completed all the requirements as provided in the new Trade Union Act. These are:

+ Tanzania Social Industry Workers Union (TASIWU);
+ Industrial and General Workers Union of Tanzania (IGWUTA; and
+ Tanzania Union of Journalists (TUJ).

The 11 trade unions that were formally affiliated to TFTU formed a new federation, the Trade Union Congress of Tanzania (TUCTA), on 29th April 2001. Ms. M. Sitta (President of TTU) was elected President while Mr. N. Ngulla (General Secretary of RAAWU) was elected to be the Secretary General of TUCTA.

The 1998 Trade Union Act and Challenges Ahead

As pointed out earlier on, the new 1998 Trade Union Act, which de-registered OTTU came into operation on July 1st, 2000. The challenges that this Act imposes on the trade union movement are many. They include the following.

First, although the Act provides for freedom of association, it nevertheless gives a lot of powers to the Registrar and the Minister for labour to effectively control the unions to be registered. The new Trade Unions will have to fight for review of the Act to reduce some of these powers.

Second, according to the Act, 20 or more employees can form and register as a trade union and in one workplace it is possible to have several unions. This being the case, it is quite possible that a multitude of trade/craft unions will be formed. This might not be in the best interests of the workers since it will lead to weak unions both financially and otherwise. Trade unionists in the country have the challenge of making sure that such a situation does not arise.

Third, two or more unions can form a federation. Thus, it is quite possible that many trade union centres or federations may be formed which may weaken the trade union movement as a whole and erode trade union unity and solidarity. The challenge before the new unions is thence how to maintain unity and solidarity under the present situation. This, in my opinion can best be achieved if the unions will opt for having only one centre or federation.

3

THE HISTORY OF WORKERS' PARTICIPATION IN TANZANIA

OFFICIAL ADOPTION OF WORKERS' PARTICIPATION

Workers' participation as practiced in Tanzania today, has its origins in the Presidential Circular No.1 of 1970. The entire programme of participation, as set out in this directive, was intended to involve workers in the management of the enterprises that employed them. It was a conscious move imposed from above to contain the new challenges and expectations that developed after the attainment of political independence, particularly following the adoption of the policy of socialism and self-reliance (Musa, et al 1994:22). It was this policy that transformed both the political and socio-economic direction in Tanzania, and it was the same that laid the foundation for workers' participation (see Mapolu, 1976; Besha, 1982).

However, some forms of workers' participation did exist even prior to the issuing of the Presidential Circular, the principal one being through Workers' Committees. Thus, we first discuss, albeit briefly, the history of these Committees.

History of Workers' Committees in Tanzania

Following the industrial unrest after the general strike of 1947, the colonial government in Tanganyika took some measures aimed at containing industrial unrest. This included the establishment of a statutory machinery for fixing minimum wages and terms and conditions of employment under the Regulations of Wages and Terms of Employment Ordinance of 1951. This Ordinance was introduced not only to substitute collective bargaining but also to defeat the then growing trade union strength and pressure. Thus, the minimum wage bill of 1951 contained provisions for setting up of workers' or staff committees in every industry and would be involved in the negotiations for wages and terms of employment at factory level. This set-up as stated by the Labour Commissioner had three main objectives (Mihyo, 1983: 81):

+ To give employees a wide interest and a greater responsibility for the conditions under which their duties are performed;
+ To provide a recognised and direct channel of communication between employees and employers on all matters affecting their joint and several interests; and
+ To promote throughout the undertaking a spirit of cooperation in securing the efficiency of the undertaking and the contentment of staff.

To enforce the formation of workers' committees, a circular, which required the formation of such committees, was issued to all heads of departments, companies and all incorporated bodies in 1953. As a result of this circular the number of workers' or staff committees shot up from 11 in 1952 to 80 at the end of 1956, involving 35,000 workers. From 1952 to 1955 workers' committees formed an important organ in the collective bargaining machinery and for sometime managed to substitute trade unionism. But later, in 1956, when TFL was formed, it took over the collective bargaining function and through its federated unions became the chief spokes-organ of most of the employees.

After independence, workers' committees, which had been set up during the colonial period began to wane and finally became defunct by the end of 1962. However, due to industrial conflicts that occurred between 1960 and 1964, workers' committees were reintroduced (through the Security of Employment Act). They were seen as basic industrial relations units for solving industrial problems at grassroots level, thereby averting gross industrial action by workers. The Security of Employment Act of 1964, among other things, required the establishment of workers' committees at every work place with ten or more employees. Exceptions to this rule were only in armed forces, i.e. the military, the police, prison services, National Service and the then East African Common Services Organization. The workers' committees were given the following statutory functions:

+ To consult the employer on issues pertaining to the disciplinary code which, was made a schedule to this Act outlining possible offences and permissible penalties that an employer could impose for those offences;
+ To discuss with the employer from time to time means and ways of promoting efficiency;
+ To appoint an employee who would accompany the factory inspector in all factory inspections. This person was supposed to act as a watchdog of the employees by pointing out unprotected areas or machinery that were required

by the Factories Ordinance, to be protected. He would also help in explaining to the factory inspector various problems faced by the workers in the factories;

◆ To give advice to the employer on matters relating to the safety and welfare of the workers; and

◆ To investigate and report non-compliance with the wage regulations, advice employer on rules to govern the place of work, and furthering good industrial relations.

In spite of the fact that the above functions do not give the committees powers of decision-making but rather provide only an opportunity for consultation, section 6 (2) of the Security of Employment Act specified matters which the workers' committees were prevented from consulting or advising the employer. These included the following:

◆ Termination of probationary employment within one month of such employment, unless such termination is for the breach of the disciplinary code

◆ Termination of seasonal or casual employment, except when such termination is for the breach of the disciplinary code

◆ Recruitment of new staff unless such recruitment comes immediately after dismissal on grounds of redundancy

◆ Promotions and demotions, and

◆ Transfer of employees to another place under the same employer to perform work of a similar nature.

It must however be stressed that the workers' committees were established outside the trade union structure. Thus, from 1964 to 1975 there were both trade union (NUTA) field branches and workers' committees.

From 1964 to 1967, workers' committees mainly acted as checks against the arbitrary exercise of managerial power as regards discipline and the like. After 1967, however, the committees went beyond discipline. They became cell organisations for the protection of workers' rights. Indeed, they performed some functions that had not been intended let alone foreseen by the architects of the Security of Employment Act. In 1970, there were about 12 strikes in the whole country whose demands were political and not economic and which were organised by these committees. The demands were mainly for the removal of racist managers, arrogant nationals in management, equal opportunities for both management and shop/office floor workers. From 1971 to 1974 these committees also played a very significant role in drawing the attention of Tanzanian workers to issues of national importance.

Early in 1973 workers' committee were involved in factory takeovers. For example, on 29 March, 1973 under the leadership of the workers' committee, the workers at the Rubber Industries (Dar es Salaam) locked out their management officials, appointed their own managers and invited the government and the party (TANU) to recognise this take-over. Another take-over soon followed, "the Night-Watch Security Force in Dar es Salaam, took-over the premises of the force and converted them into a cooperative property with elected management. This was a second take-over which was also recognized by the government" (Mihyo, 19981: 106). These takeovers were neither staged with the consent/blessing of NUTA nor were they prepared and accomplished under the auspices of TANU. On 25 May 1973, workers at the Mount Carmel Factory in Dar es Salaam attempted to take-over their factory and drive out the management officials. It was at this juncture that workers' committees were abolished and Union Field Committees took-up their functions. This abolition was effected early in 1975 through an Act of Parliament, the Labour Laws (Miscellaneous Amendment) Act, 1975 which provided for the replacement of workers' committees with NUTA committees. This said, it is important to take note of three things here.

First, when they were formed in 1964, workers' committees were not incorporated in the trade union structure. Second, when the committees were disestablished in 1975, their successors were incorporated into the union structure, and in 1979 they also became organically entrenched within the Party structure because the then new union, JUWATA, was a mass organisation of the ruling party, CCM. Thirdly, workers' committees and their successors, the JUWATA Branch Committees were supposed to exist in every enterprise employing ten or more people (ICPE, 1981).

THE PRESIDENTIAL DIRECTIVE ON WORKERS' PARTICIPATION

In Tanzania, where from 1967 to mid 1980s, the goal was to build socialism, workers' participation was an attempt to remove unnecessary bureaucratic tendencies in the management of the peoples' institutions. Indeed, the Presidential Directive (No. 1 of 1970) on workers' participation aimed at achieving the following objectives:

a) To give the working class power, thereby solving the contradictions that existed between the management and the workers. The management and the workers (the managed) all should be seen as workers belonging to the same enterprise. "In particular the top management must have an attitude which regards the workers and the lower levels of management as partners in a common enterprise, and not just tools like the machines they work with" (Nyerere 1970, in Maseko, 1976: 234);

b) To allow workers' involvement in deciding the affairs of their lives and in the development process of their enterprise;

c) To increase efficiency in the socialised enterprises. In other words, through workers' participation the workers will increase their dedication and love for work, build up a sense of pride and satisfaction, end workers' alienation and hence increase efficiency (see Maseko, 1976:233-235).

The 1970 Presidential directive also directed that in all public corporations employing more than 10 workers, a Workers' Council, Workers' Council Executive Committee, and a Board of Directors had to be formed by the end of 1970. A description of the main features of these three bodies, according to the Circular, follows.

Workers' Council: Composition and Functions

The Workers' Council should consist of the following:

+ The Chairman of the Party Branch of the enterprise;
+ The General Manager or Manager, who in the first year of office and/or the first three-year period of the Council becomes also its Chairman, but subject to election to the chair after the first year like all other members;
+ All heads of departments or sections in the enterprise;
+ All the members of the Workers' Committee and representatives from departments or sections who are elected by the workers themselves. But to be eligible, these must be members of TANU. They were also subject to re-election after three years. The elected workers' representatives together with members of the Workers' Committee should not exceed 25 percent of the whole Workers Council;
+ Representatives from the Trade Union; and
+ Other members can be co-opted onto the Workers' Council from outside the organisation. However, their co-optation had to be determined by an agreement between the Trade Union and management.

Although the secretary of the workers' council was appointed by management, the council was empowered to regulate its own procedures for conducting its meetings.

The Workers' Council met at least every six months (twice a year). But, when necessary, emergency meetings could be called. The functions of the Workers' Council were mainly advisory to the Board of Directors on such issues as: government wages policy, marketing of goods and services, quality and quantity of the goods and products produced and services rendered. The Council was also empowered to discuss and analyse the balance sheet of the enterprise and advise on planning as a whole and on all relevant aspects of production.

Workers' Council Executive Committee: Composition and Functions

The Workers' Council Executive Committee consisted of the following members:

+ The Manager or General Manager as chairperson;
+ Heads of departments and/or heads of sections; and
+ Workers' representatives from the Workers' Council who should not exceed more than one third of the total membership of the Executive Committee.

The main function of the Executive Committee was to scrutinize the reports and proposals furnished both by the management and the workers' council on matters concerning finance, production, productivity, promotion, training programmes, marketing and the daily running of the enterprise.

The Board of Directors

The President appoints the Chairman of the Board of Directors (the Board) while the Minister of the enterprise's parent ministry, appoints the other Board members. At least one member has to be from the trade union. The main function of the Board was to establish the kind of policy the organisation should follow in accordance with the aims of the nation.

IMPLEMENTATION OF THE CIRCULAR ON WORKERS' PARTICIPATION

The initial implementation of the 1970 Presidential Circular on workers' participation was haphazard. Workers' councils were formed indiscriminately in each parastatal organisation that had a separate legal existence. As a result holding corporations and their subsidiaries had each their own councils. This led to duplication in the decision-making structure and locus of power and responsibility was greatly blurred. This forced the Prime Minister to issue a complimentary circular in December 1974 directing that workers' councils should be only established at the level of holding corporations and drawing membership from the subsidiaries. Subsidiaries were directed to form only management committees. The structure was passed as a law in 1976 through the Parastatal Organisation Act No. 16 of 1976. Under the Act, the management committees of the subsidiaries comprised of a 40 percent membership drawn from among the employees of the enterprises in question while 60 percent would be drawn from among citizens of the United Republic especially from the party (CCM), trade union (JUWATA) and research institutions nationwide. Those from outside had to be appointed by the Minister of a particular corporation's parent ministry. Even so, APADEP research in Tanzania has revealed that, to a large extent, the complimentary circular issued by the Prime Minister was ignored. That is, implementation of workers' participation in the subsidiaries of holding corporations was governed by the Presidential Directive No. 1 of 1970. (Chambua,1995; Chambua and Semkiwa, 1995).

The above regulations on workers' participation were, however, confined to public corporations and Parastatal organisations up to 1976. In 1977 the government extended the participatory process to Government Ministries and Departments. A participatory structure was instituted which required creation of sub-councils in government departments and councils in ministries. The objectives of this participatory structure were outlined as follows:

♦ To let civil servants participate in the implementation of government orders;
♦ To advise government to ensure its services are rendered in accordance with the policy of socialism and self-reliance;
♦ To advise the government on issues concerning benefits and working conditions of civil servants;
♦ To advise the government on changes on civil service regulations and orders; and
♦ To advise government on promotion procedures and discipline.

One other major attempt at the transformation of labour organisation came from the ruling party in the form of the "Party Guidelines of 1971" popularly referred to as Mwongozo. Its basic objectives were:

♦ To increase the say of peasants and workers in determining their own affairs (para. 20);
♦ To build equality among people; that is resolving the power and status of differentials between leaders and the led (para. 15); and
♦ To eliminate the attitude of bossism and the habit of relying on issuing commands, to eliminate false consciousness and instill a sense of security and responsibility among both leaders and workers.

Mwongozo came in the wake of a wave of strikes that started in 1967. Managers had considered the firms as their own personal property and that they could not be removed. This led to absence of democracy in the industries. Clause 28 of Mwongozo states:

> For a people who have been slaves or exploited by colonialism and capitalism, 'development' means 'liberation'. Any action that gives them more control of their own affairs is an action for development even if it does not offer them better health or more bread. Any action which reduces their say in determining their own affairs or running their own lives is not development and retards them even if the action brings them a little better health and a little more bread. . . . If development is to benefit the people, the people must participate in considering, planning and implementing their development plans.

In addition to this, clause 15 further states:

> There must be a deliberate effort to build equality between leaders and those they lead. For a Tanzanian leader it must be forbidden to be arrogant, extravagant, contemptuous, and oppressive. The Tanzanian leader has to be a person who respects people, scorns

ostentation and who is not a tyrant. He should epitomize heroism, bravery, and be a champion of justice and equality.

Mwongozo ignited the workers further and between 1971 and 1974 workers all over the country rose in the heroic attempt to take over not only the management but also at times, the ownership of the factories. In most, if not all cases, they quoted parts of clauses 15 and 28 to justify their actions. That is, being aware that these clauses condemned in no uncertain terms all practices involving arrogance and humiliation they:

> ... put these out first. But behind these, lay their grudge against terrible working conditions, industrial insecurity, lack of an agreement between them and the employer on wages and fringe benefits, leave allowance, sick-leave and funeral leave with pay, and so forth (Mihyo, 1981: 113).

The growing labour instability ignited by Mwongozo was not anticipated by neither the party nor the government. In fact Mwongozo, just like the Presidential circular on worker' participation, was aimed at promoting industrial peace, harmony and stability. Consequently, the state moved quickly to suppress not only the strikes but also to expel the protesting workers themselves.

The APADEP research in Tanzania shows that Mwongozo was meaningful but not very effective in furthering workers interests. In other words, the Workers' Councils played a useful advisory role and provided avenues for workers to air their grievances (Musa, 1992; Chambua and Semkiwa, 1994; Chambua, 1995). In the following sections we discuss workers participation in one enterprise, the Morogoro Canvas Mills, which in our view was typical of many state owned enterprises in Tanzania. The information provided is based on a case study conducted in 1994.

WORKERS' PARTICIPATION: THE CASE OF MOROGORO CANVAS MILLS

The specific objectives of the case study were to:

+ Gain insight into the functioning of workers' participation in the enterprise, thereby complementing information collected through other APADEP research methods;
+ Investigate or analyze the achievements and problems of workers' participation at the enterprise being studied; and
+ Provide the trade union in Tanzania (OTTU) with empirically based information on the conditions for the development of an effective and more meaningful participation of workers' and trade union representatives.

Research Methodology

The main methods of data collection were interviews using prepared questions and direct observations. The interviewees included 30 ordinary workers (both sexes); four members of the Workers' Council, four members of the Workers' Council Executive Committee (WCEC), five trade union branch committee members/representatives; and five members of the company's management. The interviews were both formal and informal. This method was supplemented by analysis of various documents, including those of the enterprise and official documents together with published and unpublished materials from both the University of Dar es Salaam Library and the Institute of Development Studies .

History of the Enterprise

Morogoro Canvas Mill (MCM) was established following a feasibility study in 1975, which was undertaken and financed by the World Bank, for the Morogoro Industrial Complex. That study's principal recommendation was that the Morogoro Industrial Complex should begin with a tannery that would process raw hides and skins into leather to be supplied to the shoe industry. Prior to the establishment of MCM, the local shoe factories either imported canvas from abroad or bought drill produced (that was not primarily produced for canvas making) by local textile mills.

Initially, the mill was under the National Development Corporation (NDC) but later Tanzania Leather Associated Industries (TLAI) took over the ownership of the company in January 1979. Thus, MCM became one of TLAI's companies and was incorporated in December 1978. The construction of the factory commenced in April 1980, and was completed in December 1983. However, delays in the supply of water and electricity led to postponement of the start of the factory for half a year. Trial test runs were carried out and completed in March 1984. Actual production (spinning and weaving) began in May while the processing and finishing commenced in June 1984 with a total workforce of 700 employees working in two shifts. In 1986 the mill started to operate with three shifts. At the beginning of 1993 the company had a total of 1,032 employees working in three shifts for six days per week.

Cotton, which is locally supplied, is the basic raw material for the manufacture of canvas. The factory normally got 50 percent of its cotton requirements from Mwanza and Shinyanga regions and another 50 percent was from within Morogoro region. Other inputs such as yarn were occasionally bought from local textile mills to supplement weaving requirements. Dyes, chemicals, auxiliaries and other finishing products were imported, as were most spares for plant and machinery, but some spare parts were made locally whenever possible. MCM has had foreign management since its inception in which M/S Hebox Holland Engineering BV, was initially entrusted with the task of managing the project. At first, Hebox seconded 15 expatriates for various management positions including those of: General Manager, Plant Manager, Electrical Engineer,

Financial Controller, Production Manager, Marketing Manager and Spinning Manager. By December 1993 the number of expatriates had been reduced to only six. The current contract expired in December 1993 but was renewed and extended (for six months) to 30 June 1994, with three expatriates to allow the smooth handover to the next management team under the Parastatal Sector Reform Programme (PSRP). PSRP was formed to deal with the selling of public institutions to private entrepreneurs or to arrange for joint ventures with the private sector. At the time of study, MCM was for sale under the privatization policy.

MCM's Performance

This section restricts itself to a discussion of production and financial performance of the company. The company has a rated installed capacity of producing 6.0 million linear metres of various types of canvas per annum which can be used for a wide range of applications such as: tarpaulins (for lorries, wagons, pick-up trucks, professional covers, grain storage covers); tents (heavy, medium, light); filter cloth; sails (heavy); mailbag; raincoats and workwear; upholstery and curtains; shoe cloth and lining; tyre cords; and other technical applications.

The company's cotton-canvases were produced in accordance with internationally recognised standards, grades and weight classes set by the American Society for Testing and Materials. The original plans were for MCM to cater mainly for the domestic market (to meet the demand for local shoe and bicycle factories and various other local customers - individuals and institutions). However, production started at a time when Tanzania faced serious economic difficulties. This resulted in first, poor performance of many local firms including the shoe and bicycle factories; and second, low purchasing power for MCM products in the domestic market.

Faced with these local market constraints, the company had to make drastic changes in the product mix. It entered the export market as early as 1985, after less than one full year of operations. Export markets were found in USA, Canada, United Kingdom, Netherlands, Germany, Italy and Saudi Arabia. With the exception of Saudi Arabia, which imported finished products from MCM, the rest of these overseas customers preferred to buy unfinished grey canvas (not dyed) and do the processing and finishing (including dying) on their own. Estimates for 1993 put exports at about 70 percent of MCM production.

The company faced stiff competition in foreign markets from other developing countries, especially India, Pakistan and Brazil. Hence, there was still the need for the company to develop a large domestic market for its products and to win local competition from imports, which have risen as a result of the trade liberalization policy adopted in July 1986.

Major local customers for heavy and medium finished canvas were: the army, prisons, medical stores, and other local converters of the products into tarpaulins, tents, and so on; while the light heavy canvas for twills, school uniforms, bed sheets, curtains and cushion materials were bought by general customers. Production and financial performance of MCM are shown in Tables 3.1 and 3.2 respectively.

Table 3.1: *Production Performance of MCM 1984 - 1992*

Year	Production ('000 L. Mts)	Capacity utilisation (%)	Sales domestic ('000 L. Mts)	Exports ('000 L. Mts.)	Exports as % Total Production
1985	2,723	45.4	2,054	464	17.0
1986	3,923	65.4	1,678	1,603	40.9
1987	4,270	71.2	1,568	2,770	64.9
1988	4,278	71.3	1,191	2,707	63.3
1989	4,885	81.4	2,669	2,266	46.4
1990	4,813	80.2	1,660	2,985	62.0
1991	3,774	62.9	1,238	2,257	59.8
1992	3,482	58.0	1,018	2,004	57.6

Source: Financial Controller, MCM.
Notes: L.Mts. = Linear Metres.

Production increased slowly from 2.0 million linear metres in 1984 to 4.885 million linear metres in 1989 before dropping gradually to 3.774 million linear metres in 1991. Exports increased from 0.5 million linear metres in 1985 to a high of 2.77 million linear metres in 1987 (representing about 65 percent of total production), thereby fluctuating in a downward trend (Table 3.1). Capacity utilisation increased annually from 33 percent in 1984 to 81 percent in 1989. Thereafter, it started to go down to 58 percent in 1992 (Table 3.1 is indicative). The financial performance is shown in Table 3.2.

Table 3.2: Financial Performance of MCM 1984 - 1992 ('000 TShs)

Year	SALES			Profit (Loss) Before Tax	Exports as (%) Total Sales+
	Domestic	Exports	Total+		
1985	158,965	10,973	169,938	7,350	6.50
1986	237,689	89,909	327,598	1,496	27.4
1987	317,336	298,494	615,830	2,801	48.5
1988	414,708	477,951	892,659	2,104	53.5
1989	874,918	539,545	1,414,463	8,352	38.1
1990	726,574	1,076,561	1,803,135	18,400	59.7
1991	759,372	877,121	1,636,493	(50,008)	53.6
1992*	722,069	967,250	1,689,319	(186,742)	57.3

Source: Financial Controller, MCM
Notes: (i) + Figures calculated by the author
        (ii) * Figures as per Draft Accounts.

Working Conditions and Problems Faced by MCM Workers

The terms and conditions of work and employment in the enterprise (MCM) were governed by the employment regulations laid down by the Presidential Standing Committee on Parastatal Organisations (SCOPO). Although SCOPO was dissolved in early 1993, many parastatals continued to apply the terms and regulations as laid down by SCOPO.

Salaries and Wages

All the respondents complained that the wages and salaries were low. For the majority of them, the monthly wage/salary could not meet the monthly requirements of the worker, let alone his/her whole household. In order to ease this problem, the management decided to pay workers (as from 1990) a non-refundable salary advance of 50 percent of the employee's monthly salary at the middle of every month. Workers were happy with this arrangement. Also the workers, on request, were given reject products and materials and many sold them to augment their income.

Job Security

All the employees interviewed were permanent workers, therefore, their employment was secured by the Security of Employment Act of 1964 and other terms and conditions set by SCOPO. Furthermore, employees who were/are involved in accidents and suffer(ed) losses while on duty were/are compensated. Indeed, the majority of workers at MCM were content with their job security.

Medical Welfare

The enterprise provided medical services to all its employees from its own dispensary on the premises. Only serious cases were referred to the regional hospital for further treatment, the cost was met or paid for by the company. All the respondents were happy with those arrangements. However, some respondents (11, or 37 percent of those interviewed) complained that the dispensary lacked some of the important basic medical equipment. This lack of adequate medical equipment prevented proper treatment at an early stage of a disease.

Transport

The company provided its workers with transport services to and from the factory. However, this service was not reliable because most of the vehicles were worn out and in unreliable operating condition.

Food Provision

The canteen on the company premises provided an important service of giving workers a reliable lunch. However, many workers interviewed claimed that the food served in their canteen was not well prepared. Although some of them showed some satisfaction with the quantity of the food, but not the quality, few of them (5, or 17 percent) were not happy at all.

Recreation and Entertainment

Formerly, the company had both football and netball teams but they were abandoned due to the company's financial constraints. Unfortunately, this was at a time when the teams were progressing well. For example, in 1990 the netball team's initial rounds of victory led it to join the final games in Arusha. However, the team was abandoned before the final games, thus preventing the team from participating.

Workers' Participation at MCM

MCM, being a public enterprise, introduced workers' participation when it was formed in 1984, despite being under foreign management. We now discuss the objectives of workers' participation at MCM as they have been implemented.

Objectives

The 1970 Presidential Circular gives three underlying principles of workers' participation in the management of public enterprises in Tanzania. These are: to provide a proper work environment so that the majority of workers can become more creative and hence, produce more; to treat workers as the very purpose of production and not as just 'factors of production;' and, to incorporate workers in decision-making so as to bring about industrial discipline and harmony as workers will know fully why and how production is carried out (Mapolu 1972).

The objectives of workers' participation at MCM are in line with these principles; that is, to bring the workers close to the management of the enterprise and to promote better industrial relations by giving workers some say in the formulation of company policies through their involvement in decision-making. However, when it came to the issue of the importance of workers' participation, there was still a divergence of views on the part of MCM management. The majority of management officials (managers and heads of department) interviewed were of the opinion that workers' participation was both necessary and beneficial to the enterprise because:

a) Workers' grievances are accommodated through it and management could effectively use these participatory structures to solicit a common understanding between management and workers for the smooth running of the enterprise;

b) When workers are involved in decision-making they become aware of the challenges (as well as prospects) facing the enterprise. This awareness would enable them to make reasonable demands;

c) Increasing labour productivity needs a better working environment, which could be attained through workers' participation.

Seen in the light of the foregoing, workers' participation is an essential element by which management can realise increased profit. For example, in 1988 workers were able to advise the management to confront the relevant authority to solve the problem of purchasing cotton from far away Dar es Salaam instead of off-loading the cotton at Morogoro Railway Station on the shipment's way to Dar es Salaam, thereby making huge savings. This is but one example of the benefits of workers' participation and it shows that, given the chance, ordinary workers can contribute to productivity other than through their labour.

Two other managers believed that workers' participation at the enterprise was not very effective and therefore a waste of time. They argued that shop-floor workers were not in the position to contribute viable ideas for the betterment of the company. Many issues discussed in the Board of Directors (hereinafter referred to as the Board), or other participatory structures, need professional skills (which ordinary workers lacked) to be able to participate effectively. Since these are administrative and technical issues, they should be entrusted to management as the only body capable of making sound decisions. According to this view, managers are professionals, knowledgeable in their field; therefore, there should be no interference in their work of considering matters and deciding what to do for the benefit and prosperity of the company.

To the majority of ordinary workers, workers' participation is vital. Although the majority of the respondents could not clearly explain what workers' participation means, they were able to say at least something about the objectives of workers' participation, thereby implicitly explaining the meaning of workers' participation as:

a) The attendance of workers at meetings in which they are given a chance to air their views and be listened to by management; and
b) The opportunity provided to workers to join workers' organisations and elect their representatives to various participatory structures.

These were considered indicators of workers' participation. The importance of workers' participation was seen in the same light as by management; that is, to increase productivity, harmonize industrial relations and to create a forum whereby workers' grievances can be heard and acted upon. Another importance of workers' participation mentioned by the respondents is to defend workers' rights and interests against those of the employer.

Similar views were also held by the majority of workers' representatives: the departmental representatives and OTTU Branch Committee members. However, some of them were able to point out the weaknesses of workers' participation as was then being practiced at MCM. By then, workers' participation was not effective, they argued, because the management was not legally bound to create participatory structures and adhere to the agreed regulations and procedures. Instead, management paid only lip service to the participatory structures. For example, in many cases the management called workers' council meetings merely to inform workers what has already been decided, rather than to hold a real discussion over an issue that required discussion. Real workers' participation, it was argued, should be considered at all levels of the enterprise so that workers are empowered to discuss issues, make decisions and suggestions to higher participatory structures without interference from the management. Workers' participation should involve workers at the shop-floor level to plan for their sections, departments and finally at the enterprise level. Sections and departments must be the source of information for Workers Council meetings and not otherwise. Such a practice would eventually facilitate the attainment of the organizational goal of reaching maximum efficiency.

This said, we now turn to discuss the composition and functioning of four participatory structures established at the enterprise: the Workers' Council; the Workers' Council Executive Committee (WCEC); the General Assembly; and, the Board.

COMPOSITION AND FUNCTIONING OF THE PARTICIPATORY STRUCTURES AT MCM

The Workers' Council

The Workers' Council was composed of two types of membership: membership by virtue of one's position (General Manager, heads of department and OTTU Branch Committee members), and membership by election or appointment. Each department elected one representative and the OTTU regional office appointed one representative. Membership lasted for a three-year period, continuity being subject to re-election or re-appointment. The following was the composition of the Workers' Council at MCM:

Membership by Virtue of Position

a) Management team (8 members): the General Manager, Financial Controller, Production Manager, Technical Manager, Plant Engineer, Manpower Development & Administrative Manager, Marketing Manager, and the Materials Manager.
(b) 20 OTTU Branch Committee members.

Elected and Appointed Members

Seven workers' representatives one from each department and one appointed member from OTTU regional office.

Workers' Council at MCM had a total membership of 34 (at the time of the study only two of them were women). Two members represented their fellow workers in their departments and were at the same time members of OTTU Branch Committee. The Chairman of the Council had always been the General Manager. During the first year this was by virtue of his position, and thereafter by election. The functions of the Workers' Council included the following:

a) To discuss work plans and how best to implement them;
b) To discuss income and expenditure statements of the company;
c) To discuss manpower development programmes in the company (education and training);
d) To discuss labour motivation and the best ways to implement the wages policy;
e) To receive and discuss the company's balance sheet; and
f) To advise the management and the Board accordingly.

During its first meeting, normally held at the beginning of each production year, the Council discusses and recommends for further action the company's budget plan to the Board. The second meeting, which was held at the end of that year, reviewed and evaluated the performance of the company in line with the approved budget.

The Chairman of the Workers' Council was, as discussed earlier, the General Manager, elected by Council members. Although there was no formal agreement that the General Manager should be the Chairman, it had always been so in practice. The expectation was that if the General Manager is the chairperson, then Council decisions would be binding. It is the Chairman who initiates discussions in the meeting and who can stop any member who prolongs discussions unnecessarily or dwells on irrelevant issues.

The agenda for Workers' Council meetings was prepared by the General Manager and/or the WCEC, whose chairperson was also the General Manager. Therefore, it is management who determine what is to be discussed in the workers' council.

The status of workers' council meetings was only advisory to the Board and management. Decisions were reached by consensus. The atmosphere of these meetings was normally friendly except when it came to disciplinary issues. There was no formal method of ensuring that workers in the company had access to information on issues discussed in this participatory forum. The majority got information by word of mouth from friends who happened to be members of the council. Rarely was information communicated through notice boards or departmental meetings. Moreover, members of the workers' council normally received information only one day before the meeting, contrary to the laid down procedure by which such information was supposed to be given at least two weeks before the workers' council meeting.

The Workers' Council Executive Committee (WCEC)

The WCEC is meant to improve the efficiency and effectiveness of the workers' council. The WCEC is required to prepare and digest information to facilitate discussions in the workers' council. The WCEC at MCM was made up of the following 12 members:

* General Manager (1);
* Heads of department or heads of section (7);
* Elected worker representatives (3); and
* Chairman of the OTTU Branch Committee (1).

This composition was in line with the 1970 Presidential Circular on workers' participation.

The WCEC was dominated by the management who comprised of about 67 percent of the total membership, while workers' representatives were a mere 33 percent. The functions of the WCEC were:

* To review income and expenditure plans as prepared by management before being discussed in workers' council;
* To review work plans, education and skills training programmes as prepared by management and the OTTU Branch Committee before they are discussed in the Workers' Council;
* To advise on daily work performance;
* To advise management on policy issues proposed by the Workers' Council before they are sent to the Board for approval, adoption or rejection;
* To advise on better ways of motivating workers to increase productivity;
* To approve the agenda for the Workers' Council meeting; and
* To make a follow-up of issues resolved in the Workers' Council.

Departmental Meetings

Heads of department were encouraged to hold departmental meetings. These meetings were chaired by the heads of department and attended by heads of section and supervisors. Ordinary workers were not represented in the departmental meetings. The main objective of these meetings was to discuss, among other issues, the progress of work and issues related to both production problems and workers' welfare at the departmental level. They were to advise management and were held according to the will of the head of each department. Therefore, while some departments held meetings monthly, others did not. They instead preferred to accommodate workers' views and opinions through consultation at any given time, to lodge grievances or consider feelings without necessarily following a bureaucratic hierarchical procedure. In such cases, one manager argued, management comes closer to the workers than by convening a meeting, which does not include all workers or their representatives.

The General Assembly

The General Assembly was held twice a year. This was the only participatory forum which brought together the management, OTTU Branch Committee members and workers to discuss the problems and achievements of the company. General Assembly meetings are chaired by the General Manager. In most cases they are informative and decisive, especially on matters concerning workers' welfare that fall within the competence of the management. Those issues that cannot be immediately solved by management were forwarded to the Board for a final decision.

Board of Directors

Based on Presidential Circular No.1 of 1970, Clause 18, an agreement was made between OTTU Headquarters and MCM management to provide for workers' participation on the Board. This was the highest participatory forum in the company, enjoying final authority. It is endowed with powers to make decisions binding throughout the company, even on management. Therefore, the endeavor to bring workers close to management should ensure that workers are represented in this body. Nevertheless, there was no worker representative on the Board. All the directors represented the interests of the shareholder, the Government. There was not a single director on the Board who was a worker representative from the enterprise. This was despite the insistence by OTTU to have at least one worker representative who could have defended the interests of the workers.

The Board was, by then, composed of eight directors: the Chairman who was appointed by the President and seven others who were appointed by the Minister of Industries and Trade for a three year term. Management was represented on the Board by the General Manager (who also served as the Secretary), Financial Controller, Manpower and Administrative Manager and the Technical Manager. These were not directors themselves but they participated in the discussions and were able to defend the interests of management. Workers did not attend Board meetings, not even as invited observers. Their interests were defended by a representative from OTTU Headquarters (who was based in Dar es Salaam). Minutes of Board meetings were confidential.

The Board met quarterly. The first three meetings mainly reviewed the performance of the company. The last meeting discussed mainly the budget plan of the company for the next year. Management prepared all relevant documents and information for the Board meetings. It was at the first and last meeting of the Board that the minutes of the workers' council meetings are discussed and final rulings are issued where appropriate.

The Chairman of the Board normally initiates the discussions. After the normal business of adopting the agenda and confirmation of previous minutes, the Chairman invited the Secretary (the General Manager) to present the report of the management on the financial performance of the company and on other issues. Directors and other invited or attending members (the three heads of major departments) were then given an opportunity to discuss and contribute to the tabled agenda items. The invited members could participate in the discussions but they were not allowed to vote whenever there was a need to do so. Otherwise, many decisions were reached by consensus. Not only had the Chairman a casting vote but she/he also had the power of veto, although this had never been used in the friendly atmosphere of the meetings. In a few cases, however, the Board refers final authority to the Government through TLAI.

The meetings of the Board were conducted in strict confidence so that workers had no access to the Board proceedings, the only forum with final authority in making organisational policy. It is the only body that made strategic decisions to be followed by the management in order to realise organisational goals. Only a few Board decisions, and in most cases those related to workers' welfare, were to be disclosed by the General Manager during a General Assembly or in Workers' Council meetings.

EVALUATION OF THE WORKER'S PARTICIPATION STRUCTURES

Our earlier discussions on the structure of the participatory forums indicated that employees in MCM had access to five participatory forums. These were the workers' council, WCEC, departmental meetings, general assembly and Board meetings. The mere existence of participatory forums where workers themselves could attend or be represented is indicative of the existence of workers' participation, even if workers or their representatives had little opportunity to influence decisions. Nevertheless, what is apparent from our discussion so far is that the participatory forums have inherent limitations for the full realisation of effective workers' participation.

First, the Workers' Council could only make recommendations to the management and the Board, given the advisory status accorded it. It could not make final decisions. To make it more meaningful and effective as a participatory forum, it should be given the power to make final decisions on issues that do not require the formal approval of the Board. After all, there was nothing to fear as the General Manager and all heads of departments were members of the workers' council.

The functions of the workers' council, as outlined above, indicate clearly the importance of the Council for the realisation of effective workers' participation. The fact that Workers' Council meetings preceded the Board's meetings is also an indicator of the importance attached to the workers' council. Yet, it was not democratic in that only about 21 percent of the membership was elected workers' representatives and it met only twice a year. However, if you include the 20 (including two who were also elected workers' representatives) OTTU Branch

Committee members, then the Workers' Council was dominated by representatives of the workforce. The General Manager and/or the WCEC (whose Chairman was also the General Manager) prepared the agenda for Workers' Council meetings. It was therefore the management who determined what was to be discussed in the workers' council.

Late receipt of information was a hindrance to the effective participation of workers' representatives. The practice of giving information to workers' representatives only one day before the meeting had two main but related limitations. One, there was no enough time to digest the issues to be discussed and thus participate effectively. Two, there was hardly any time for workers' representatives to consult other workers on what was to be discussed at the workers' council meeting.

Those members of the workers' council who come from the management side went into the meeting with full information, and presumably a prior stand on the matters to be discussed and decided upon, while the workers' representatives lacked all of this.

Another serious setback to the functioning of workers' council as a participatory forum was that, in practice, its members did not go through the minutes of the workers' council meetings and approve them before they were sent to the Board. The Chairman approved them on their behalf. Given the fact that the minutes of Board meetings were confidential, the above practice was indefensible. In practice, the workers' council did not even fulfill the advisory role accorded to it simply because whatever advice it gave the Board would not be outside what the management would have advised.

In addition, the capacity of workers' representatives to participate effectively in this participatory forum had been severely limited by their generally low level of education. Worse still, the use of the English language in the documents and in meetings rendered some of the worker representatives as permanent listeners, nodding or shaking their heads to indicate approval or disagreement.

The fact that the General Manager was the chairperson weakened their resolve to challenge management. This situation would not necessarily have existed if the workers' council had consisted only of workers, excluding the management. Had this been the case, discussions then could be in Kiswahili, more lively and without fear of being misunderstood or labeled by the management.

These limitations notwithstanding, workers' representatives (elected representatives and OTTU Branch Committee members) wanted to participate in the workers' council so that they could get a chance to defend workers' interests. That was why many workers related the effectiveness of workers' participation to the extent to which management had been able to solve their problems. Management, on the other hand, considered the effectiveness of workers' participation in relation to raising productivity and promoting smooth (that is, peaceful) industrial relations.

Second, the WCEC, which prepared the agenda for workers' council's meetings was dominated by management. Workers' representatives faced the limitation of being a minority, which affected their ability to influence decisions. The fact that the WCEC was dominated by members from the management means that it was less democratic and so its effectiveness in promoting workers' participation was highly questionable. The General Manager remained powerful because he was also the Chairperson of the WCEC. He/She had the final authority to determine which issues were to be discussed and decided upon. Consequently, the WCEC was not a body of the workers, for the workers and by the workers. But it never was meant to be so, according to the original objectives of the 1970 Presidential Circular on workers' participation.

The participatory nature of the WCEC could be significantly improved if the workers' council itself, through its secretary and chairperson, was given the task of preparing for its own meetings including drawing up the agenda. Then, the WCEC could truly function as a task force of the workers' council to ensure implementation of Workers' Council decisions.

Third, although heads of department are encouraged to hold departmental meetings, these were on an ad hoc basis and ordinary workers were not represented. These meetings were therefore undemocratic. These meetings should be more formalized and all workers in the department or at least departmental worker representatives should attend. In other words, they should be seen as and function as General Assembly meetings at the departmental level.

Fourth, MCM workers were not represented on the Board by their fellow workers. As workers are not represented, the whole question of workers' participation in this forum was a mockery. It is true that in two out of its four annual meetings the Board went through the minutes of the workers' council meetings for discussion and action. But the absence of workers and/or elected workers' representatives means that management was in a better position to influence decisions in their own favour, as they were even more knowledgeable of what was happening in the company than the directors themselves.

To make the Board a more effective and meaningful forum for workers' participation, employees should be represented by at least two elected representatives from the enterprise. Alternatively, both the chairperson and secretary of the workers' council should represent the workers in the Board meetings, provided that the General Manager is not the chairperson of the workers' council.

Fifth, in general, workers showed more enthusiasm towards the General Assembly than any other meeting. Many saw workers' participation in terms of their participation in this forum. They were happy with the way these meetings were conducted, and in most cases decisions were made by consensus. Ordinary workers considered these meetings to be valuable and informative. Although in most cases General Assembly meetings were friendly, the atmosphere sometimes was tense, especially when management was faced with a genuine challenge from the workers.

In summary, MCM lacked effective workers' participation in decision making, although a wide range of issues were discussed in the Workers' Council and the Board. This was because the degree of participation was limited, in practical terms, to the level of 'consultation' in the case of the workers' council where workers are represented. Furthermore, workers' participation had been inhibited not only by the fact that workers in the company were denied the right of representation on the Board but also because they were under-represented (at 33 percent) in the formally established WCEC. Worse still, as we have observed, members of the Board received information and the necessary documents five days before the meeting was to take place. One of these pieces of information was the minutes of the workers' council meetings. But workers' council meetings are called or held, normally, six days before the Board meeting. The agenda of the workers' council meeting is drawn up by management through the WCEC. This, coupled with the fact that the General Manager chaired both the workers' council and the WCEC meetings, leads us to the conclusion that workers' participation in MCM had been all but hijacked by the management. This was also the conclusion of another case study on workers' participation in another public enterprise in Tanzania, the Mbeya Farm Implements factory, commonly known as Zana za Kilimo Mbeya (see Musa, et al, 1994).

Management and Workers Opinions on Workers' Participation

There was general agreement among MCM managers that workers had been able to participate effectively in making decisions. The company had set up various participatory forums such as departmental meetings, the workers' council and the General Assembly where workers' views and opinions were accommodated. Asked about the absence of workers representatives in the Board meetings, they argued that even there the discussions held and decisions made were based on what had first been discussed in the workers' council. This implies that workers' ideas were discussed in the Board although workers were not physically represented. Furthermore, as management was part of the workers' council and its Chairman, the General Manager, is the secretary of the Board there is no basis to argue otherwise, that is, that workers were not represented on the Board.

Employees, particularly workers' representatives, agreed that they did not really participate in the decision-making process for several reasons: One, although workers in the company were represented by fellow workers on the workers' council, the council had only advisory status. Therefore, its decisions were not binding on the Board. Two, the highest body with the most authority to make crucial decisions for the company (the Board) lacked representation of the workers. Three, workers had not been able to participate in making decisions because of their low level of education, coupled with their inability to communicate effectively in English language, a medium of communication used during the meetings. Some workers' representatives admitted that the majority of them were unable to participate effectively because of the technicalities associated with discussions of some issues and their inability to communicate fluently in English. Even so, the majority of ordinary workers shared the view that workers' representatives had been able to participate in the decision making process. Two reasons were given to support this position. One was the mere attendance of these workers' representatives (elected and OTTU branch members) in the company participatory forums. Being members of these participatory forums, they automatically participated in meetings where decisions are made. Two, the benefits workers have been able to achieve were related to or reflect the effectiveness of workers' participation. It was through workers' participation that workers' representatives were able to give their opinions and lodge their demands for a better working environment. The fact that some of the demands that they lodged were met by the management symbolized the effectiveness of workers' participation.

ACHIEVEMENTS OF WORKERS' PARTICIPATION AT MCM

There was no doubt on the part of MCM management that workers' participation objectives, as stated in the Presidential Circular of 1970, had been met. Since it was formed up to the time this study was conducted, MCM had not experienced any strikes by workers. In this case, the objective of bringing about smooth industrial relations had been fulfilled. The other objectives of increasing motivation and raising labour productivity were hard to evaluate because of other confounding contextual factors such as lack of markets, low wages, frequent power cuts and so on. These contributed more to poor financial performance, and with it low productivity, than anything else.

Management had been able to utilise the participatory structures to inform the workers about the financial and other problems confronting the enterprise. In so doing, they successfully restrained workers from calling strikes. As workers grievances were aired in these participatory forums, tranquility was encouraged and industrial harmony was maintained. The participatory forums were also used to educate the workers on the importance of taking proper care to safeguard the equipment of the company, as they were an integral part of the company. Therefore, workers' participation imparted, to the workers, a sense of belonging to the company, and the need to protect and defend not only the interests of workers but also those of the enterprise as a whole. In general, management believed that the company benefited well from workers' participation.

The majority of workers shared the belief that they were able to achieve some benefits through the functioning of workers' participation, although they were not satisfied with what they had achieved. They believed that if workers' representatives were given more power in the participatory forums conditions would have changed more in their favour. In addition, employees wanted the right of information and access to the proceedings of the Workers' Council, the WCEC and the Board meetings, as well as to be represented on the Board by a full director elected by the workers themselves, apart from the representatives from OTTU Headquarters. These demands indicate clearly that workers were not fully satisfied with the then existing participatory structures in terms of the stated objectives.

The objective of workers' participation in terms of decision-making had not been fully realised because workers were not represented in the bodies that make final and binding decisions. Nevertheless, through workers' participation they were able to get a platform to air their views and make suggestions while enjoying the status and benefit of being listened to by the management. Therefore, to some extent, workers' participation had managed to secure them (workers) a status of being 'consulted' by the management in matters of importance and be able to get some information about the performance of the company. Some benefits, directly related to social welfare, such as the mid-month non-refundable 50 percent salary allowance, loan advances during public holidays and getting reject materials had also resulted.

To honour the benefits that workers had achieved through workers' participation, they had showed a keen interest in strengthening it and extending it to cover not only public enterprises but also those in the private sector. They strongly suggested that workers' participation should be given a legally binding force in empowering workers to participate effectively in the decision making process. In short, workers' participation at MCM had been meaningful although not very effective.

CONCLUSION

Based on the Presidential Circular of 1970, workers' participation was imposed on the workers from the highest authority, the state President. As a result, the structures of the forums of participation have been set in favour of management as this is the section representing the interests of the Government in the participatory structures. Workers have only been involved in the endeavour to harmonise industrial activities and make workers feel that they are an integral part of the enterprise concerned many managers argued. The Government was preoccupied with creating an ideal type of working environment that would stimulate more production and hence maximise profit in the interest of national development. Thus, it is not surprising that the Presidential Circular, pointed to earlier, directed the management of public enterprises to set up the machinery for workers' participation so as to permit workers to contribute their ideas in the development of their enterprises. Following the Presidential directive, Workers' Councils were set up, in many cases, just to satisfy and fulfill requirements of the circular, without any serious commitment to an effective application of those councils. Even so, in the process, management discovered that the participatory forums directed by the President could be employed effectively to promote the interests of management. Management has utilized the existence of workers' participation to increase efficiency in production while at the same time solving some of the workers' problems. However, partly due to the fact that the structures and participatory forums have no legal force, the effectiveness of workers' participation has not been achieved.

Nevertheless, the existing practice of workers' participation has not all been meaningless. Workers became aware of their rights partly due to the existence of this participatory machinery. It is through these participatory forums that workers express their views and opinions. True, many workers, especially workers' representatives were/are not happy with the 'consultation' status accorded to their participatory forums such as the Workers' Council and WCEC, but given the fact that they are now (by then) questioning the rationale of being excluded from participating in Board meetings, this indicates that workers have benefited from workers' participation not only in terms of access to information and the opportunity to air their views on a wide range of issues but also in increasing their consciousness of having the right to participate effectively in the decision-making process.

The Presidential Circular No.1 of 1970 had been an important document for the implementation of workers' participation in Tanzania during the era of state control/ownership of major means of production, its weaknesses and limitations notwithstanding. The achievements of workers' participation in Tanzania are attributable to that document. But this document is now out of date since many public enterprises have been privatized and the directive is only applicable to the public/state owned enterprises. Thus, enactment of a law that will make Workers' Participation obligatory in all enterprises, whether public or private, is highly desirable. That law should also take into account the social, economic and political changes that have occurred in Tanzania since the abandoning of the socialist (Ujammaa) ideology. Since the government claim that it is committed to build a democratic society, then the place to strengthen, promote and sustain democracy is at the workplace. Both, the workers and employers are going to benefit from an effective and meaningful participation. Otherwise, there is a danger of not only participation dying but also re-emergence of labour unrest.

4

WORK PLACE CONDITIONS

Co-authored with Godwin Naimani

INTRODUCTION

In this chapter an overview of the general economic conditions prevailing in Tanzania will first be given before discussing the conditions that prevailed at workplaces during the 1990s. Discussion on workplace conditions will focus on first, job characteristics and working conditions. Six groups of variables were utilized to collect the data:

- Employment record;
- Employment contract;
- Conditions of employment;
- Working conditions;
- Job characteristics; and
- Education and training at workplace.

Second, satisfaction with job/work conditions, i.e. satisfaction with different dimensions of work/job: work in general and character of work; social relations at work, working conditions; employment security; personnel policy; and enterprise management.

Third, satisfaction with economic conditions, i.e. wage/salary and employment related benefits, household income, and household income supplementing/generating activities.

The main source of information was the questionnaire surveys. However, in order to get a deeper insight of the results presented in this chapter, we first briefly discuss the general economic situation in the country before and during the 1990s when the surveys were conducted.

General Socio-Economic Conditions in the Country

Following independence in 1961, the newly formed government identified 'poverty', 'diseases' and 'illiteracy' as being the major enemies. But the initial development strategy (between 1961 and 1967) was directed at promoting growth without addressing distribution of resources to the majority. The then President J.K. Nyerere, categorized this as a period of "growth without development" as it emphasized development of things not people.

Early in 1967, Tanzania through the Arusha Declaration, adopted the policy of Socialism and Self-Reliance, which put people at the centre of the country's development process. Thus, for the period between the late 1960s to the early 1980s, national efforts to tackle the three problems (ignorance, diseases and poverty) were channeled through centrally directed medium-term and long-tem development plans. The implementation of the Arusha Declaration demanded massive investment in the improvement of the quality of life of the majority of Tanzanians. This resulted in a significant improvement of per capita income and access to education, health and other social services until the end of the 1970s (United Republic of Tanzania - URT, 2000a: 1). The achievements resulting from the Arusha Declaration include:

a) Primary school enrolment reached almost 100 percent (by 1979);
b) Approximately 80 percent of the population had access to health care;
c) Almost 90 percent of children of one year old had access to immunization services;
d) Approximately 60 percent of population had access to clean drinking water;
e) Government introduced preferential seats which increased the proportion of women participation in the Parliament; and
f) Government further introduced a quota system aimed at enhancing female transition rates to secondary school education.

From 1980 severe economic crisis made it difficult for Tanzania to sustain most of the above- mentioned achievements. Economic problems started from mid 1970s and became much more serious during the early part of the 1980s. The GDP annual growth rates were low and actually negative for three consecutive years 1980/81, 1981/82 and 1982/83 while per capita income declined and up to 1990 it has not reached the 1976 level measured in real terms (*see* Table 4.1 which illustrates some of the aspects of the severe economic crisis which Tanzania experienced during the period indicated). The crisis manifested itself in the form of:

• Widespread shortages of consumer goods and manufactured products;
• Debt crisis, balance of payment problems, and deteriorating terms of trade;
• Production declines for both industry and agriculture;

* Scarcity of foreign exchange, hence failure to import necessary industrial goods and inputs;
* Growing government deficit;
* Growing donor dependency in financing development projects as well as part of recurrent expenditure;
* Erosion of many of the social gains from the progressive policies of Ujamaa and Self Reliance; including subsidies for basic necessities; and
* During the 1970s, particularly after the 1973/74 drought, the country's food security position started to deteriorate.

Table 4.1: *GDP, GDP Annual Growth Rates and GDP/Capita (at 1976 constant prices)*

Year	GDP (million Tshs)	Annual Growth Rate (%)	GDP per capita	Per Capita Index, 1976=100
1976	21652	n.a	1328	100
1978	22142	1.10	1303	98
1979	22943	3.60	1306	98
1980	23888	4.10	1295	98
1981	23666	- 0.9	1249	94
1982	23439	- 1.0	1217	92
1983	22886	- 2.4	1152	87
1984	23656	3.40	1154	87
1985	24278	2.60	1172	88
1986	25070	3.30	1181	89
1987	26345	5.10	1189	90
1988	27460	4.20	1203	91
1989	28558	4.0 0	1223	92
1990	29904	4.70	1262	95

Source: *Economic Survey:* 1986,1992 , 1994 and *Statistical Abstracts* (various issues).
Note: Growth Rates and Index Calculated by the Authors.

From 1981 to 1985, the government of the United Republic of Tanzania (URT) pursued several measures in an attempt to resolving the economic crisis. From 1981 to 1982, a National Economic and Survival Programme (NESP) was initiated by the government in an attempt to address the external sector imbalances. It aimed at increasing exports, marketed food crops, control government expenditure and improve production of essential industrial goods. The policies for attaining these targets were not spelt out clearly and failed to resolve the crisis.

From 1982 to 1985, a Structural Adjustment Programme (SAP) was designed to reinstate a balance in government and external sector accounts, reduce inflation and restore output to pre crisis level, while maintaining the social services and rehabilitate the economic infrastructure. The programme failed to even take-off because it was based on the assumption that external resources would be forthcoming. But this (home grown) SAP was not supported by donors because of what they called the failure of the government to adopt adequate adjustment measures.

Due to the inability to restructure the economy and as a result of donors who were gradually withholding their support to a government that was excessively dependant on aid, the government of the United Republic had no option but to sign the agreement with the IMF/World Bank. The major elements of the World Bank structural adjustment reform programme under the name 'Economic Recovery Programme' (ERP) were: liberalization of prices and domestic trade; import liberalization; government budget cuts; devaluation of local currency; public service reforms including reduction of the size of civil service through worker retrenchment; privatization of public enterprises; and, to encourage private (foreign and domestic) investments into the economy.

The thrust of this exercise was to move away from a centrally controlled and state planned economy to a more market driven economy. This factor affected public expenditure patterns in favour of those sectors that were considered to have direct and short term impact on production.

The crisis and the SAPs, which forced the government to cut its investments in the social service sector, had the following socio-economic effects:

- A significant cost of social reproduction transferred to the household level, with women carrying a heavier burden;
- Real income for the majority declined, a factor that negatively affected the quality of life of the majority of the people;
- Increasing inequalities among the people, between and within geographical regions;
- Disintegration of families, leading to a greater number of internally displaced persons, such as abandoned children, street children, street vendors and prostitutes;
- Increased rates of unemployment especially due to retrenchment of civil servants resulting in increased crime rates, which have been threatening the personal security of the people, especially the employed population;
- In terms of social services delivery, there are two parallel systems: public sector and private sector. This has provided NGOs particularly religious organizations with an opportunity to play a greater role in service delivery particularly in education and health. But has also raised other concerns related to the quality of the services offered both within and between the two systems;
- Shift from the Socialist or Ujamaa philosophy, which emphasized on development with equity and equality, to a market driven model, which emphasizes on competition and the role of the market in determining resource allocation and use;

Box 4.1: Major Structural Changes in the Economy of Tanzania, Mid-1980s-1999			
	Mid 1980s	Mid-1990s	July 1999
Parastatal sector	Trade in more than 50 commodities restricted to parastatals.	Trade completely liberalized; more than 400 parastatals identified for divestiture.	More than 200 parastatals divested; preparations startedfor divestiture of utilities /other large monopolies.
Financial sector	Government-owned banks control more than 90% of deposits	New privately-owned banks licensed; main government banks being restructured.	Main government owned banks privatized or put under private sector management.
Price controls	Most prices government controlled.	All prices market-determined except petroleum products.	All prices market determined.
Import/ export regulations	Imports subject to quantitative restrictions and exports to licencing	Imports/exports liberalized quantitative restrictions on petroleum products imports only	Remaining restrictions on petroleum products imports scheduled to be eliminated by January 2000
Access to foreign exchange	Holding of foreign illegal; exchange rate set by the Govt.	Exchange rate market determined; no restriction on holding foreign exchange for current account transactions	Exchange rate market determined; no restrictions on holding or acquiring foreign exchange for current account transactions
Monetary policy	Policy nonexistent as banks had liberal access to BoT financing	BoT financing terminated with restructuring of state owned banks	BoT operations strictly for monetary policy focussing on reducing inflation
Fiscal policy	High deficit financed by BoT credit	High deficits financed by BoT credit during 1993/94 -1994/95	Strict cash control system in place
Tax system	Tax base consists of parastatals; targets met by ad hoc levies on parastatals	Tax base eroded as the tax net fails to include new private and informal sectors as well as many descretionary excemptions; dependence on trade taxes increased	Tax administration improved and discretionary exemptions removed; VAT has replaced cascading sales taxes, and reform import duties and personal income taxes implemented
Civil serivice reforms	Civil service employment increasing; real wages eroded	Govt employment reaches highest level of 354,000 in 1993; comprehensive civil reform begun	Govt employment reduced to 264,000; wage reforms begun

Source: IMF/IDA (1999: 4)
Notes: BoT = Bank of Tanzania; and VAT = Value Added Tax.

+ Shifting away from medium and long term planning to rolling plans and forward budgeting strategies; and
+ Deepening of external dependency.

Regarding retrenchment of public employees, a comprehensive civil service reform programme started in 1993 at a time when government employment was at its highest level of 354,000. As a result of this reform programme, the number of public employees has since 1993, steadily declined every year and by the end of 1999 the number of public servants had declined to 259,846 people, 38.4 percent of whom were women. From 1993-99, retrenchments claimed 25,953 people (Table 4.2) while "about 68,813 public employees decided on their own to retire from the civil service to join the non-governmental sectors while several others died" (Economic Survey, 1999: 73). Apart from the civil service reform programme, the government has, since 1993, taken a variety of measures to spur private investment. These included adoption of the Tanzania Investment Act, the privatization of public enterprises, and the establishment of the Tanzania Investment Centre. Despite these measures, the response of private investors has fallen below expectation (except in the mining and tourism sectors).

Table 4.2: *Retrenchment of Civil Servants*

Year	Gender	Number	Percent	Total
1993-1996	Females	3,189	28.20	11,310
	Males	8,121	71.80	
1997	Females	3,685	38.15	9,958
	Males	5,973	61.85	
1998	Females	150	26.98	556
	Males	406	73.02	
1999	Females	1,942	43.85	4,429
	Males	2,487	56.15	
Total	Females	8,966	34.55	25,953
	Males	16,987	65.45	

Source: Economic Survey, 1999

The economic reforms created and/or increased the pressure for the liberalization of the political system as well as democratization. This entailed, *inter alia*:

+ Moving away from a monolithic political system to political pluralism as symbolized in the emergence of various political actors including many political parties;
+ Growing intensity of associational life;

- Creation of independent media including press, TV, radio etc.;
- Enhancement of an independent judiciary;
- Strengthening of human rights movement;
- Strengthening of civil society; and
- Holding of multi-party elections at local government level late in 1994 and presidential and parliamentary elections in October-November, 1995. The CCM party won both presidential and parliamentary elections.

However, as a result of the above socio-economic reforms, Tanzania has progressed significantly towards re-establishing macro-economic stability. Annual growth of the GDP recovered to an average of 3.8% during 1986-1992; inflation however remained close to around 30 percent per year during the same period, reflecting continued financing of the economy by the Bank of Tanzania. Macro-economic management deteriorated significantly between 1992 and 1995 and annual inflation rate increased from 21.8 percent in 1992 to 35.8 percent in 1994. The reform and stabilization effort, however, regained momentum following the election of a new government in 1995 and annual rate of inflation declined to 7.8 by 1999 (Table 4.3); and to 6 percent in 2000. Performance in terms of GDP per capita and poverty reduction has remained below expectation (see Table 4.3), partly due to rapid population growth and low economic growth.

Absolute poverty is still persistent in Tanzania, and the country remains one of the poorest in the world. Based on the 1991/92 Household Budget Survey (HBS), about 27 percent of the people live in households whose total expenditure is insufficient to obtain enough food to meet nutritional requirements, and about 48 percent are unable to meet basic requirements, including food. The results from the updated estimates for the year 2000 show that poverty levels may have actually increased during the period 1991/2 - 2000 from 48 per cent to well over 50 per cent for Mainland Tanzania (URT, 2000a: 5-6).

The level of poverty steadily declined in the 1980s and early 1990s, but rose during the 1993-1998 period. Major causes of the post 1993 increase in the level of poverty were widening income inequality and relatively low rate of economic growth, particularly in the rural areas (URT, 2000a: 8). Two factors were responsible for this, namely: unequal growth in the per capita incomes and changes in the distribution of income. In other words, average household incomes appear to have increased faster than indicated from the macro-economic statistics, thence, the decline in the level of poverty reported during 1983-1993. Thereafter, income growth slowed down significantly, leading to increased poverty levels in 1990s.

According to the government (see URT, 2000a), income poverty in Tanzania has four main characteristics. First, poverty is largely a rural phenomenon. Incomes are lower in the rural areas and the extent and depth of poverty is greater than in urban centres. "According to the 1991/92 HBS, basic needs rural poverty incidence is estimated at 57 percent, and the food poverty incidence is about 32 percent" (URT, 2000a).

Second, although poverty is less acute in the urban areas, it is still a serious problem, especially in urban areas other than Dar es Salaam. According to the 1991/92 HBS the basic needs poverty incidence for Dar es Salaam was 5.6 percent and for the other urban areas it was 41 percent. Results from updated estimates for the year 2000 show that poverty incidence levels for Dar es Salaam may have increased to 9.2 percent and for the other urban areas it may have risen to 48 per cent. The urban poor are concentrated in the informal sector.

Third, poverty has a clear intergenerational dimension: the young and the old are likely to be poorer than Tanzanians in the 15-64 age group. In addition, older women are more likely to be poor than older men as a result of lower lifetime earnings, lower social status and more limited access to poverty and inheritance.

Fourth, poverty in Tanzania has a clear gender dimension; women are generally poorer than men, own less land and livestock and have less years of schooling. Women's poverty is often associated with unequal access to productive resources and control of assets, together with poor health, inequality in access to education, personal insecurity and limited participation in public life.

Available evidence also suggests that the poor are more likely to be less educated (literacy rate for rural poor is 54.3 percent as against 61 percent for rural population as a whole).

The Government of Tanzania has recognized that the improvements in macroeconomic performance have so far not really benefited the poor. In 1998 the Government launched its Vision 2025 and the National Poverty Eradication Strategy (NPES) aimed at making Tanzania middle-income country by the year 2025. In addition, the Government has embarked on a series of reforms in the civil service sector, local government and regional administration, education and health sectors; all with the aim of promoting economic growth and improving the quality of life of Tanzanians.

Tanzania has also prepared a Poverty Reduction Strategy Paper, PRSP (see URT, 2000a). The PRSP is one response to the enhanced Highly Indebted Poor Countries (HIPIC) initiative, under which framework, the country has been declared eligible for debt relief. Decision point to that effect was reached in April 2000. Total relief will translate into debt service relief over time of US$ 3 billion. This implies a 54.7 percent reduction on the debt of multilateral and bilateral commercial creditors outstanding at the end of June 1999. The Government agreed to target the debt relief to those sectors such as education and health that have the largest impact on poverty and human development and to specific poverty initiatives. This means that the resources to be freed from this relief will be channelled towards poverty reduction.

Table 4.3: Selected Economic Indicators for Tanzania

	1985	1986	1987	1988	1989	1990	1991	1992	1993	1994	1995	1996	1997	1998	1999
GDP at constant 1992 prices (Tshs million)	983221	1001349	1071540	1119017	1147745	1219236	1253134	1277917	1281006	1298943	1345246	1401711	1448090	1505827	1577291
GDP Annual growth rate		1.8%	7.0%	4.4%	2.6%	6.2%	2.8%	1.8%	0.4%	1.4%	3.6%	4.2%	3.3%	4.0%	4.8%
GDP per capita at 1992 constant prices (Tshs)	47499	47012	48929	49514	49472	51014	50940	50431	49270	48650	48918	49530	49767	50194	51045
GDP per capita at current prices (Tshs)	5221	6613	9150	12675	25093	31799	40227	50432	61837	79600	101696	121999	147134	170844	193724
GDP per capita at current prices (US $)*	295	199	140	126	174	161	181	167	149	156	177	210	241	257	258
Imports (US$ million)	865	920	910	808	1015	1227	1270	1362	1275	1309	1341	1213	1148	1366	1411
Exports (US$ million)	241	338	259	270	365	408	362	397	439	519	683	762	753	589	541
Balance of Merchandise Trade (US$ million)	-624	-582	-651	-538	-650	-819	-908	-965	-836	-790	-658	-451	-395	-777	-870
Overall Balance of payments (US$ million)	-395	-384	-281	-258	-249	-200	-260	-408	-737	-461	-386	-245	-556	-616	--
Exchange rate (Tshs/US$)	17.67	33.25	65.20	100.06	144.49	197.59	222.61	301.91	414.53	509.63	574.76	580.0	609.9	664.7	752.1
Inflation (annual average)	33.3%	32.4%	30.0%	31.8%	30.3%	35.8%	28.7%	21.8%	24.0%	33.8%	27.4%	21.0%	16.1%	12.9%	7.8%

Source: Economic Surveys, 1997; 1998; 1999 and Bank of Tanzania, Economic and Operations Report – various years
Note: * GDP per capita in US $ calculated by the authors.

Conditions at Workplaces

As pointed out at the beginning of this chapter, six groups of variables were used to collect information on job/work conditions: employment record; employment contract; information on employment conditions; job characteristics; and education and training at workplaces. Total number of worker representatives (the respondents) was 1116.

Employment Record

Employment record is described by five variables which were captured by asking the respondents to state: their age when they started working; how long (number of years) they have been working with their present employer; if they ever changed their employer and if yes, how many times; and if they have been unemployed and if yes, how often.

About 35 percent of the worker representatives started working at the age of 18 to 20 years and 39 percent started working at the age of 21 to 23 years. Only about 23 percent of the respondents indicated that they started working when they were over 23 years old. Thus, the majority of the worker representative (74 percent) started working when they were young, at the age of 18 to 23 years old.

The majority of the worker representatives (926 out of 1116) have worked with, by then, their present employer for over 6 years. Of this, 27 percent had remained with their employer for six to 10 years; 32 percent for 11 to 15 years; 23 percent for 16 to 20 years; and 18 percent for over 21 years. This indicates a high degree of stability of work.

Stability at work is further confirmed by the fact that over 60 percent of the respondents have not changed their employer at all. Only about 21 percent have indicated changing employer once; eight percent twice; six percent thrice; and three percent more than three times. In addition to this, most of the worker representatives (77 percent) indicated that they have never been unemployed. However, for most of those who have been unemployed, they have been in that situation only once. The duration of being unemployed varied from less than three months to more than four years as follows: less than three months (40 respondents); three to six months (43); six to nine months (23); nine months to one year (54) one to two years (42); two to three years (31); and four or more years 49 respondents)

Employment Contract

Insofar as the nature of the respondent's employment contract is concerned, most of the worker representatives were employed under indefinite public contract (53 percent) and civil service contract (33 percent). Few (less than 2 percent) were employed without any employment contract (Table 4.4). For about 69 percent of the respondents, their employment contracts were regulated by a collective agreement. Even so, few of the respondents (9 percent) did not know if or not a collective agreement applied to their employment contract.

Table 4.4: *Nature of Current Employment Contract*

	Number	%
Civil service contract	370	33
Written contract under public company	583	53
Written contract under public company for a specified period of time	`27	2
Written contract under private company	60	5
Written contract under private company for a specified period of time	8	1
Verbal Contract	2	0
No contract	16	1
Other	42	4
Total	1,108	99

From the above discussion, it is clear that over 90 percent of workers in our sample had written contacts, almost none (2 out of 1108) had verbal contracts and only about one percent of the respondents worked without any contract.

Information on Employment Conditions

This section discusses data on whether a respondent had information on: the employment regulations for his/her industry; labour laws; and the availability of copies of labour laws for consultation by workers. Of the 1105 respondents who replied to the question on whether they knew the employment regulations in their place of work, 89 percent answered 'yes'; seven percent said 'no'; and four percent answered 'I don't know'. If we interpret the response 'I don't know to also mean 'no', then it follows that 11 percent of the respondents did not know the employment regulations in their work places. Taking into account that these are worker representatives it can safely be assumed that a significant number of workers have no knowledge of the employment regulations in their work places. In Tanzania, at the time of our survey, there were several different pieces of labour legislation or labour laws in force. These included:

* Employment Ordinance (1955) Cap. 336 of the Revised Laws;
* Trade Union Ordinance (Amendment) Act, No. 51 of 1962;
* Civil Service (Negotiation Machinery) Act, No. 52 of 1962;
* Severance Allowance Act, No. 57 of 1962;
* National Provident Fund Act, No. 34 of 1964;
* Security of Employment Act, No. 62 of 1964;
* Permanent Labour Tribunal (Amendment) Act, No. No. 3 of 1990;
* Organisation of Tanzania Trade Unions, No. 20 of 1991; and
· Industrial Court Amendment Act, No.2 of 1993.

Respondents were asked to write down up to four different pieces of labour legislation that they knew; had personal copies of; copies were available at their local trade union branch and at their workplace. The results were as shown in Tables 4.5 to 4.8.

Notice that in all multiple responses tables in this book (for instance table 4.5), each respondent was allowed to provide more than one answer. The implication of this is that the percentages do not add up to 100. Thus, the tables should be read as follows (taking table 4.5 as an example): 542 or 54 percent of all the 1000 respondents (Base de %) who answered the question, indicated that they knew the 'Security of Employment Act'.

Table 4.5: *Tanzania Labour Laws that Respondents knew*

Multiple responses, exclusive non responses	N	%
Security of Employment Act, No. 62 of 1964	542	54
I do not know any labour law	352	35
Employment Ordinance Cap. 366	199	20
Workman's Compensation Act	96	10
Permanent Labour Tribunal (Amendment) Act	43	4
Severance Allowance Act	37	4
Others	96	10
BASE DE %	1000	100

More than one third (35 percent) of the respondents indicated that they did not know any labour laws. For those who indicated to have knowledge of labour legislation, 54 percent were aware of the Security of Employment Act; followed by Employment Ordinance (20 percent); Workman's Compensation Act (10 percent), the Permanent Labour Tribunal Act/Industrial Court Act of 1993 (4 percent), and Severance Allowance Act, 4 percent (Table 4.5). From these results it is obvious that the degree of ignorance regarding labour laws was relatively high among the respondents. Considering that these are worker representatives it is apparent that they were not effective in the different forums in which they represent workers. The assumption here is that if you are ignorant of labour laws then you also do not know the rights of workers.

Ignorance of labour laws is further aggravated by the fact that majority of the respondents (65 percent) did not have personal copies of any labour legislation/law. Only 30 percent have indicated to have personal copies of Security of Employment Act; Employment Ordinance (7 percent); Workman's Compensation Act (3 percent); Permanent Labour Tribunal (Amendment) Act (2 percent); and Severance Allowance Act (1 percent) (Table 4.6).

Apart from personal copies, workers can consult labour laws through copies of the same if they are kept either at their workplace or local trade union branch. But this is hardly the case since very few of the worker representatives indicated that their local trade union branch and work place had such copies. Actually 50 percent of the respondents indicated their local trade union branch had not even a single copy of any labour law and 14 percent of them answered, "I don't know." For those trade union branches with copies of labour laws, Security of Employment Act was mentioned by 28 percent of the respondents, followed by Employment Ordinance, 4 percent (Table 4.7).

Table 4.6: *Labour Laws that Respondents had Personal Copies*

Multiple responses, exclusive non responses	N	%
No Copies	610	65
Security of Employment Act, No. 62 of 1964	283	30
Employment Ordinance Cap. 366	67	7
Others	36	4
Workman's Compensation Act	30	3
Permanent Labour Tribunal (Amendment) Act	20	2
Severance Allowance Act	12	1
BASE DE %	932	100

From these results, it is obvious that to a large extent, respondents cannot consult the various labour laws because copies were not available either at their local trade union branch or at their work place. The implication of this is that knowledge of labour laws is low among both the workers and their representatives. In our opinion, this is a disturbing finding and something need to be done to rectify the situation. To be effective, worker representatives have no choice but to be knowledgeable about the labour laws of their country. Thus, future trade union action and sensitization need to be directed to educating workers about the labour laws of Tanzania.

Table 4.7: *Copies of Labour Laws at Trade Union Branch*

Multiple responses, exclusive non-responses	N	%
No Copies	511	50
Security of Employment Act, No. 62 of 1964	286	28
Don't Know	145	14
No trade union branch	53	5
Employment Ordinance Cap. 366	41	4
Workman's Compensation Act	15	1
Permanent Labour Tribunal (Amendment) Act	11	1
Severance Allowance Act	6	1
Others	30	3
BASE DE %	1,025	100

Regarding availability of copies of labour laws at work places, more than one third (39 percent) of the respondents indicated that no copies of any labour law were available at their work places while another 20 percent did not know whether or not their work place had any copies of any labour legislation or law. For those workplaces with copies of labour laws, copies of Security of Employment Act was mentioned by 34 percent of the respondents; Employment Ordinance (8 percent); Workman's Compensation Act (4 percent); Permanent Labour Tribunal Act (2 percent); and Severance Allowance Act (1 percent)(Table 4.8).

Table 4.8: *Copies of Labour Laws available at Workplace*

Multiple responses, exclusive non responses	N	%
No Copies	383	39
Security of Employment Act, No. 62 of 1964	337	34
Don't Know	200	20
Employment Ordinance Cap. 366	75	8
Others	67	7
Workman's Compensation Act	35	4
Permanent Labour Tribunal (Amendment) Act	17	2
Severance Allowance Act	14	1
BASE DE %	979	100

Working Conditions

Information about working conditions was collected on the following aspects: time taken to go to work, distance between home and workplace, means of transport, transport assistance by employers, availability of canteen at workplace, and availability of toilet.

Regarding time taken to go to work, out of 1098 respondents who answered this question, 42 percent took less than 30 minutes, 30 minutes to one hour (47 percent), one to two hours (10 percent) and three hours and more (1 percent). Thus, most of the workers (89 percent) can reach their places of work within one hour. This indicates that most of the workers live within the vicinity of their work places. Actually, most of them (66 percent) were not more than four kilometers from their working places.

As for means of transport used by the respondents to go to work, most of them (46 percent) go by foot and about 19 percent use bicycles. Again this is an indication that they are not far away from their work places. Even so, 26 percent go by bus, personal vehicle (4 percent), and motorcycle (3 percent).

It seems that many workers (64 percent) are provided with transport assistance such as office bus (14 percent of the respondents), a bicycle (2 percent), a motorcycle (1 percent), a vehicle (5 percent), and transport allowance (42 percent). However, about one third (33 percent) of the respondents indicated that they were not being provided with any transport assistance from their employers.

Regarding availability of canteen on the enterprise premises, over one-half

(53 percent) of the respondents indicated that there was no canteen at their work place. In most government offices, the working day lasts for eight hours from 7.30 am to 3.30 pm or from 8.00 am to 4.00 pm without a lunch break. This might explain why over half of the respondents had no canteen at their work place. Unofficially, however, many workers take a lunch break from 1 pm to 2 pm. For many private companies, there is an official lunch break of one hour and the working day lasts from 8.00 am to 5.00 pm. These are the ones most likely to have a canteen within the company premises. As for the availability of toilet/washroom facilities, only 4 percent indicated that these facilities did not exist at their workplace.

JOB CHARACTERISTICS

In this sub-section, the job characteristics of respondents will be described by four variables (i.e. the nature of job performed, enterprise ownership, enterprise numerical size and economic sector in which the enterprise belong). The objective here is to capture the immediate environment of the workers.

Job Performed and Enterprise Ownership

The respondents were asked to give a brief description of the nature of work they were doing for living. The responses were then coded and grouped into four categories as follows:

* Manual work (such as farming, artisan, etc.);
* White collar job (such as civil servant, primary court magistrate, office clerk, office secretaries, bookkeeping, nursing, etc.);
* Professional work with high level education (such as engineers, doctors, judges, lecturers, charted accountants, etc.); and
* Highly placed work (such as highly placed civil servants, e.g. directors, and commissioners).

The majority of the worker representatives (70%) were engaged in white collar jobs, followed by professionals (15%), and manual work (14%). Few were in highly placed jobs (1%). As for enterprise ownership, most of the respondents were working in the public enterprises, civil service (29%) and parastatals (56 %). Some of them were also in trade union offices (9%) and very few were working in private enterprises (5%). However, given the major structural changes in the economy of Tanzania, from mid-1980s-1999 (see box 4.1 above), the pattern of ownership has now changed drastically in favour of private ownership. That is, most of the respondents who by then indicated working in parastatals are now working in private enterprises.

Size of the Enterprise and Economic Sector

A sizable number of the worker representatives (21 percent) were working in enterprises having less than 25 employees; 34 percent of them were in enterprises having 25-100 employees; and 39 percent in enterprises with more than 100 employees. However, about six percent of the respondents indicated that they did not know the size of their enterprise. We considered this to be a valid response and thus not treated as missing data.

Insofar as economic sectors are concerned, the majority (51 percent) of the respondents were employed in the service sector, about 7 percent were in the agricultural sector; manufacturing sector had 19 percent of the worker representatives; commerce, marketing and banking had 13 percent of the worker representatives; while transportation and mining sectors had less than 10 percent of the respondents working in them.

IN-HOUSE EDUCATION AND TRAINING BY EMPLOYER

Another aspect which is related to the working environment of workers is education and training offered and/or paid for by the employer. As a matter of fact, most jobs require special skills in order to perform them effectively. Such skills can either be obtained through in service training or by sending employees to particular training centres to acquire such skills. It is of paramount importance that employees are regularly trained so as to perform their work more skillfully and efficiently. This in turn has an effect on the quality of service or products offered by the enterprises. In the case studies conducted in Tanzania through APADEP there is an indication that workers in different enterprises need training in different aspects related to their work. The questionnaire surveys also support this finding in that a substantial number of the respondents (37 percent) indicated that they had not received any education/training that was paid by the employer (Table 4.9).

For those saying 'no' (i.e. they had not received any education/training which was paid by the employer), there were differences according to gender, size of the enterprise and level of education. Insofar as gender is concerned, a large proportion of females (40 percent of all female respondents) indicated to have had received no education/training, while the proportion for male was 35 percent of all male respondents.

As for the numerical size of the enterprise, the number of respondents saying 'no' decreased with increasing size of the enterprise with the exception of only very small (employing less than 25 workers) enterprises (Table 4.10). This seem to indicate that the larger the size of an enterprise the higher the chances of it having education/training programmes for its employees. In deed education/training seem to have significant statistical association with size of enterprise at 5 percent level (chi-square=24.2 and p= 0.004)

Table 4.9: *Have You Received any Education/Training paid by Employer?*

	Number	%
No	405	37
Yes, of one week or less duration	79	7
Yes, of one week to one month duration	155	14
Yes, of one month and above duration	466	42
Total	1105	100

Table 4.10: *Size of Enterprise by Education and Development Training by Employer*

Count (N) Row % Column %	No	Yes, 1 week or less	Yes, 1 week to 1 month	Yes, 1 month & above	Row Total
Very small, less than 25 employees	95 41.9 25.1	16 7.0 21.3	15 6.6 10.1	101 44.5 22.9	227 21.8
Small enterprise, (25-100 employees)	150 39.6 39.7	26 6.9 34.7	64 16.9 43.0	139 36.7 31.5	379 36.3
Medium (101-500 employees)	80 29.5 21.2	21 7.7 28.0	44 16.2 29.5	126 46.5 28.6	271 26.0
Big (more than 500 employees)	53 31.9 14.0	12 7.2 16.0	26 15.7 17.4	75 45.2 17.0	166 15.9
Column Total	378 36.2	75 7.2	149 14.3	441 42.3	1043 100.0

With regards to level of education, a large proportion (53 percent) of all the respondents with low level education (primary school or adult education) indicated 'no' compared to: 31 percent for all the respondents with middle level education (secondary school education and or basic technical education); and 28 percent for those with high level education (university education and/or higher level technical training). This implies that those with higher level of education have a higher chance of receiving education and training paid by the employer than those with low level of education (Table 4.11). This is further confirmed by the observed strong association between education level and receiving education/ training paid by the employer (chi-square = 90.9 and p =0.00).

There was no significant relationship between education/training paid by the employer and type of ownership. Even so, 37 percent of all the respondents from public own enterprises indicated that they received no education/training paid by the employer as compared to 35 percent of the respondents from private owned enterprises. This, to some extent, reflects the extent of government budget cuts as a result of implementation of SAP measures.

Table 4.11: *Education Level of Respondents by Education/Training Paid by Employer*

Count (N) Row % Column %	No	Yes, 1 week or less	Yes, 1 week - 1 month	Yes, 1 month & above	Row Total
Low Education	159 53.0 39.5	39 13.0 50.0	28 9.3 18.1	74 24.7 15.9	300 27.2
Middle Education	213 30.8 52.9	31 4.5 39.7	105 15.2 67.7	343 49.6 73.8	692 62.9
High Education	31 28.4 7.7	8 7.3 10.3	22 20.2 14.2	48 44.0 10.3	109 9.9
Column Total	403 36.6	78 7.1	155 14.1	465 42.2	1101 100.0

SATISFACTION WITH WORK/JOB CONDITIONS

The questionnaire surveys also gathered general information on the extent to which respondents were satisfied or not with 19 different dimensions of work/job. The values used for the two aspects of each dimension were:

+ Very satisfied
+ Satisfied
+ Not satisfied
+ Very unsatisfied.

Even so, during the analysis these were collapsed into two values only, satisfied and not satisfied for purposes of convenience. The results were as shown in Table 4.12.

Table 4.12: *Satisfaction With Different Dimensions of Work*

Satisfaction with the following at your workplace:	Satisfied (%)	Not satisfied (%)	N*
1. Canteen	48	52	522
2. Toilet/Washroom facilities	70	30	1068
3. Your work	82	18	1113
4. Hygiene	65	35	1115

Table 4.12: *Continued....*

Satisfaction with the following at your workplace:	Satisfied (%)	Not satisfied (%)	N*
5. Health and safety	62	38	1115
6. Transport	46	54	1113
7. Security (stability) of work	61	39	1105
8. Promotion procedures/chances	38	62	1113
9. Disciplinary procedures	68	32	1112
10. Personnel policy in general	54	46	1106
11. Education/training opportunities	35	65	1103
12. Maintenance of machines/equipment	50	50	1103
13. Availability of machines/equipment	44	56	1105
14. Social relations with fellow workers	96	04	1100
15. Social relations with supervisors	82	18	1095
16. Social relations with management	75	25	1098
17 Social relations with directors	62	38	1083
18. How interesting/worthwhile your job is	83	17	1100
19. The procedures for work distribution	66	33	1107

* The number of respondents include valid cases only, thus the NA categories (such as no canteen) and no response were treated as missing cases.

The 19 dimensions were grouped into six categories: intrinsic job satisfaction; satisfaction with social relations at work; satisfaction with working conditions; satisfaction with employment security; satisfaction with personnel policy; and satisfaction with enterprise management.

Intrinsic Job Satisfaction

Two dimensions/variables (3 and 18 in Table 4.12) were used to assess the degree of satisfaction with the actual work the respondent was doing: satisfaction with the work in general and satisfaction with the character of the work (i.e., how satisfying and worthwhile was the job for the respondent). 82 percent of the respondents were satisfied with their work in general while 83 percent were satisfied with the character of their work (Table 4.12). Since the two questions appeared at different parts of the questionnaire, this shows that the degree of satisfaction with work is not only high (over 80 percent) but also was the extent of reliability of the responses.

Satisfaction With Social Relations at Work

Four dimensions/variables (14-17) were used to define social relations at work, i.e., satisfaction with social relations with:

• Fellow workers;
• Supervisors;

* Management; and
* Directors (members of the Board of Directors).

These variables/dimensions were used in assessing the extent to which the respondent was satisfied with her/his social relations at work since these dimensions are part of the humanization aspect of participation. The degree of satisfaction with fellow workers was the highest (96 percent of the respondents), followed by satisfaction with supervisors (82 percent), with management (75 percent), while 62 percent of the respondents indicated that they were satisfied with social relations with their directors (Table 4.12). Thus, for 75 percent and over of the respondents are satisfied with the social relations with those they work close with at the work place. As for satisfaction with directors (Board members), this received the highest percentage of those indicating not satisfied perhaps because of little interaction between the workers and members of the Board.

Satisfaction With Working Conditions

Satisfaction with working conditions was assessed using five variables (dimensions 1, 2, 4-6 of table 4.12), i.e., satisfaction with:

* Canteen at workplace;
* Toilet/washroom facilities;
* Hygiene;
* Health and safety; and
* Transport.

The majority of the respondents were satisfied with toilet/washroom facilities (70 percent), hygiene (65 percent) and with healthy and safety (62 percent). Strangely though there about 4.2 percent of workers who have indicated that they have no toilet/washroom at their places of work. More than half (53 percent) of the respondents indicated that there was no canteen at their work place. However, for those who indicated existence of a canteen at their workplace, the majority of them (52 percent) were not satisfied with their canteen. The implication of this is that canteens were not common in many work places and where they are found workers are not satisfied with their services. In the case of transport, 64 percent indicated that their employers provided transport assistance to them. Even so, 54 percent of the respondents were not satisfied with transport. This seem to indicate that either the means of transport provided by the employers were not reliable or the transport allowance was not enough to meet the fare to-and-from work. All in all, the majority of the respondents (over 60 percent) were satisfied with three out of the five selected work conditions while over 50 percent were not satisfied with the remaining two, i.e. canteen and transport.

Satisfaction With Employment Security

About six out of ten (61 percent) of the respondents expressed satisfaction with the security or stability of their work (Table 4.12). Perhaps this is due to the fact that 69 percent of the respondents had employment contracts that were regulated by a collective agreement, and the Security of Employment Act protects such agreements. Otherwise, one would have expected a lower degree of satisfaction with security of work in view of the rentrenchment programme implemented from 1993 to 1999 (see Table 4.2).

Satisfaction With Personnel Policy

The following variables were used to assess the extent to which respondents were satisfied with the personnel policy of their work places, i.e., satisfaction with:

* Personnel policy in general;
* Promotion Procedures/chances;
* Education/training opportunities; and
* Disciplinary procedures.

The majority of the respondents expressed satisfaction with disciplinary procedures (68 percent) and with personnel policy in general (54 percent). Most of them were, however not satisfied with education/training opportunities (65 percent) and with promotion procedures/chances (62 percent) (see Table 4.12).

Disciplinary procedures are governed by the Security of Employment Act, thus it is not surprising that of all the four aspects of personnel policy, it scored the highest proportion of respondents expressing satisfaction. The low degree of satisfaction with education and training opportunities reflects the fact that the Structural Adjustment Programme (SAP) did not put emphasis on education and the other social services in general. Dissatisfaction with promotion procedures/chances emanate from the fact that during periods of economic difficulties chances of being promoted tend to be low.

Satisfaction With Enterprise Management

The extent of satisfaction with enterprise management was assessed through three variables (i.e. dimensions 12, 13 and 19 of table 4.12):

* Satisfaction with procedures for work distribution;
* Satisfaction with availability of machines/equipment; and
* Satisfaction with the maintenance of machines/equipment.

The majority of the respondents (66 percent) were only satisfied with the procedures of work distribution. On maintenance of machinery/equipment, the assessment was even in that 50 percent of the respondents were satisfied while another 50 percent were not. But when it came to availability of machinery/equipment the majority (56 percent) of the respondents indicated that they were not satisfied. This implies that working tools are either not sufficient for everyone or are out-dated. The overall assessment, however is that the majority of the respondents were not satisfied with the overall enterprise management.

Satisfaction with Economic Conditions

The term 'economic conditions' as used in this section, essentially refers to the purchasing power of the respondents. A statement of salary earned and household income gives only an idea of the level of these resources. Consequently the questionnaire survey also included variables aimed at assessing the extent to which a respondent was satisfied with his/her individual earnings and with particular economic conditions. The latter was captured indirectly by asking a respondent to indicate the extent to which the household income was sufficient to meet certain necessary costs (transport, education for children, medical care, etc.). A respondent was asked to choose one of the following three values: Yes, household income is sufficient; Household income is not very sufficient; and No, household income is not sufficient. As for satisfaction with individual income (salary), the respondents had to choose one of the following four values: very satisfied; satisfied: not satisfied; and very unsatisfied: We deliberately avoided what Adams and Schvaneldt (1985: 152) refer to as 'escape value' of "not satisfied, not dissatisfied" or "as much satisfied as dissatisfied." During the analysis we found it convenient to combine 'very satisfied' and 'satisfied' to mean satisfied and 'not satisfied' with 'very unsatisfied' to imply not satisfied.

Earning Levels

The questionnaire survey results indicate that 85 percent of all the (1116 respondents) worker representatives were not satisfied with their levels of earnings. There was no significant relationship between satisfaction with level of earnings with type of ownership, gender or size of the enterprise. The salaries ranged from Tshs. 1302/= to Tshs. 202,230/= per month, with an average salary of Tshs 18559.09 and a standard deviation of Tshs. 17532.5452 (see Table 4.13a). This shows that the salaries were heterogeneous, indeed, the coefficient of variation (CV) was 94 percent. Women's salaries were generally lower than those of men. The average salary for women was Tshs 17946.00 with a standard deviation of Tshs. 16617.3241, while the average salary for men was Tshs 19166.59 with a standard deviation of Tshs 19149.1162. The salaries of both women and men varied greatly but variation in women salaries (CV= 92.6 percent) was low as compared to those of men (CV=99.9 percent) (table 4.13b).

On average private, parastatal and trade union workers had higher salaries than those in civil service (Table 4.13a). There was a wide variation of salaries in

Table 4.13a: *Type of Enterprise Working for and Monthly Salary (Tshs.)*

	Mean	Std Dev	Cases
1. For Entire Population	18559.0948	17532.5452	1087
2. Civil Service	15138.3567	10762.1384	314
3. Private Enterprise	26623.2963	35780.4492	54
4. Parastatal Organisation	18604.4272	17346.8890	618
5. Trade Union	25335.9888	18893.6062	89
6. Other	19182.9167	11132.7746	12

general, where the coefficient of variation for the entire group was 94.4 percent those in private and parastatal organizations were over 90 percent. This shows that there was a wide gap between individual salaries in all the enterprises. Private organizations had the highest salary gap (coefficient of variation was 134.4 percent) compared to other enterprises. The variation in levels of monthly salary by gender/year and type of ownership were as summarized in Tables 4.13b and 4.13c.

Considering the changes in salaries over the years in Tanzania shillings it can be noted that there has been an increase in salaries from Tshs. 8760 in 1992 to Tshs. 41,328 in 1996 for men. For women the trend has been the same, whereby in 1992 the average salary was Tshs. 8896/= and in 1996 the figure was Tshs. 33,239/=. It can be observed that women's average salary in 1992 was slightly higher than that of men. Again total variation of salaries differed between those received by men and women. Whereas the coefficient of variation for women's salaries ranged from 37.9 percent in 1992 to 74.9 percent in 1996 that of men ranged from 44.9 percent in 1993 to 123.9 percent in 1994.

Table 4.13b: *Summaries of Monthly Salary ((Tshs.)) by Year of the Survey and Gender*

	Mean	Std Dev	Cases	CV
MALE	19166.5865	19149.1162	757	99.9%
1992	8760.4503	3322.4731	151	37.9%
1993	11501.4631	6731.7657	149	58.5%
1994	14733.5251	10990.6020	179	74.4%
1995	25716.2000	18169.4724	170	70.7%
1996	41328.7500	30965.6534	108	74.9%
FEMALE	17946.0000	16617.3241	340	92.3%
1992	8896.2340	4584.3980	47	51.5%
1993	10612.5507	4768.7624	69	4.9%
1994	14412.4783	17860.8958	92	123.9%
1995	23075.3067	15424.5615	75	66.8%
1996	33239.5614	19108.2478	57	57.5%

There was a general increase in absolute (mean) salaries in all the sectors. For example, for workers (respondents) who were in the civil service, the average monthly salary changed from Tshs. 8,043 in 1992 to Tshs. 33,042/= in 1996; for the private sector employees, the average monthly salary increased from Tshs.5,164/= in 1992 to Tshs. 58,575/= in 1996; and for respondents who were in pararastatals, the average monthly salary increased from Tshs. 9,315/= in 1992 to Tshs. 34,667/= in 1996. The private sector employees seemed to have had more variation in salaries than employees in public/parastatal sector. Furthermore, average monthly salaries for respondents who were in the parastatal sector were higher than those who were in the civil service for the entire period under review (Table 4.13c).

Table 4.13c: *Summaries of Monthly Salary (Tshs) by Year Of the Survey and Type Of Enterprise*

		Mean	Std Dev	Cases	CV
Civil Service		15138.3567	10762.1384	314	71.1%
	1992	8043.4000	2931.2596	55	36.4%
	1993	8528.8594	3079.5742	64	36.1%
	1994	10997.7765	4999.2969	85	45.4%
	1995	21038.1791	8891.2790	67	42.3%
	1996	33042.8140	10618.8578	43	32.1%
Private		26623.2963	35780.4492	54	134.9%
	1992	5164.2727	1771.5501	11	34.3%
	1993	10917.5714	4421.1772	7	40.5%
	1994	17530.6250	10928.7597	8	62.3%
	1995	18915.6667	9129.6838	12	48.3%
	1996	58574.6875	52567.7441	16	89.7%
Parastatal		18604.4272	17346.8890	618	93.2%
	1992	9415.0547	3864.9103	128	41.0%
	1993	12280.0299	6983.0230	134	56.9%
	1994	16802.5466	16745.6794	161	99.7%
	1995	28604.8222	21515.2242	135	75.2%
	1996	34667.0667	20466.0754	60	59.0%
Trade Union		25335.9888	18893.6062	89	74.6%
	1993	13742.2222	6959.9035	9	50.6%
	1994	10777.8667	6161.2701	15	57.2%
	1995	19879.6552	6912.2763	29	34.8%
	1996	38695.6944	22347.1744	36	57.8%
Other	1991	82.9167	11132.7746	12	58.0%
	1992	9400.0000	1555.6349	2	16.5%
	1993	15000.0000	.0000	1	0.0%
	1994	10657.5000	993.4850	2	9.3%
	1995	13847.5000	1424.8202	2	10.3%
	1996	29477.0000	10208.3419	5	34.5%

However, in real terms the increases were not impressive given the high levels of inflation aggravated by the devaluation of the Tanzanian shilling as already discussed. Actually, real average monthly salaries for respondents who were in the civil service declined from Tshs. 369/= in 1992 to Tshs. 355/= in 1993 to Tshs. 325/= in 1994; for trade union employees, the decline was from Tshs. 573/= in 1993 to Tshs. 319 in 1994. Private sector respondents had the lowest mean monthly real wages in 1992 but the wages increased annually and in 1996 had the highest real monthly wages. All respondents (except those in the private sector) the real average monthly salaries in 1994 were lower than in 1993 (see Table 4.14). The most severe declines in real salaries in 1994 were with respondents who were trade union employees and those in the civil service (Table 4.14). In that year (1994) OTTU called for a general strike involving all employees in the country to pressure the government to increase wages for employees in the public sector (see Chambua and Naimani, 1996a).

Since the workers' salaries were low in real terms, it compelled the workers to engage themselves in other income generation activities. Even with these income-generating activities there were still some indications that family income for a large proportion of the workers (the respondents) was not sufficient for house rent, buying food, buying clothes, etc. This is why 85 percent of the respondents were not satisfied with their levels of earnings.

Table 4.14: *Real Monthly Average Salary (Tshs.) by Year, Sex and Type of Enterprise*

	1992	1993	1994	1995	1996
Male	401.86	479.23	435.90	938.55	1,968.04
Female	408.08	442.19	426.40	842.16	1,582.84
Civil service	368.96	355.37	325.38	767.82	1,573.48
Private	236.89	454.90	518.66	690.35	2,789.27
Parastatal	431.88	511.67	497.12	1,043.97	1,650.81
Trade Union	--	572.59	318.87	725.54	1,842.65

Source: Calculated by the author from Table 4.13b and 4.13c taking into consideration the annual rate of inflation.

It is known through the theory of relative deprivation that satisfaction with level of earnings (salary) is affected by the assessment of what other people earn. This so-called relative deprivation is regarded as an indicator of whether somebody is 'class conscious' or not. To test this theory, the questionnaire survey asked the respondents to indicate whether, in their opinion an employee in each of the eight chosen occupations earns: more than s/he should; a just salary/wage; and less than s/he should. The occupations selected and the wage/salary category in which they are perceived to fall were the following:

- Lowest wage/salary: domestic worker   office messenger
- Low wage/salary: mechanic   office clerk
- Higher wage/salary: teacher   medical doctor
- Highest salary: manager   university lecturer/professor

Table 4.15: *Respondents' Perception of Salary Structure*

Earns:	More than s/he should (%)	A just wage (%)	Less than s/he should (%)	N
Domestic worker	1	25	74	1096
Office Messenger	2	41	57	1099
Mechanic	3	39	58	1090
Office clerk	2	43	55	1096
Teacher	2	41	57	1098
Medical doctor	5	46	49	1097
Manager of a company	42	41	17	1096
University lecturer/professor	12	51	36	1093

The results as shown in Table 4.15 did not support the theory. For all of the above occupations (except three), over 50 percent of the respondents indicated that employees in these occupations earned less than they deserve. Only in one occupation (university lecturers/professors) did the majority of the respondents (51 percent) felt that they earned a just wage. As for company managers, this received the highest percentage (42%) of the respondents who indicated that they earned more than they should and the lowest number (17 percent) indicating that they earned less than they should. These results are consistent with the fact that salary scales in Tanzania were generally very low during the period when the questionnaire surveys were conducted. A discussion of the 1994 general strike is now in order.

THE 1994 GENERAL STRIKE IN TANZANIA

Background and Objectives

In his May Day speech of 1993 at Mtwara, the President of the United Republic of Tanzania (URT), promised that the Government would raise wages and salaries effective from 1st July 1993. During the budget session (for the 1993/94 budget), the Minister for Finance announced that the government will not raise wages/ salaries during the period 1 July 1993 to 30th June 1994 as promised by the President due to lack of funds. Instead of salary increases, government employees were given a hardship allowance of 2,000/= per month. This resulted into discussions and confrontations between the Government and OTTU over the issue.

The government stand was that the economy could not afford salary increases without escalating or fuelling inflation. OTTU's stand was that the salaries/wages were so low that workers could not meet most of their basic needs for physical survival and called for the URT to raise wages/salaries as already promised by the President. Other demands made by OTTU to the Government included: raising the minimum wage from 5,000/month to 45,000/= per month; making workers' participation a law and workers should have their own representatives in Boards of Directors, and review of the privatization policy since its contrary to workers' interests. After long confrontation the Executive Committee of OTTU's General Council decided to call for a general strike involving all employees from 1st - 3rd March 1994 if by then the salaries were not raised. The salaries were not raised and hence the decision by OTTU to carry out the strike.

However, a strike is a collective action by workers in general (solidarity strike) or by workers in a particular industry, institution, etc. against the employer or employers. Thus, a strike is also a test case of organisational ability of the trade union/leadership in question and its acceptability by members. This implies that before calling for any strike there ought to be close consultations between the trade union leadership, its various branches and members in general to ensure that most, if not all of them, will support/join the strike. Careful planning, preparations and assessment of the strengths and weak points are but mandatory to ensure success.

Success or failure in this case has to be measured against the extent to which the objectives of the strike were met and/or the gains to workers and the TU as a result of the general strike. The general strike had the following intended objectives:

◆ To force employers to raise the salaries/wages of workers/employees in Tanzania particularly those in the Civil Service and also forcing the URT to make various allowances a real wage increase; and
◆ To soften, in the course of the strike, the stand of the Government/employers on the issue of salary/wage increase.

The unintended or indirect objectives of the strike included:

◆ To test the organisational ability of the trade union movement
◆ To test the acceptability of OTTU by the working people in Tanzania.

Negotiations Prior to the 1994 Workers' General Strike

As mentioned earlier, the President of the Ununted Republic of Tanzania promised that the government will increase wages effective from 1 July 1993, a promise which was not honoured. Instead the government offered an allowance of Tshs.

1,500/= to 2,000/= per month to all employees in the public sector effective from July 1, 1993. The minimum wage/salary by then was Tshs. 3,500/= per month which was not enough for daily necessities of the worker. OTTU leaders pressed for the government to increase wages as the President had earlier promised. But the government refused arguing that it had no money to do so. Dar es Salaam workers confronted OTTU and requested the leadership to organise a demonstration by Dar es Salaam workers to the State House to ask the President to force the government to carry out his promise. OTTU agreed and the demonstration was to take place on 17 July 1993.

At this stage the Government invited OTTU to discuss the issue. OTTU agreed and presented its demands to the government for discussion. OTTU held two separate discussions with the Prime Minister and also met with the Minister for Labour twice in September 1993. The demands of OTTU during the negotiations/discussion were:

a) Salaries/wages to be increased as promised by the President and the minimum wage to be increased from 5,500/= to 45,000/= per month;

b) Benefits to retrenched workers to be paid on the date they receive letters informing them of their being laid off, again a promise made by the President but which was not honoured;

c) Workers' Participation to be enforced by law in every work place and workers should have their representatives even in the Boards of Directors; and

d) The Civil Service (Negotiating Machinery) Act of 1962 is outdated and should be reviewed.

The initial stand of the government was that: (a) the government has no money to increase wages because of the poor performance of the economy; (b) the 2000/= per month allowance is enough; (c) the government has given the workers one full day (Saturday, which was previously a working day) to engage in income generating/saving activities to supplement their meagre salaries. Even so, the discussions/negotiations ended with the following agreement: OTTU to call off the planned demonstration to the State House and on its part the government promised/agreed to implement the following:

a) To review its budget (with OTTU's involvement) and effect salary adjustments by December 1993;

b) To ensure that the workers are represented in the Boards of Directors of public enterprises as per Presidential Directive No. 1 of 1970;

c) To review the Civil Service (Negotiating Machinery) Act, No. 52 of 1962;

e) To adhere to the Tripartite principle among Social Partners, i.e. of involving employers, the government and workers in dealing with workers issues;

f) To take into consideration the recommendations of the Minimum Wage Board before effecting salary/wage revisions; and

g) To pay promptly, the benefits of those workers affected or are going to be affected by the exercise of retrenching workers.

But the government did not honour the above agreement. Yes, the budget was reviewed and the government came up with a mini-budget effective from January 1994. The mini-budget increased the minimum wage for employees in the private sector from Tshs. 3,500/= to 5,000/= per month to make it at per with the minimum wage for public sector employees. Ironically, the majority of private sector employers within the formal sector were already paying a minimum wage that was above the government set minimum wage for the public sector. Other measures taken by the government included increased prices for petroleum products (diesel, petrol, kerosene, etc.) and electricity as well as introducing new taxes for small vehicle owners (private car saloons, taxis and station wagons). The measures led to price increases due to, inter alia, increases in transportation costs. This implied that the living conditions were becoming even more unbearable in so far as the workers were concerned. OTTU informed the government about this and demanded for wage increases as per September 1993 agreement. The government maintained that it had no money to do so.

On January 17, 1994 the National Executive Committee of OTTU met to discuss the matter and decided that negotiations with the government on salary increases should continue but if by 28 February 1994 no agreement had been reached regarding salary increases, then OTTU would call for a General Strike involving all workers in Tanzania from 1 - 3 March 1994. This decision was endorsed by the organisation's General Council on 18 February 1994.

Negotiations between OTTU and the government continued on 17 February 1994. OTTU's delegation consisted of:

1) P. Nyamhokia   National Chairperson (OTTU)
2) B. Mpangala   Secretary General (OTTU)
3) J. Nasib   Vice Chairperson (OTTU Zanzibar)
4) J. Mwambuma   General Secretary of TUICO
5) Rutatina   General Secretary of TUGHE
6) P. Nyindo   General Secretary TPAWU
7) T. Kasilati   Secretary, Department of Economics and Research
                       (OTTU Headquarters)
8) S. Chala   OTTU's Lawyer

The government delegation included five Ministers and their Principal Secretaries:

1) H. Diria   Minister for Labour
2) K. Malima   Minister for Finance

3) F. Alli   Minister of State for Civil Service (President's Office)
4) J. Makweta   Minister for Agriculture
5) M. Nyanganyi   Minister of State (Prime Ministers' Office).

OTTU presented its demands which this time were basically two: (a) Salary increases so that the income of the worker is enough to meet the basic necessities of the worker and his/her family. Based on prices for food items in Dar es Salaam, OTTU recommended a minimum wage of Tshs. 93,000/= per month. When this was rejected it proposed another figure of 84,020/= per month. This was also rejected, then OTTU asked the government to offer a minimum wage of 45,000/= per month as recommended by the IMF/World Bank. This was also refused. OTTU also gave the government yet another option of offering a national minimum salary of Tshs. 26,000/= per month, which by then, was the minimum wage for members of the police force. OTTU was not prepared to accept anything below this figure.

The second demand concerned salary increases to match with the level of inflation. The government rejected both demands on the grounds of lack of funds and that such massive wage increases would only fuel inflation which by then (1993) was 24% per annum. But it was prepared to offer a minimum wage of 10,000/= per month as per minimum wage recommendation of late 1993. This was rejected by OTTU. At this stage, the government negotiators asked for adjournment of the meeting to 27 February to give the entire cabinet sufficient time to study more closely OTTU's demands and find ways to implement them. The government arranged yet another meeting with OTTU on 25/2/94 but it had nothing new to offer except telling OTTU to call off the strike. It was at this stage that OTTU withdrew from the negotiations with the government. The meeting of 27 February never took place and thence the General Strike.

Preparations for the Strike

After the January 17th 1994 decision by the Executive Committee calling for a three day general strike starting on 1st March 1994, the leadership realized that given the vastness of the country, it would require extra efforts in so far as preparations for the strike were concerned. Thus, on 16th February 1994, the General Secretary of OTTU appointed a task force of eight (8) people to prepare for, and make follow-up of, the strike to ensure its success. The preparations included:

a) Preparation and Distribution of Documents/Papers

One of the tasks of the Task Force was to prepare documents/papers in connection with the general strike and distribute them throughout the country to all OTTU leaders from the national to the branch level. The leaders would then distribute the same to all trade union members and other workers in their respective workplaces. The following three basic documents were prepared and their distribution started on 19/02/94, ten days before the date of the strike.

a) Mgomo wa Wafanyakazi wa Tanzania Tarehe 01 Machi, 1994

This was an 11-page document addressed to all OTTU leaders: national, regional, district and branch. It explained OTTU's demands and why the decision for a general strike and urged all workers to take part in the strike. The leaders were told to make sure that they distributed the same to all workers in their place of work before 28/02/94.

b) Statement of OTTU on Discussions With the Government

This three-page statement carried the message that the government was not serious during the discussions and called for the workers to start preparing for using their last weapon, i.e. staging a strike.

c) Discussions on Salary Increases

This 19-page document essentially showed the basis for OTTU's demands for salary increases as well as for the minimum wage proposed by OTTU. It argued that the government has the ability to pay even higher salaries than those proposed by OTTU. The problem and or failure to do so, according to OTTU, was due to bad use and/or misuse of government funds and failure to collect taxes coupled with allowing tax exemptions. This paper did not give details on the actual negotiations/discussions between OTTU and the government.

These three documents were sent through DHL and up-country bound private buses. One thing to be noted here is the extremely short time interval between their dispatch on 19 February and 1 March 1994, the date for the strike. We shall come to this aspect later when we evaluate the success or failure of the strike.

Meetings With Leaders of TU Branches in Dar es Salaam

The Task force also held meetings with trade union branch leaders of TUGHE based in Dar es Salaam. The purpose was to inform them of the strike and in mobilizing their workers to support and take part in the strike. Time was too short to arrange meetings with all trade union branches even in Dar es Salaam. Thus, the task force had to reach other union leaders (at regional and district levels) by telephone.

Educating and Mobilizing Workers

Educating the public on the general strike as well as mobilization of workers to ensure they take part in the strike was through the media: the OTTU Newspaper

'*Mfanyakazi*,' private newspapers, and foreign radios like BBC & VOA (Voice of America) whose programmes (in Kiswahili and English) are very popular in the country.

Various posters were also prepared and distributed in many places in Dar es Salaam and in several other places that could be reached easily. OTTU leaders in other places were reached by phone and the messages contained in those various posters were read to them and asked to prepare similar posters. In addition to that, OTTU was compelled to postpone a seminar involving all Regional OTTU Secretaries that had just started on 21 February 1994. These Regional Secretaries were ordered to go back to their respective regions to prepare for the strike.

GOVERNMENT THREATS AND OTTU'S REACTION

On 25 February 1994 the government announced that: (a) the General Strike called by OTTU was illegal under the Civil Service Act (No. 52 of 1962); (b) disciplinary measures will be taken to all workers who will take part in the strike; (c) it will continue to negotiate with OTTU and salary increases will definitely be effected in 1994/95 financial year; and (d) the dispute was between OTTU/government employees and the government. In other words, private and parastatal sector employees are excluded in the dispute although OTTU's call for a strike was for all employees or workers in the country: private and otherwise.

OTTU's reaction was immediate. On 26 February it issued a statement to challenge the above announcement by the government. That statement pointed out, among other things, that:

* The strike was for all workers and not government employees only;
* The 1962 Civil Service (Negotiating Machinery) Act was out of date and OTTU had earlier asked for its review; and
* The government did not even say/mention that salaries will be increased by how much in 1994/95, if it failed to honour the Presidents' promise for the same what guarantee is there to trust it now.

Placards/posters were also prepared and distributed with the following messages:

"OTTU Maintains That the Strike is on, Fair and Just
Governments Threats Amount to Dictatorship
Workers You Must not be Swayed, Unity Forever"

Of course the government, through the state owned radio stations (Radio Tanzania Dar es Salaam and Zanzibar), the state owned newspapers (*Daily News* and the *Sunday News*) and the CCM Kiswahili newspapers (*Uhuru* and *Mzalendo*) continued to issue threats to suppress the strike. OTTU also used the private media to both challenge the government's position and to mobilize workers to go on strike as planned.

Execution of the General Strike

The strike took place as planned. It is difficult to establish how many workers really took part in the strike but it is widely known that the number decreased as the days passed. One OTTU official who was in the Task Force estimated that about 15 percent, 10 percent and 5 percent of government employees took part on the $1,^{st}$ the 2nd and the 3rd day of the strike respectively. This included those who actually did not go to work as well as those who did go to work but did not work. There was no independent confirmation on these estimates. Even so, according to OTTU, the execution of the strike was as shown in Table 4.16.

Table 4.16: *Number of Branches/workplace That Took Part in the Strike*

Place	1 March 1994 On Strike	Go slow	2 March 1994 On Strike	Go Slow	3 March 1994 On Strike	Go Slow
Dar es Salaam	36	6	34	6	34	6
Morogoro	4	-	4	-	4	-
Kilosa	5	2	5	2	5	2
Iringa	1	-	1	-	1	-
Tabora	12	-	12	-	12	-
Arusha	20	-	20	-	20	-
Babati	6	-	6	-	6	-
Mbulu	8	-	8	-	8	-
Monduli	4	-	4	-	4	-
Moshi	9	5	9	5	9	5
Singida	1	-	1	-	1	-
Coast Region	11	4	11	4	11	4
Lindi	4	-	4	-	4	-
Rukwa	1	5	1	5	1	5
Kigoma	7	-	-	7	-	7
Tanga	1	-	1	-	1	-
Dodoma Region	6	1	6	1	6	1
Mtwara	2	-	2	-	2	-
Mwanza Region	24	2	23	3	23	3
Shinyanga	3	1	3	1	3	1
Mara Region	16	-	16	-	16	-
Mbeya	44	1	44	1	44	1
Kagera Region	12	6	12	6	12	6
Ruvuma	3	-	3	-	3	-
Zanzibar	-	-	-	-	-	-
Pemba	-	-	-	-	-	-

Source: Extracted from OTTU (1994)

Notes: "Go Slow" means that workers did report to their respective workplaces but did not work.

It is obvious from Table 4.16 that the strike was spread all over the country except in Zanzibar. Even so, the majority of the workers did not take part in the strike not because they were satisfied with their salaries but because they feared to be fired. We shall come to this point later but first there is need to mention several incidences connected with the strike in few selected places.

Dar es Salaam

* At Urafiki Textiles, workers debated on weather to go on strike or not. They failed to reach a consensus on this issue and as a result, 25 percent decided not to strike and 75 percent were on strike;
* Some trade union branch leaders participated in convincing the workers not to take part in the strike on grounds that regional OTTU leaders did not involve them during the preparations;
* The Secretary of the Mwananyamali Hospital trade union branch was arrested and taken to Osterbay Police Station for questioning regarding the strike, and released thereafter. The workers there were on strike for all the three days;
* The Principal Secretary, Ministry of Foreign Affairs personally supervised the registration of workers at the Ministry's head office who reported to work during the strike period;
* The Prime Minister gave orders to Radio Tanzania Dar es Salaam not to broadcast any information concerning the execution of the strike in the regions.

Arusha

* The Regional Commissioner summoned the OTTU Regional Secretary and told him to stop making preparations for the strike;
* The chairperson of the Sunflag trade Union branch was arrested and sent to Police Station for questioning, and released thereafter.

Mbeya

* Three Hi Soap trade union Branch leaders, among them the chairperson and secretary, were expelled from work on charges of inciting workers to go on strike;
* Two workers of the Water Department were taken to court to answer charges of causing water shortage during the strike. Another worker, Mr. Elias R. Mkisi, of the same department was arrested by Police on 2 March 1994 at 2 pm.

Ruvuma

* Police were deployed outside government offices to intimidate workers.

Kagera

* Members of the notorious Field Force Unit were deployed in all streets of Bukoba town to intimidate the workers
* Workers of the Regional Hospital were followed in their homes and forced to go to work on the first day of the strike. This action angered them and they did not go to work from 2 - 3 March 1994. Patients had to be transferred to Kagondo Mission Hospital.

Musoma

* OTTU posters/placards were confiscated by the government. All copies of the TU newspaper 'Mfanyakazi' were bought by security agents and no copies were sold to the general public in Musoma. This was not limited to Musoma alone.

What we want to stress here is that the government spent a lot of time and resources to suppress the strike by intimidating workers, monopolizing the state media and making it to provide one-sided and biased coverage of issues relating to the demands of the workers and the General Strike. This said we now turn to evaluate the success of the strike.

THE GENERAL STRIKE: SUCCESS OR FAILURE?

To asses the success or failure of the general strike one has to consider, among other things, the following: (a the fact that for about 28 years the trade union movement in Tanzania was under the control of the state/ruling political party; (b) it was the first strike organised/supported by the trade union since the formation of NUTA in April 1964; and (c) the extent to which the objectives of the strike were realised.

The mere fact that it was the first strike to be called by the trade union in Tanzania after 30 years in spite of government threats must be translated as a historic and success story in the country's trade union history since 1964. The act of daring did bring to an end the more than 30-years legacy of submissiveness. It also showed that unlike NUTA and JUWATA, OTTU was capable of opposing the government. This was important in view of the fact that OTTU was formed through an Act of Parliament and because of this, some people were of the opinion that it is incapable of taking actions not approved by the government just like NUTA and JUWATA. Even so, the question still remains, to what extent were the objectives behind the strike realised?

The first objective was to force employers, especially the government, to raise wages/salaries for their employees. This objective was not met immediately but in July 1994 the government increased the minimum wage by 100 percent, i.e. from Tshs. 5,000/- to 10,000/- per month. In July 1995 the minimum wage was increased by 75 percent to 17,500/- and in 1996 it was increased by 71 percent to 30,000/- per month effective from the 1st of July 1996. Percentage wise, these were huge increases although far below OTTU demands and the minimum wage was inadequate to meet the basic/daily necessities of life. What is significant here is the softening of the initial government's stand and change of attitude towards salary/wage increases. Thus, the second objective was realised. Indeed, the government (after the strike) also changed its initial stand of expelling all those who participated in the strike to only taking disciplinary measures of reprimand and a 3-day salary cut.

The other two objectives of testing the: (a) organisational ability of the trade union movement and (b) acceptability of OTTU by the workers in Tanzania are dependent on two factors. First, the extent to which the call for a general strike by the centre managed to reach all the workers in time and how the workers were mobilized to support the call. Second, the number or proportion of workers who were actually on strike.

Organisationally, the task of educating/mobilizing the workers for the general strike was severely constrained by lack of time. One has to recall that the task force was formed on 16 February 1994 and important documents/information were dispatched from Dar es Salaam on 19 February 1994 while the strike was to commence on March 1, 1994. Because of time constraints it was not possible for OTTU leadership to determine actually how many trade union branches and or workers were going to take part in the strike. Even meetings of OTTU leaders with union branch leaders/members did not take place except in some Dar es Salaam branches. The leadership simply assumed that workers would take part in the strike because of low wages.

According to trade union leaders we interviewed, some union branch leaders did not take any measures to prepare, educate and mobilize their workers to take part in the strike. There were also numerous reports of some union branch leaders actually taking part in discouraging workers from taking part in the strike. Although the seminar for OTTU Regional Secretaries in Dar es Salaam was postponed on 21st February1994 to allow them to go to their respective regions to prepare workers for the general strike, they did not have enough time to do so and some never reached their regions in time. In short, there was lack of effective communications between the Centre, which called for the strike, and the union branches. The flow of information was one-way, from top to bottom. As a result a lot of questions on the part of workers remained unanswered. For example, questions related to security of employment given the government threats to expel all those who would take part in the strike; after three days of strike what next if the government did not change its position; what gains will result from the strike; what will happen to those who would not take part in the strike; etc. Given the fact that the strike was the first to be called by the trade union movement in more than 30 years, these and other issues needed to be clarified to ensure its success. Because this was not done, the response to it was not impressive (Table 4.16).

Regarding the number of workers who actually took part in the general strike this is not known except that the majority did not. Interestingly enough: (a) the majority of those who actually participated in the strike came from the private sector although for them this was a solidarity strike and (b) within the public sector, the majority of employees who were actually on strike were primary and secondary school teachers who had earlier on participated in a strike, which was not endorsed by OTTU, to press for better pay and working conditions. The strike was forcefully suppressed by the government and some of the leaders were arrested while others were suspended (Rutinwa, 1995: 21). Other groups of employees with relatively higher proportion of their members directly taking part in the strike were medical doctors, employees of water (Maji) and construction (Ujenzi) government departments.

It is obvious from the above discussion that both the organisation and response to the general strike were not impressive. Even so, the strike proved or demonstrated that it takes more than restrictive legal provisions and/or threats to prevent industrial action by dissatisfied/demoralized workers.

LESSONS FROM THE STRIKE

From our discussion so far, it is obvious that salaries/wages in Tanzania have remained too low, at least from the 1980s, to meet basic necessities of the worker. Even the government did not deny this. Thus, OTTU was justified to demand for wage increases. But since salaries/wages have been kept very low for a long time the amount of increase demanded by OTTU was very big, i.e. to raise the minimum wage by at least more than 500 percent at a go at the middle of a financial year was unrealistic. Thus, one lesson to be learned is that the strike should have been called much earlier than 1994. Of course legal strikes were virtually impossible in Tanzania but even this one was also illegal from the point of view of both the government and existing labour laws.

Secondly, one can say that OTTU's demand for wage increases had the support of the majority of employees in the country but few heeded the strike call for fear of loosing their jobs. OTTU failed to reach the majority of workers in Tanzania due partly to time constraints and the vastness of the country. Thus, another lesson to be learned by the trade union movement is twofold. First, is the need for adequate preparations and involvement of union branches at workplaces. Second is the involvement of union leaders and workers' representatives at all levels in educating and mobilizing workers to support decisions taken by their leaders. The general strike showed clearly that OTTU by then had not yet reached the ordinary workers. This should now be the main drive of all unions in the country.

Thirdly, apart from trade union newspapers there is a need for trade unions in the country to have a joint radio station which will play a useful role insofar as information, education and communication is concerned. Of course money here is involved but they can approach donors to help in purchasing the basic equipment. The strike also showed lack of solidarity among workers and commitment among some union leaders and workers' representatives. Radio programmes can be used to educate the workers and leaders as well on the need for solidarity, commitment and unity of purpose in fighting for workers' interests. From what happened in the early 1960s, which led to the ban of TFL and creation of NUTA by the government, the trade union movement should be more critical and suspicious of all those who want to use it for personal political gains.

Trade union leadership lacked experience in organising strikes and this became obvious from the way the strike was executed. It is our hope that the general strike gave the leaders an opportunity to experience what it means/takes to organise and stage a strike.

On the part of the government, it ringed to many that perhaps the days of submissiveness on the part of Tanzanian workers and their unions were over. In the past, partly because of free social services, government subsidies and price control by the government, workers were able to survive in spite of low wages. With all these things now becoming history, the workers will definitely become more militant unless they get a living wage. Given the fact that the government eventually increased the wages shows that it has learned this important lesson. Indeed, if the government will fail to find ways and means of at least paying a living wage to its employees, another industrial action is imminent. This said we now turn to discuss other workplace conditions

Entitlement to Benefits

Apart from wage or salary, monetary income for employees can consist of considerable benefits. Thus, in order to have a full picture of the respondents' income from their work, and to know whether these benefits existed or not, the respondents were asked to indicate whether or not they were entitled to each of the six benefits selected. The selected benefits and the results were as shown in Table 4.17. Over 80 percent of the respondents indicated that they were entitled to all but one of the benefits (child care). But even with this one benefit, still the majority of the respondents (63 percent) were entitled to them (Table 4.17). These results tend to be inconsistent with the various satisfaction results. The explanation to this is definitely the fact that being entitled to a particular benefit does or did not imply actual enjoyment of that benefit. For instance, many workers are entitled to company house but not all of them have a company house. They are thus compelled to rent houses and pay the house rent. Only senior officials who are most likely to either be provided with a company house and or to have their house-rents be paid by their respective companies.

Table 4.17: *Entitlement to Benefits*

Are you entitled to the following:	Yes (%)	No (%)	N
Company house	80	20	1116
Company loan	90	10	1116
Pension scheme/Provident fund	89	11	1109
Company medical care assistance	93	7	1114
Company transport/allowance	91	9	1112
Child care	63	37	1105
Others benefits	65	35	1088

The next section assesses the degree of sufficiency of the monetary income of all members of a respondent's household in meeting basic needs of the household.

Sufficiency of Household Income

Household income is used to meet expenses for various household requirements. Eight items were selected to represent the basic needs of any household: rent, food, clothes, children's education, electricity and water, firewood and/or charcoal, medical care, and transport. The majority of the worker representatives indicated that their household's income was not sufficient to meet expenses for these basic needs (Table 4.18).

Table 4.18: *Sufficiency of Household Income to Meet Basic Needs Expenses*

Is Household income sufficient for:	Yes (%)	Not very sufficient	No (%)	N
Paying house rent	18	47	35	1097
Buying food	11	52	37	1096
Buying clothes	8	52	40	1097
Paying children's education	5	43	52	1054
Electricity and water bills	16	44	40	1011
Buying firewood/charcoal/kerosene	18	51	31	1095
Paying medical care expenses	8	41	51	1097
Transport expenses	8	44	48	1097

The above results indicate that many of the respondents fell under the category of 'the working poor.' This is true even if the value 'not very sufficient' were to be taken to imply 'household income is sufficient' or vice versa. Slightly more than 50 percent of the respondents indicated that household income was not sufficient for paying children's education and medical care expenses. As mentioned earlier, the government used to offer free medical services and education before it adopted the IMF/World Bank sponsored SAPs in the mid-1980s. From there on to date, people have to pay for these services. Worse still, government budget cuts in the financing of social services have had the effect of lowering the quality of services, particularly education and health, offered by the government. This in turn has had the effect of making many people to prefer to go to private hospitals (for medical care), and send their children to private schools. The fees charged by private hospitals and schools are very high since many operate profit-making ventures. The same also is true of transport in that before SAPs, the transport of people was mainly by public owned companies and hence, fares were set/fixed by the government. The situation changed after the adoption of SAPs to private domination by private companies, which raised transport charges. This, to a large extent explains why only between 5 to 8 percent of the respondents indicated that their household income was sufficient to meet medical care, education of children and transport expenses.

Insofar as buying food was concerned, another variable was included in the questionnaire to assess the extent to which food for a household is provided, either by only the monetary resources or by cultivation. The results were as follows: of the 1099 worker representatives who answered the question, 23 percent of them said they bought all their food in the market; 30 percent indicated that they bought most of their food; another 30 percent indicated that they buy half and produced half of their food; 15 percent said that they produced most of their food themselves; and only two percent indicated that they produced all the food themselves. Thus, nearly all of the respondents (98 percent) depended partly or wholly on the market to meet their household food requirements.

Household Income Generating Activities

Practically in all African households, one does not depend on wage/salary alone for a living. This is true even in urban areas. Most of the respondents (they and/or members of their households) were engaged in other informal income-supplementing/generating activities. Respondents were asked if they and or members of their households were engaged in the following activities to supplement their wage/salary earnings:

+ Agriculture: cultivating beans, maize, fruits, vegetables, rice, cotton, coffee, and other crops
+ Craft work: tailoring, basketry, pottery carpentry, and other crafts;
+ Animal husbandry: cattle, sheep, goats, chickens, pigs, other animals;
+ Fishing; and
+ Commerce: shoe repairs, kiosks, transport, and other small businesses.

The respondents were also asked to indicate whether or not they were selling some of the products from the income-supplementing activities, i.e. agriculture, craftwork, animal husbandry, and fishing activities. A count was made of those saying 'yes' (they were engaged in a particular income-supplementing activity) and another similar count for selling some of the products. The results showed that of all the 1116 respondents, 86 percent were (and/or some members of their households) engaged in at least one of the eight agricultural activities mentioned above; 64 percent in hand craftwork; 15 percent in fishing; and 57 percent in commerce. The percentage of those engaged in selling at least one of the products was as follows: agriculture (51 percent); handcraft (42 percent); animal husbandry (42 percent); and fish (11 percent) (see Table 4.19 A1 to E).

Table 4.19: *Count of Engagement in Income Supplementing/ Generating Activities*

A1: *Count of Engagement in Agricultural Activities*

Value Label	Value	Frequency	Percent	Cum Percent
None	.00	161	14.4	14.4
One crop	1.00	117	10.5	24.9
Two crops	2.00	134	12.0	36.9
Three crops	3.00	171	15.3	52.2
Four crops	4.00	195	17.5	69.7
Five Crops	5.00	184	16.5	86.2
Six crops	6.00	98	8.8	95.0
Seven crops	7.00	35	3.1	98.1
Eight crops	8.00	21	1.9	100.0
Total		1116	100.0	

A2: *Count of Selling Agricultural Crops*

Value Label	Value	Frequency	Percent	Cum Percent
Not selling any	0.00	453	40.6	40.6
Selling one crop	1.00	202	18.1	58.7
Selling two	2.00	123	11.0	69.7
Selling three	3.00	97	8.7	78.4
Selling four	4.00	90	8.1	86.5
Selling five	5.00	80	7.2	93.6
Selling six	6.00	32	2.9	96.5
Selling seven	7.00	16	1.4	97.9
Selling eight	8.00	23	2.1	100.0
Total		1116	100.0	

B1: *Count of Engagement in Handcraft Work*

Value Label	Value	Frequency	Percent	Cum Percent
Not engaged in any	.00	397	35.6	35.6
Engaged in:				
One craft	1.00	360	32.3	67.8
Two	2.00	198	17.7	85.6
Three	3.00	75	6.7	92.3

Table 4.19 B1: *Continued....*

Value Label	Value	Frequency	Percent	Cum Percent
Four	4.00	51	4.6	96.9
Five	5.00	21	1.9	98.7
Six	6.00	14	1.3	100.0
Total		1116	100.0	

B2. *Count of Selling Handcraft Products*

Value Label	Value	Frequency	Percent	Cum Percent
Not selling any	.00	642	57.5	57.5
Selling: One product	1.00	293	26.3	83.8
Two	2.00	109	9.8	93.5
Three	3.00	39	3.5	97.0
Four	4.00	23	2.1	99.1
Five	5.00	10	0.9	100.0
Total		1116	100.0	

C1. *Count of Engagement in Animal Husbandry*

Value Label	Value	Frequency	Percent	Cum Percent
Not engaged in any	.00	316	28.3	28.3
Engaged in: one	1.00	232	20.8	49.1
Two	2.00	199	17.8	66.9
Three	3.00	172	15.4	82.3
Four	4.00	119	10.7	93.0
Five	5.00	49	4.4	97.4
Six	6.00	29	2.6	100.0
Total		1116	100.0	

C2: *Count of Selling Animals*

Value Label	Value	Frequency	Percent	Cum Percent
Not selling any	0.00	649	58.2	58.2
Selling: One type	1.00	241	21.6	79.7
Two types	2.00	121	10.8	90.6
Three	3.00	58	5.2	95.8
Four	4.00	30	2.7	98.5
Five	5.00	17	1.5	100.0
Total		1116	100.0	

D1: *Engagement in Fishing*

Value Label	Value	Frequency	Percent	Valid Percent	Cum Percent
YES	2	169	15.1	15.5	15.5
NO	3	922	82.6	84.5	100.0
No Response	0	25	2.2	Missing	
Total		1116	100.0	100.0	

Valid cases 1091   Missing cases   25

D2. *Selling Fish*

Value Label	Value	Frequency	Percent	Valid Percent	Cum Percent
YES	2	124	11.1	24.1	24.1
NO	3	390	34.9	75.9	100.0
No Response	0	602	53.9	Missing	
Total		1116	100.0	100.0	

Valid cases 514   Missing cases 602

E. *Count of Engagement in Commerce/Small Business*

Value Label	Value	Frequency	Percent	Cum Percent
Not engaged in any	0.00	476	42.7	42.7
Engaged in: One	1.00	317	28.4	71.1
Two	2.00	171	15.3	86.4
Three	3.00	91	8.2	94.5
Four	4.00	61	5.5	100.0
Total		1116	100.0	

These results imply that members of a typical household of the worker representatives were engaged in several income supplementing/generating activities. This in turn is a reflection of the fact that we are dealing with workers who get very low wages/salaries as already discussed in this chapter. In order to manage their living, they have no choice but to engage in these activities. But even those getting relatively higher salaries were also engaged in such activities.

RECAPITULATION

Tanzania, like many other African countries, was confronted with a serious economic crisis unprecedented in her history during the 1980s. In its efforts to deal with the crisis, the government was compelled to adopt and implement the IMF/World Bank sponsored SAPs from the mid-1980s. The measures taken included price decontrol, trade liberalization, devaluation of the Tanzanian shilling, government budget cuts especially to social services, privatisation and retrenchment of civil servants.

The SAP reforms were vigorously applied. For example, whereas during the mid-1980s prices of about 50 commodities were determined by the government, by 1999 all prices were market determined; exports and imports were completely liberalized; and more than 2000 parastatals were divested. From 1993 to 1999 about 26,000 civil servants were retrenched in efforts to reduce government expenditure and devaluation of the Tanzanian shilling has been massive, i.e. from about Tshs.18/= per one US $ in 1985 to Tshs. 752/= per one US $ in 1999.

Implementation of SAPs and other measures managed to restore economic growth and stability and inflation has been brought down from over 35 percent in 1990 to 6 percent in 2000. But at the same time there has been growing unemployment and income differentials. For instance, absolute poverty levels increased during the period 1991/92 - 2000 from 48 percent of the population (earning less than 1 US $ per day) to well over 50 percent. This means that it was the workers and the peasants who had to pay dearly for the economic reforms.

Working conditions did not improve significantly during the period under review, partly due to low level of knowledge of their rights e.g. labour laws. Although satisfaction with work and with social relations at work was high, satisfaction with conditions of work (wage/salary, canteen and transport) was very low. Over 50 percent of the respondents were not satisfied with them. Wage/salaries have remained very low and workers were forced to engage in other income supplementing/generating activities. Yet, in spite of this engagement, sufficiency of household income to meet expenses of basic needs is very low, ranging from 5 percent (income sufficient for paying for children's education) to 18 percent (income sufficient for paying house rent and purchasing firewood/charcoal/kerosene respectively).

Since 85 percent of the respondents came from the public (civil service parastatal) sector that has now shrinked considerably, perhaps things have changed now. This, together with the government's commitment to poverty eradication by 2025 calls for another study to find out how the situation has changed and its impact on poverty reduction. Otherwise, thus far the conclusion to be drawn from the data presented in this chapter is clear: in spite of restoration of economic growth and success in fighting inflation, the majority of the people have not benefited from the implementation of SAPs.

5

TRADE UNIONS AND THE PARTICIPATION OF WOMEN IN DECISION-MAKING BODIES

INTRODUCTION

This chapter is intended to give a realistic impression of the trade union structure in Tanzania and the conditions in which the unions operated. The issues of 'workers' education/training' by trade unions as well as that of 'gender, employment and participation in decision-making bodies' will be given extra weight by drawing both from case studies (2) and questionnaire surveys.

It may be recalled that the Organization of Tanzanian Trade Unions (OTTU) was established in 1991 through an Act of Parliament. Unlike its predecessor, JUWATA, OTTU was not affiliated to any political party. As already pointed out in chapter two, the process of forming industrial unions took place between 1992 and 1995. By 1995, eleven (11) sector-based trade unions had been formed. They were all OTTU affiliates (by law) and they were deemed registered along with OTTU, i.e. they had no separate registration. In 1995 OTTU together with its 11 affiliates decided to change the name of the federation from OTTU to Tanzania Federation of Free Trade Unions (TFTU). Again, as discussed in chapter two, officially this change of name was not possible unless the OTTU Act was repealed/reviewed to allow such changes. Thus, from 1995 up to June 30th, 2000 (the day OTTU/TFTU ceased to exist), the organisation had two names, OTTU (the officially recognized name) and TFTU (unofficial but popular name with many people). The 11 trade unions affiliated to OTTU/TFTU were as shown in Box 5.1.

Box 5.1: *Trade Unions that were Affiliated to OTTU/TFTU*

Conservation, Hotels, Domestic and Allied Workers Union (CHODAWU)
Communication and Transport Workers Union of Tanzania (COTWU)
Research, Academic and Allied Workers Union (RAAWU)
Tanzania Railway Workers Union (TRAWU)
Tanzania Union of Industrial and Commercial Workers (TUICO)
Tanzania Mines and Construction Workers Union (TAMICO)
Tanzania Teachers Union (TTU)
Tanzania Union of Government and Health Workers (TUGHE)
Tanzania Local Government Worker's Union (TALGWU)
Tanzania Plantation and Agriculture Workers Union (TPAWU)
Tanzania Seamen Union (TASU)

OTTU/TFTU and its affiliates operated at a time of implementing social, economic and political reforms in line with the IMF/World Bank structural adjustment programmes (SAPs). The main concern of trade unions, insofar as SAPs were concerned, was their impacts on workers especially as they relate to employee retrenchment, privatisation and the introduction of cost sharing in social service deliveries.

ATTITUDE OF TRADE UNION OFFICIALS TO SAPs

It has been argued that the retrenchment exercise has endangered the incomes of workers and therefore their welfare and that of their dependents. Moreover, since retrenchment in most cases involves low cadre employees (the rank and file members of trade unions) it has greatly reduced the size and strength of the trade unions. In its endeavour to reduce the rate of inflation the government did not increase the real wages/salaries of workers. This, in turn, meant that the income of many workers was not consistent with their living standards. Whereas the battle against inflation has been won (inflation has been reduced from over 30 percent in 1987 to 6.5 percent in 2000), unemployment and poverty increased during the same period. Introduction of the cost-sharing programme in social service delivery has further aggravated the problem of poor living standards of the workers. Workers have been made to pay for the services when their salaries are not sufficient to feed their families. Below we discuss some of the attitudes of trade union officials to SAPs as well as what they consider to be the effects of some of the measures implemented under SAPs.

Privatization

According to the trade union officials we interviewed, privatization is viewed to be a good thing but the way it has so far been implemented leaves a lot to be

CHAPTER FIVE

112

desired. For instance, neither the workers nor their trade unions were involved in the privatization exercise. Thus, workers were ignorant of their rights and many of them were not paid their terminal benefits in time. Privatization led to loss of members, about 1000 in total in the case of CHODAWU. The hardest hit union appeared to be TUICO whose membership decreased from 92,430 in 1996 to 60,000 in 1997 and to 39,000 in 1999. The reasons for this decline were mainly retrenchments and privatization. Although new employment opportunities were created, the number was smaller than the ones that vanished. This loss in membership translated into loss of revenue for the unions. Furthermore, privatization also led to a situation whereby a good number of Tanzanians who held middle to top cadre positions being replaced by foreigners.

Workers' Education/Training

According to the General Secretary of CHODAWU, many Tanzanian workers were trained under parastatal structure and management style. With new technology/management style, a good number of them lack the new skills needed and thence the pretext for foreign investors to employ foreigners. He further pointed out that new/private employers are not interested in educating/training of workers. They prefer to employ those who have already been trained and posses the required skills. According to him, the trade unions in Tanzania must pressure the government and other employers to invest in workers' education/ training for the benefit of all.

Worker's Securuty of Employment

There was also a general feeling among trade union leaders that many private investors were not in favour of the 'Security of Employment Act' since, in their opinion, it makes it very difficult to dismiss a worker. But all the trade unions are in favour of it and in their opinion, the Government should do more to enforce the Act. Furthermore, in the Export Processing Zones, workers' rights appeared to have been neglected, in fact trade unions were/are not allowed to operate in these zones.

Regarding security for workers, health and safety for workers was/is still a problem in some workplaces. Truly, there are some areas where the new private investors have improved the working conditions but there are many areas yet to be improved. The trade union challenge, therefore, is to pressure the management to take the appropriate measures to protect the health and safety of their workers at workplaces.

Workers' Participation

There was a general consensus among the trade union leaders that the form of workers' participation through Works Councils (as per Presidential Circular of 1970) is difficult to sell to foreign investors. Many see it as unnecessary interference with management prerogatives. Thus, since this form of workers' participation was introduced in the country through a Presidential directive (No. 1 of 1970), there is a danger that it is going to be defunct or less effective unless it is given a legal basis and extended to cover the private sector as well. The unions themselves are in favour of this form of participation and would like the Government to enact a law to enforce and extend it to also cover the private sector.

Trade union leaders (on behalf of their members) responded to SAPs by communicating to the government on the negative impacts of the reforms on the welfare of the working population and they made several proposals to ameliorate the plight of the working people. Some of the trade union proposals are summarized below and involve:

+ *Labour Laws*: There are many labour laws and, therefore, in many different documents. Some of these laws are out of date and oppress workers. The proposal made was to update the labour laws, have a single law book/ document, make the industrial court function as an independent court and to have laws that protect and motivate the employees;

+ *Economic Policies*: The created enabling environment to attract investors was not adequate and transparent. Also, there was/is concentration of investment projects in few regions (Dar es Salaam, Mwanza, and Arusha) and in few sectors (tourism and mining). The proposal made was to increase the extent and magnitude of enabling environment and transparency. Investment policies need to indicate the expected gains from a given project. They also proposed that decentralization of investment promotion centres to the regional levels would increase the magnitude of the investment potentials of the country. It has been pointed out that privatisation aimed at making the private sector more market oriented. Increased productivity and efficiency are, therefore, crucial for the sector in the short run (and sometimes even in the long run). The issue of employment generation was not of importance in this exercise. Retrenchments have made the situation worse. As a solution to this problem, the unions proposal was/is to make the informal sector more attractive to those who loose their jobs in the formal sectors. Further, payments for the retrenched should be made promptly to enable them find an alternative job.

+ *Institutional Framework*: According to the trade union officials interviewed, institutions dealing with workers' welfare (The National Provident Fund - NPF, The Parastatal Provident Fund -PPF and the Local Government Provident Fund -LGPF) do not function in the best interests of the workers. They appeared to be more concerned with the generation of government revenues with minimal benefits to the workers who made the contributions. The proposals made centred on the need to restructure these institutions by making them to be more oriented towards the workers' (contributors') welfare; involve the workers in decision-making through their representatives; and to create institutions that will deal with social welfare.

THE TRADE UNION STRUCTURE

In this section we intend to look at the structure of OTTU/TFTU, how the trade unions were accommodated in this structure, their own structure and their link to TFTU. But, first there is need to recall that following changes in the trade union movement due to withdrawal of direct state control of the trade union movement, the 1995 OTTU Congress resolved to form a Federation of Trade Unions with 11 affiliated unions. As a result of the changes, the structure of the trade union movement in Tanzania, up to 30th June 2000 was as follows:

a) At the federation level there was OTTU/TFTU. Although TFTU was never legally registered it did prepare grounds for its operations and it had its own constitution approved by its affiliates; and

b) The national leadership of TFTU was elected during the OTTU Congress held in Dodoma in 1995. The national Chairperson of TFTU was Mr. Peter Nyamuhokya and the Secretary General was Mr. Bruno Mpangala. According to the TFTU constitution there was also the deputy chairperson from Zanzibar and two deputy Secretary Generals: one from Zanzibar and the other one from Tanzania mainland. The main bodies of the Federation were:

A: The Executive Committee

This consisted of all the top leadership of the elected leaders of the Federation, that is, Chairpersons and Secretary Generals and the treasurer of TFTU; and all Chairpersons and Secretary Generals of the 11 unions which were affiliated to TFTU. This was the executing body of TFTU. Its functions included:

a) To implement directives issued by the Congress and the General Council;
b) To be answerable to the functioning of TFTU to the General Council;
c) To recommend to the General Council disciplinary measures to be taken to top officials of TFTU if and when necessary;
d) To take disciplinary measures to employees appointed by the Executive Committee of TFTU and to remove leaders who have been elected by the General Council if they prove to be incompetent and fail to perform as expected; and
e) To present the annual budget to the General Council.

The Executive Committee meets at least four times per year.

B. The General Council

This consisted of all members of the Executive Committee of TFTU and three members elected from each union affiliated to TFTU. The constitution provided positions for female members to the General Council. Each union affiliated to TFTU elected one female representative to the Council. The functions of the General Council included:

a) Electing the deputy Secretary Generals and national treasurer;
b) To implement policies and decisions of TFTU;
c) To discuss recommendations on changes of the Constitution whenever necessary;
d) To approve national strikes; and
e) To promote trade union activities in the country.

C: The Congress

The Congress consisted of:
a) All elected national leaders of TFTU, i.e. the chairperson, the deputy chairperson, the secretary general, and the two deputy secretary generals;
b) All general secretaries and chairpersons/presidents of all the unions affiliated to TFTU;
c) The treasurer;
d) 18 members from each of the affiliated unions;
e) One female representative elected from each union affiliated to TFTU; and
f) Three members from each union affiliated to TFTU.

The functions of the Congress are to:
a) Discuss TFTU plans;
b) Discuss and approve the five year income and expenditure reports of the Federation;
c) Elect chairperson, Secretary Generals and Vice Chairpersons of the Federation;
d) Approve the TFTU constitution.

D: Departments in TFTU

To execute its activities the TFTU initially had five departments; but in an efforts to cut down expenses these were reduced to three departments, namely: Women and Youth; Education; Workers' Participation and Research; and Health and Safety at Work Environment.

ORGANISATION STRUCTURES OF THE INDUSTRIAL UNIONS

In our study we discovered that the organisation structures of the eleven trade unions resembled each other with a few exceptions especially when it comes to the zonal distribution, nature of the hierarchies from the grassroots to the national level, and the number of members constituting the boards, to mention but a few. The following organisational structure was found to be common to all the trade unions in the country.

Trade Union Branch (Workplace Level)

Under the branch there are four different committees as follows:

a) *General Members Meeting:* This meeting is constituted by all the members of the branch and is chaired by the branch's chairperson. The functions of this committee included:

1) To receive and adopt the development reports of daily activities of the Union; and
2) To elect representatives to various organs at higher levels, regional or zonal. The committee normally meets quarterly.

b) *The Branch Committee*: The branch committee is composed of the branch chairperson, branch secretary and other members the number of which is determined by the number of members constituting the branch. The criterion is as follows: if the size of the branch is between 10-50 people, then the committee total membership is 5 people. On the other hand if the size of the branch is between 51-100 people, then total committee membership is 10 people. If however, the size of the branch is between 101-500 people, then total committee membership is 15 people.

If the size of the branch is between 501-1000 people, then total committee membership is 20 people. If the size of the branch is over 1000 people, then total committee membership is 25 people.

The branch Committee was elected by the whole branch membership and had the following functions:

- In charge of the day to day activities of the union at the branch level
- Implementing all directives from regional, zonal to national levels
- Negotiating with management on issues that concern the workers at the branch level, and
- Under the branch committee leadership various representatives were elected or appointed to various bodies at the regional level.

(c) *Women Committee*: This committee was found only in two unions: TPAWU and RAAWU, and is mainly concerned with gender issues.

d) *All Workers Meeting* (unionised and non-unionised): These meetings are held annually and are chaired by the chairperson of the trade union branch. The meeting discussed general issues concerning the conditions of work prevailing at the enterprise but also it was a means of convincing workers/non members to join the union.

Regional Level

At the regional level, the trade unions' structure consisted of the following organs:

a) *Regional Executive Committee*: This is composed of the regional chairperson, regional secretary and other members elected by the general meeting.

b) *Regional General Meeting*: This is conducted/held annually and its functions/ purposes are to:

+ Coordinate the development of the trade union;
+ Plan and help in the implementation of all trade union programmes and activities;
+ Propose ways of improving working conditions of members;
+ Elect regional chairperson and the other members of the executive committee; and
+ Elect representatives to the zonal and national meetings of the union.

A trade union region did not necessarily coincide with the political administrative region. For instance, the General Secretary of TALGWU noted that if at the level of the district there are 2500 members and above then the district acquired a regional status with a regional chairperson and regional secretary. Furthermore, some unions such as TPAWU had/have an Area Office level which comprising of several neighbouring regions. This office acts as a referral office to the offices from the grassroots to the regional levels. There are no specific organs at the Area office and the Area Secretary is directly linked to the Zonal Secretary.

Zonal Level

Normally this is above the regional level but in some trade unions it was the level immediately after the branch level. At the zonal level the leadership constituted of the Zonal Chairperson, Zonal Secretary and members elected from branch and regional levels. While the chairperson had/has the responsibility of chairing the zonal meetings, the zonal secretary handles the day-to-day operations as they come to him/her from the branch/regional and national levels. At the zonal level (as TRAWU details) there was the Zonal Executive Committee, Zonal General Council and Zonal General Meeting as different organs of the zone. The functions of these organs related to policy formulation, budgetary and execution issues.

National Level

At the national level of the unions there are three organs: the National Congress, the General Council and the National Executive Committee.

The National Congress is the biggest forum and top most decision-making organ. It is composed of the president who chairs the congress, the vice president who in the absence of the president chairs the congress, general secretary, treasurer, regional chairpersons and regional secretaries, and elected members from the branch, regional and zonal levels as the case may be.

It meets after every five years and elects the president, vice president, the general secretary and the treasurer. It also elects members or the union's representatives to the Congress (of the federation of trade unions). It also has the power to accept and reform the constitution of the trade union. The Congress also discusses issues related to improving the conditions of the workers at workplaces.

The General Council is composed of the national chairperson, the general secretary, the two deputy general secretaries (one for the Mainland and the other for the Islands), all the members of the National Executive Committee and other members as stated in the trade union's constitution. It meets annually and its functions are to:

* Draw-up the budget;
* Formulate short-term policies;
* Monitor the financial trend of the union;
* Elect representatives to the General Council of the trade union federation.

The National Executive Committee comprises the chairperson, the general secretary and other representatives as stipulated in the union's constitution. The functions of this committee are to run the day-to-day operations of the union, prepare programmes for the National Congress and the General Council. In most unions the national executive committee is the sole employer of the union.

It is of significant importance to mention here that some trade unions such as TPAWU have departments at national level which include: (a) Administration and Finance; (b) Education, Women and Youth; and (c) Economics, Research and Audit. TRAWU on the other hand has only two departments: Accounting and Education. In general we would like to reiterate that most of the trade unions have three to four levels/stages in their organisational structure as follows:

* Branch, regional, zonal and national (CHODAWU and TUICO);
* Branch, district, regional and national (TTU);
* Branch, district, zonal and national (TAMICO);
* Branch, regional and national (TALGWU and TUGHE); and
* Branch, zonal and national (COTWU, RAAWU, TRAWU and TPAWU).

However, there is need to point out that as a result of the coming into effect of the new 1998 Trade Union Act, the number of industrial unions is now more than eleven and the then existing eleven unions had to apply for registration with new constitutions (while retaining their former names). In view of this and given the fact that the new unions cover only one part of the United Republic, then there are some changes in the union structures. For instance, the office of the second deputy General Secretary (from Zanzibar) is no longer needed since Zanzibar has its own trade unions.

THE TRADE UNIONS' LINK WITH OTTU/TFTU

As indicated earlier, all the trade unions had similar links with OTTU/TFTU. The links hinged on the fact that:

a) They all had to contribute 5 percent of their income (membership fee) to TFTU;
b) As affiliate members of TFTU, they were represented in the different organs of the former;
c) They participated in, and benefited from, the different seminars, workshops and conferences organised by TFTU;
d) There are some issues that can be better handled at the national level such as national strikes (c.f. the 1994 national strike);
e) In a many cases, international communications were made by TFTU on behalf of the unions and in some cases external financing to industrial unions was made via TFTU since the unions had no independent registration.

These issues made the unions and TFTU to work together and/or adopt a common strategy.

The questionnaire survey contained also many questions that solicited information on the characteristics of the trade unions' structure and the conditions in which they operated during the 1990s. The questions covered the following areas:

- Position of respondent in the trade union structure;
- Trade union election and accountability;
- Trade union activities;
- Resources/means available to trade union;
- Trade union information and communication; and
- Trade union education/training.

Respondent's Position in The Trade Union Structure

The respondents included in our sample were workers' representatives. A total of 1094 or 98 percent of them were trade union members and only 22 (or 2 percent) did not belong to any trade union. In addition to this, when the questionnaire was drawn the industrial unions were not yet established. Consequently instead of asking the respondents to indicate which particular union they belonged, they were asked to state which section of the trade union (by then OTTU) they belonged. Slightly more than one-third (35 percent) of the respondents belonged to industry and commerce; 15 percent belonged to central government and hospitals; 8 percent to hotels and domestic workers; 7 percent to transport and communications; another 7 percent to local governments; and 5 percent to agriculture. The other sections: teachers, mines, railways and higher education and research each had less than five percent of the respondents.

Table 5.1: *Duration of Trade Union Membership*

Duration	Frequency	Percent
Less than one year	49	5
1 to 2 years	80	7
3 to 5 years	148	14
6 to 10 years	222	20
11 to 15 years	246	22
16 to 20 years	160	15
More than 20 years	189	17
Total	1094	100

Of the 1094 respondents who were trade union members, most of them (54 percent) have been trade union members for more than 10 years and only 12 percent for two years and below (Table 5.1). This means that the sample consisted of many experienced trade unionists. This is further confirmed by the fact that only 16 percent of all the respondents indicated that they were not holding any trade union office. The offices held at branch level included Chairperson (18 percent); Secretary (22 percent); and committee membership (17 percent). The median duration of holding a trade union office was 'one to two years. Even so, a good number of them (46 percent) had held trade union office for between three years and twenty years; and 2 percent for more than 20 years. At district, regional and national levels, only 22 percent; 15 percent; and 8 percent of the respondents indicated that they held trade union offices in theses levels respectively.

Election Procedures and Accountability

As for procedures used to elect office bearers at branch level, 63 percent of those respondents who held offices at this level indicated that they were elected through 'secret ballot, 27 percent through open ballot, that is 'raising hands', 5 percent were appointed to their offices, and five percent through other procedures (i.e. acclamation, designation, etc.). Duration of the mandate of an elected representative varied from one year (mentioned by 4 percent) to four years and above (mentioned by 60 percent) of all the respondents who held trade union offices respectively. A duration of two years was indicated by 3 percent; three years by 29 percent; and 4 percent of the office bearers did not know/specify the duration.

As for the possibility of controlling trade union office bearers at branch level, 19 percent of the respondents said that 'they do not know;' 55 percent indicated that such control was by the 'General Assembly of all workers'; 19 percent by 'Branch Executive Committee; and 7 percent by the 'District/Regional trade union office'. Regarding the existence of procedures of removing/recalling a representative, respondents were asked to answer 'Yes' (such procedures exist), 'No' (procedures did not exist) or "I don't know.' Of the 933 respondents who answered this question, 54 percent of them said 'Yes;' 30 percent said 'No;' and 16 percent answered 'I do not know'. These results imply that, insofar as the respondents were concerned, for over 50 percent of them mechanisms/procedures were in place for both controlling and recalling office bearers at the branch level.

Trade Union Activities

Trade union activities, as used in this section, refer essentially to the activities that a trade union member performs for his/her union. The question asked was, "Write down three most important activities you perform in your trade union." The question was open-ended and the results were as shown in Table 5.2.

Table 5.2:   *Trade Union Activities*

Multiple responses, exclusive of non-responses	N	%
Grievance handling	425	41
Organising meetings, workshops and conferences	333	32
Coordination of internal organisation	234	23
Education, training	164	16
I do not perform any activity	139	13
Promoting efficiency in production	110	11
Workers' welfare	103	10
Involvement in collective bargaining	94	9
Collection of dues	32	3
Others	85	8
BASE DE %	1032	100

The most popular activity performed by the worker's representatives included in our sample was grievance handling (41 percent); followed by organisation of meetings (32 percent); and coordination of internal organisation (23 percent). Only 13 percent of them indicated that they did not perform any activity for their trade union (Table 5.2). Although small in number, this is a bit queer taking into consideration that we are dealing with worker representatives.

Table 5.3: *Time Spent per Week During and Outside Working Hours for Trade Union Work*

	During working hours (%) (N=1071)	Outside working hours (%) (N=1069)
Don't spend any time for trade union work	21	36
Less than one hour per week	15	16
1 to 2 hours per week	28	23
3 to 4 hours per week	11	10
5 to 6 hours per week	4	4
7 to 8 hours per week	4	3
9 or more hours per week	3	8
Full time trade unionist	14	NA

For those who performed activities for their union, the time devoted for trade union work per week during working hours varied from less than one hour (15 percent) to nine hours or more (3 percent); 21 percent of the 1069 respondents who answered the question indicated that they spent no time for trade union work while 14 percent were full time trade unionists. The most popular time duration devoted to trade union work during working hours was '1 to 2 hours' (28 percent). As for time spent for union work outside working hours, ranged from less than one hour per week (16 percent of the 1071 respondents who answered the question) to nine hours or more (8 percent). Again, the most popular duration was '1 to 2 hours' (23 percent). 36 percent of the respondents indicated that they spent no time for trade union work outside working hours (Table 5.3).

From the above results one can conclude that the degree of commitment to trade union work was low for the majority of the respondents. The time outside working hours was spent on income supplementing/generating activities as discussed in chapter four.

TRADE UNION RESOURCES, INFORMATION AND COMMUNICATION AT BRANCH LEVEL

In order to function properly, there are certain things or resources that have to be made available to any trade union even at the lowest level of a branch. These resources include a room for an office, transport and a budget. Each respondent was asked to indicate whether or not each of these (and other) resources were available at his trade union branch. The proportion of the respondents who answered yes to this question was as follows: room for office (55 percent); means of transport (8 percent); a budget (25 percent); and other resources (15 percent). A count of respondents who answered 'Yes' to all, three, two, one, and to none of these resources was made. The results show that only 3 percent of the respondents indicated that their trade union branch had all the four mentioned resources; 5 percent had three; 19 percent (two); 40 percent (one); and 33 percent of the respondents indicated that their union branches had no resources (Table 5.4).

Table 5.4: *Resources Available at Trade Union Branch*

	Value label	Frequency	Percent
No resources at all	.00	372	33
1 of the four resources	1.00	451	40
2 resources	2.00	207	19
3 resources	3.00	55	5
4 resources	4.00	31	3
Total		1116	100

If we exclude those who were not trade union members, then of the 1094 remaining respondents, 43 percent came from union branches with no: room for office; with no means of transport (92%); and with no Budget (74 percent). This is a reflection of high degree of poverty within the trade union branches.

With regard to trade union information and communication, our intention was to find out how information system worked within the trade union and to what extent the respondents availed themselves of information about their union in particular and unionism in general. Two approximate indicators were chosen to inform us about the general state of information on the trade union federation (by then OTTU/TFTU): the name of the Secretary General (OTTU/TFTU) and that of the district Secretary (OTTU/TFTU). Of the 1090 valid cases, 94 percent wrote down the correct name of the Secretary General (OTTU/TFTU); 4 percent wrote down incorrect name; and 1 percent did not know the name of the Secretary General. As for the second question concerning the OTTU/TFTU District Secretary, only 998 of the respondents answered it. The majority of them (86 percent), however, knew the correct name; 9 percent wrote down a wrong name; while 5 percent did not know the name. These results seem to indicate two things: first, that the level of general information about OTTU/TFTU was high and two, the respondents were more aware of their national leaders than about their local leaders above the level of the branch. The latter is not surprising since national leaders are more often mentioned in radios, and appear in TVs and newspapers than local leaders.

As for whether or not a respondent could get access to basic information of his/her union, respondents were asked if they had personal copies of OTTU/TFTU constitution and if their union branch had the same copies. Of the 1092 valid cases, 42 percent of them answered 'Yes" to the first question, i.e. they had personal copies. The proportion of respondents who answered "Yes" to the second question was 57 percent out of the all 1094 union members. Thus, the degree of access to this basic trade union text is not very high since 43 percent of the respondents (who were union members) cannot get access to it either through personal copies or copies deposited in their trade union branches (there is need to point out that 30 percent of the respondents indicated that they did not know whether or not copies were found in their respective union branches).

Information about trade unions/unionism can also be acquired through listening to the relevant radio programme/s and reading newspapers, books, and other publications. Only 16 percent of all the respondents indicated that they never listened to the weekly trade union radio broadcast Dunia ya Mfanyakazi. Insofar as the other sources are concerned, the number of those saying 'yes' was as follows: through reading newspapers (88 percent); reading specialised books (68 percent); reading the trade union newspaper Mfanyakazi (85 percent); and reading other publications (42 percent)

TRADE UNION EDUCATION AND TRAINING

As pointed out earlier in the case of education and training paid by the employer, in-service education and training for workers is necessary to up-grade and or impact new skills. Thus we wanted to know whether the respondents were given any chance to get trade union education/training at the workplace level and beyond paid by the union. The question asked was, 'Apart from this (APADEP) seminar, have you attended any other seminar/training organised/ paid for by OTTUU/TFTU or your trade union? Three responses were allowed: 'No'; 'Yes, once'; 'Yes, more than once'. The results were astonishing. For 37 percent of the respondents, the APADEP education seminar in which the questionnaire survey was combined was their first education and training organised by/paid for by the union (Table 5.5).

Table 5.5: *Education/Training Organised and Paid for by the Union at Various Levels*

Trade union education at:	No (%)	Yes, once (%)	Yes, more than once (%)	N
Workplace level	37	29	34	1110
District level	64	20	16	1109
Regional level	77	13	10	1105
National level	88	6	6	1107
Abroad - Africa	95	3	2	1106
Abroad - outside Africa	97	2	1	1106

One of the APADEP case study conducted in 1994 in Tanzania indicated that one of the limiting factors on workers' participation was lack of proper education/ training for workers. Because of this problem workers' representatives in the enterprise studied failed to take an effective part in discussions and in decision-making due to the fact that they did not understand many of the technical issues discussed in meetings they attended (Chambua and Semkiwa, 1994: 25). This might imply that trade union movement at places of work in particular and at the national level in general lacked or had no adequate education/training programmes for workers. Alternatively, the trade union movement in Tanzania probably had no or little influence on workers' education and training. To get a clear picture of these issues, APADEP (Tanzania) conducted a study on the "Effectiveness of Trade Union Movement on Workers' Education/Training at the National and Enterprise Level" (see Chambua and Naimani, 1996). This study aimed at investigating the effectiveness of the trade union movement in Tanzania with regards to workers education/training at both the national and enterprise levels. The study looked at the content of trade unions' programmes and the resources allocated to each programme so as to determine priority areas and issues. The study also tried to find out problems that had been encountered, how they had been dealt with and how effective were the trade unions in promoting workers' education/training by their own programmes or through programmes of employers. The study's specific objectives were to:

* Identify the role played by trade unions in the provision of workers' education/training;
* Analyze trade union programmes and priority put on education/training
* Find out resources available for such programmes, i.e. human, financial, equipment and other facilities; and
* Identify what problems the trade unions faced in the provision of education/training and how they were being tackled.

The main instruments for data collection were interviews and reviewing relevant documents. The interviews were conducted using structured questionnaires for National leaders of respective industrial trade unions in Dar es Salaam (Trade Union Questionnaire), OTTU/TFTU leadership at national level (OTTU Questionnaires) and ordinary workers and management at enterprise level (Workers and Management Questionnaire). Another set of questionnaire was given to policy makers at national level (Policy Makers Questionnaire). There was also a group interview of trade union branch committee members at the enterprise level (trade union leaders at Urafiki Textile Mill) using structured questionnaire. Interviews were also administered to top officials at the Directorate of Worker's Education at the Ministry of Labour. At the OTTU/TFTU head office, interviews were held with the top officials of the directorate of Organization and Publicity, Education and Culture, Occupation Health and Safety, Women and Youth, Workers Participation, and Research and Planning.

The main documents looked at were those from industrial unions' offices, OTTU/TFTU office and workers' education directory in the Ministry of Labour. Only one trade union was not covered in this study, the Tanzania Railways Workers Union (TRAWU). Below we present a summary of the research findings of that case study.

TRADE UNIONS AND THEIR PROGRAMMES

a) Industrial unions in Tanzania were established between 1992-1995. Each trade union had its own organizational structure, power to decide on and/or establish relationships with other international organizations. Membership in these unions depended on the place of work of a worker and not profession. For example, if one is employed as a laboratory technician in a certain hospital and so is a member of TUGHE and the person has decided to change the employer and join the Kilombero Sugar Company (as a laboratory technician) where its workers are members of TPAWU, that person has to automatically withdraw his membership from TUGHE to TPAWU. This is due to the agreement/principle of "one employer one Union."

b) Most of the trade unions had members from over 130 enterprises. These enterprises were mostly government departments/ministries and parastatal organizations;

c) OTTU and five out of the 10 industrial unions covered in the study had both long (over nine months) and short (up to nine month) term annual programmes on workers education and training. Five unions were still at their infancy stage and had no annual programmes but depended on short-term seminars conducted by OTTU. Table 5.6 shows the programmes and the unions that were involved in;

d) Programmes on workers' education were the most common. Otherwise, each union had programmes relating to the specific job activities of its members;

e) Among the ten trade unions visited, only TTU produced documents for its programmes. According to TTU document on planned activities for the period January 1995 to June 1996 the education programmes were mostly on up-grading and in-service training. In that period the union was supposed to conduct two academic and professional training and five study circles;

f) In all the programmes, except for the TTU, neither the number of participants nor dates for the programmes were indicated. This in a way shows that most of the leaders of the industrial unions were not very conversant with the programmes they were running or they would be running.

Table 5.6: *Trade Unions' Annual Programmes*

Annual Programme	Trade Union Involved
Workers' education	5 unions: OTTU, TUGHE, TPAWU, CHODAWU, COTWU
Trade Union education to members	3 unions: CHODAWU, TUGHE, COTWU
Workers Participation	3 unions: OTTU, TUICO, TPAWU
Women Participation in union leadership	3 unions: CHODAWU, TUGHE, COTWU
Financial control	3 Unions: CHODAWU, COTWU, TUICO
Labour Law	3 unions: CHODAWU, COTWU, TUICO
Labour economics and statistics	1 union: TUICO

RESOURCES AVAILABLE FOR WORKERS' EDUCATION/TRAINING

Human Resources

The target groups for the programmes were mainly trade union executive committee members/officials and ordinary union members. Participants were mainly drawn in accordance with the requirements of the programme. Participants were selected by both OTTU and Workers' Education Officers at workplaces. Resource persons came from the University of Dar es Salaam and the Ministry of Labour. However, workers in their respective unions were involved in designing most of the programmes. The type of involvement ranged from putting priorities on the fields of interest to the selection of the participants.

Financial Resources

Data on financial resources attached to each of the annual programmes were not readily available. But one of the things observed was that most of the programmes were donor financed. The main financiers were ILO, Friedrich Ebert Stifng (FES) of Germany, and the Dutch Federation of Trade Unions (FNV).

Other Resources

The other resources for running the programmes include manpower resources mainly from the unions themselves, donations from Canadian Teachers Foundation and Sweden International Development Agent (SIDA). However, apart from TTU, no financial breakdown was given per programme in all the unions. The financial break down given by TTU showed that the total budget for running all TTU activities in 1995/96 was Tshs. 49,099,580/=. The total amount allocated for education/training activities was Tshs. 25,412,730/= , slightly over 50 percent of the total budget. It is thus evident that TTU gave more weight to education/training than to other activities. This finding was not surprising though due to the fact that TTU deals with educators (teachers), naturally issues of education/training will be predominant.

Materials and Equipment

Materials and equipment such as books, pamphlets and computers were used during the education/training sessions. However, it appeared that some of the equipment were not enough because some of the participants in these programmes complained of shortage of equipment.

PROBLEMS IN THE PROVISION OF WORKERS' EDUCATION/TRAINING

The major problem that confronts the unions is financial capability. Their weak financial position has led to failure to successfully carry out some of their roles as trade unions including the role of educating/training their members, the workers.

In combating this problem, union leaders thought of establishing profit-generating projects. The most popular strategy among union leaders to solve the problem pertaining to education/training of workers was to look for assistance from donors by either being affiliated to international organizations or getting financial support and human resources for their programmes.

Another problem is reluctance on the part of some members to participate in the programmes due to time constraints. The solution to this problem lies in the union leaders and the subject matter of the programmes. The leaders have to design and execute programmes that promote workers interests and the subject matter should be of interest to the workers.

The unions are also confronted with the problem of misallocation of resources meant for education/training as well as for other programmes. Together with that problem there was also a problem of lack of adequate educational/training programmes.

Other constraints mentioned were the low level of education/knowledge on trade unionism on the part of the members and the antagonistic relationship that existed between certain categories of workers (e.g. academicians and administrative staff in the case of higher learning institutions).

OTTU's/TFTU's Finances

OTTU/TFTU had a number of economic activities inherited from JUWATA. These helped the organization in generating funds. The activities include:

+ Running a press unit in Dar es Salaam called NUTA Press;
+ Running a Petrol Station in Dar es Salaam; and
+ Running Hotels, farming, renting houses, some industrial activities and social activities.

About 90 percent of the organization's total income comes from members' contributions, 2.5 percent from external donors and 7.5 and percent from other sources. Thus, the income generating activities contributed only 7.5 percent of the income of OTTU/TFTU.

The federation (OTTU) had been receiving support from various International Organizations such as the International Confederation of Free Trade Union (ICFTU), FES, Organization of African Trade Union Unity (OATUU), International Labour Organisation (ILO), Trade Union Congress (TUC) and from Sweden/Norway through ILO.

OTTU's Programmes

All the then five directorates of OTTU, including the Deputy General Secretaries offices were engaged in more than one programme. The programmes per directorate and Deputy General Secretary's office were as follows:

Directorate of Education and Culture

This has been running four programmes since 1992. The programmes are:

♦ Working environment and occupational Health and Safety (1992 to 1996). The main participants in this programme were both ordinary trade union members and leaders;
♦ Economics for Trade Unionist Structural Adjustments (1992 to 1996). Participants were trade union members;
♦ Trade Union leadership and Management Development (1993 to 1996). The participants were mainly trade union leaders at all levels; and
♦ Planning and Administration of Trade Union Training (1993 to 1996). The programme was designed for trade union leaders and educators.

What can be observed from the participants in those programmes is that most of them were trade union leaders. Ordinary workers were not involved in these programmes.

Directorate of Women and Youth

This directorate has had three programmes since 1990 when it was under JUWATA. The programmes are:

♦ AIDS/Family Planning (1990 to 1995). Participants were workers and enterprise management;
♦ Women in Plantations - OTTU MWEMA Programme (1990 to 1995). Participants were women working and living in sisal, sugar, tea and rice plantations;
♦ Child Labour (1995 to 1996). This programme involved trade union leaders, employers, parents and working children.

It can be noted that unlike the programmes in the Directorate of Education and Culture, most of the programmes under this directorate involved ordinary workers.

Directorate of Workers' Participation

The directorate was involved in only one programme (APADEP) during the period 1992-1997). This programme involved workers' representatives in workers' councils, Board of Directors, and trade union branches at work places.

Directorate of Planning and Research

This directorate had four programmes that are mostly long-term projects. The programmes are:

* Labour market information. This involved all workers and was a long-term programme;
* Company Performance Analysis. This was a continuous programme involving trade union branch members;
* Employment Restructuring Processes. The programme was a long-term one involving trade union leaders and ordinary workers;
* Evaluation of OTTU activities and data banking activities. This again was a continuous programme involving all workers.

Deputy Secretary General's Office

This had three programmes that had been running since 1988 when it was under JUWATA. The programmes were:

* Economic programme for handling trade union finance (1988 to 1995). Participants were mainly trade union officials, union secretaries, accountants, educators and staff dealing with finances at the unions;
* Economic Programme. This programme was active during the 1991-94 period involved the Assistant District Secretaries, District Secretaries, OTTU Education Officers and Regional OTTU Secretaries;
* Study Circles (1992-1995). This involved elected trade union officials, trade union secretaries and educators.

As far as education/training for workers is concerned, OTTU always gave it a high priority. It had been OTTU's motto to give education to workers on their rights. Workers were also educated/trained in order to increase and improve their performance in production, productivity and quality of goods and services they produced or offered.

One major weakness in offering the education/training programmes was that; most of them did not involve ordinary workers. Another major weakness was that the programmes were designed by the respective directorates of OTTU at the organization's head office in collaboration with the donors. Workers were not at all consulted before designing the programme.

OTTU'S SUCCESSES

Despite the weaknesses in implementing certain programmes OTTU managed to register some successes in influencing policies aimed at promoting interests of workers. This influence was possible by being active in tripartite discussions. The discussions involve the Government, Association of Tanzania Employers and OTTU. They are usually on issues related to workers. Also, OTTU had managed to have influence in the determination of the minimum wage for government employees in the country. The organization also succeeded in creating women committees at work places.

Moreover, OTTU (TFTU) was instrumental in making proposals to government to enact an Act of Parliament on Workers' Participation in which participation would have been extended to cover also the private sector. The government initially accepted the proposals and a Cabinet paper to that effect was prepared. In that sense the 1998 Trade Union Act made the trade union situation unclear and the Ministry of Labour has now a new Minister. It is yet to be known whether or not the new Minister will implement the proposal. Other influences on policy changes that were instrumented by OTTU/TFTU included:

+ Convincing the Zanzibar Revolutionary Government to form the Ministry of Labour and Industrial Court. This has helped workers in Zanzibar to have a say in running their enterprises.
+ To have a jurisdiction of having access to information of factory inspection reports and records for onward assessment if the factories have met the required standards for the safety of the workers.
+ Introduce the presidential directive on workers' participation to the private sector.

OTTU'S PROBLEMS

The major problems that confronted the organization were: a) Decline in the number of union members due to the retrenchment exercised by the government, private and various public enterprises; b) Shortage of funds in running its activities as aggravated by the decline in trade union membership; and (c) Lack of trust from some institutions, e.g. some political parties and thence some of their members that were of the view that OTTU was still affiliated to the ruling party CCM and/or received instructions from the state because of the way it was established. This in one way or another constrained the implementation of some of its activities.

Workers and Management

On the subject of education/training for workers, a total of 14 workers and management staff at the Urafiki Textiles Mill were interviewed. There were five female workers and the rest (nine) were men. Most of the workers and management staff interviewed were union members. Those who were not trade union members mentioned that they were not aware of the functions and benefits of the union at their enterprise. This indicated that the trade union branch at the enterprise was not very active in educating workers on its activities. This lack of education programmes on the majority of the workers at the enterprise level was also reflected by a number of workers who said that they had not attended any educational/training programme, their number was 6 out of 14 (about 43 percent) in the enterprise.

Workers education/training programmes at the enterprise included subjects and programmes such as:

* Rights and Obligations of workers
* Awareness workshop on family planning services
* Workshop for workers' council members, and
* Seminar on management techniques and several other seminars on labour law and workers' participation.

The main coverage for most of the programmes is on the rights of employees, obligation and responsibility of employers and labour laws. Workers' education at workplace and workers' participation in decision-making are also among the subjects covered in the education programmes. All the workers interviewed and who had attended these programmes, indicated that they had been relevant for their working environment.

Educational Facilities at the Workplace

The findings from the enterprise visited revealed that although a library and a documentation centre existed at the enterprise, they were not being fully utilized by the workers. Most workers do not have a habit of visiting the facilities. The workers interviewed mentioned the following factors as limiting their attendance to the library and documentation centre. One, low level of education for most of the workers. Two, the library/documentation centre had no relevant materials for the type of work they performed or the materials were outdated. Three, lack of time due to pressure of work.

These findings tend to suggest a call for the need to have an efficient system of securing relevant and up to date materials in the libraries/documentation rooms at the workplace. The materials sought should also cater for all workers' professions. This exercise might enhance the desire to acquire more up-to-date knowledge on the various issues pertaining to the workers' professions.

The findings also revealed that relevant/basic trade union texts were not available at the workplace. These were the OTTU constitution and the industrial trade union constitution. All the 14 respondents indicated that they were not aware of these constitutions. This can be attributed to lack of effective trade union leadership at the enterprise.

Selection of Trainees to Trade Union Programmes

The workers indicated that the selection of trainees to trade union programmes was not fair at the enterprise. They claimed that trainees were selected on the basis that they were members of the trade union branch or that a trainee was loyal to the management, i.e. those workers who are vocal in demanding workers rights at the enterprise were not selected.

GENDER, EMPLOYMENT AND PARTICIPATION

In Tanzania, the most comprehensive surveys on gender and employment are the 1990 Labour Force Survey (LFS) and the 1990/91 National Informal Sector Survey (NISS). According to the 1990 LFS, the country's total labour-force was 10,889,205 persons in 1990 out of which 5,434,106 (49.9 percent) were females. Thus, there was almost equal gender representation in the labour-force. About 55 percent of the labour-force was urban-based while 45 percent was in the rural areas. Furthermore, 52 percent of the rural based labour-force were women while the proportion of women in the urban-based labour-force was only 41percent (see also Mjema, 1999: 82).

Concerning employment in the informal sector, the 19990/91 NISS revealed that the majority of employees (60 percent) in this sector were in the rural areas and males accounted for nearly 66 percent of the total labour/work-force in this (informal) sector.

Regarding gender and employment in the formal sector, the 1990/91 NISS revealed that in all the nine sub-sectors, females were only the majority in the agricultural sub-sector both in the rural and urban areas. The sector absorbed 84 percent of all formal sector employees, 45 percent females and 39 percent males (Table 5.7). It is apparent from Table 5.7 that in the early 1990s there was some 'crowding out' of the female labour-force in the other sub-sectors especially mining and quarrying, electricity and gas, building and construction, transport and finance. Casual observations by the author tend to suggest that the situation has now changed, albeit slightly, especially in the small-scale mining sub-sector where women are also significantly getting involved.

It is a well-known fact that women occupy the relatively lower occupational positions compared to men. According to the 1990/91 LFS, for example, the proportion of the total labour-force in the; (a) 'administration and management' category was 2.0 percent (1.6 percent males plus 0.4 percent females); (b) 'professionals' category was 0.1 percent (0.1 percent males plus 0.0 percent females), and (c) 'associate professionals' category was 1.6 percent (1.1 percent males plus 0.5 percent females. The only occupational category that had a larger proportion of females (45.0 percent) than males (38.7 percent) was 'agriculture-own farms' (Table 5.8). This occupational category demands relatively low skills and is also lowly paying.

Table 5.7: *Distribution of Employees by Gender in the Formal Sectors (%)*

	Urban Areas M F T	Rural Areas M F T	Both urban & rural M F T
Agriculture	16 22 38	43 49 92	39 45 84
Mining/Quarrying	0 0 0	1 0 1	1 0 1

Table 5.7: *Continued...*

	Urban Areas			Rural Areas			Both Urban & Rural		
	M	F	T	M	F	T	M	F	T
Manufacturing	7	2	9	1	0	1	2	1	3
Electricity & Gas	1	0	1	0	0	0	0	0	0
Building/construction	3	0	3	0	0	0	1	0	1
Trade*	15	10	25	2	1	3	3	3	6
Transport	5	1	6	0	0	0	1	0	1
Finance	1	0	1	0	0	0	0	0	0
Community and PSs	11	6	17	2	1	3	3	1	4
Total	58	42	100	49	51	100	50	50	100

Source: LFS (1990/91) and Mjema (1999: 83).
Notes: F, M, and T stands for females, males and total respectively. PSs stands for personal
services.
* Includes retail and wholesale.

Table 5.8: *Employment by Occupation and Gender*

	Male	Female	Total
Administration/Management	1.6	0.4	2.0
Professionals	0.1	0.0	0.1
Associate Professionals	1.1	0.5	1.6
Clerks	0.5	0.4	0.9
Service/shops	1.4	1.1	2.5
Agriculture-own farms	38.7	45.0	83.7
Crafts	3.1	0.3	3.4
Plant/Machine Operators	1.0	0.1	1.1
Labourers	2.7	2.0	4.7
Total	50.1	49.9	100

Source: LFS (1990/91) extracted by the authors from Mjema (1999: 84, Table3).

The above male-female employment related differentials are mostly explained
by relatively low levels education among females as compared to males. This in
turn is due both to historical and cultural factors. Historically, throughout the
colonial period there were more education opportunities for men than for women.
After independence measures were taken to try to arrest this situation but success
was achieved only at the primary school level. At the post-primary education
levels there are still more education opportunities for males than for females.
Culturally, traditional norms and customs of many tribes in Tanzania confine
the role of women to household domestic work and many do not see the value of
educating girls beyond primary education.

In any society, participation of the people in decision-making is an important recipe for the realisation of development plans since they are the implementers and beneficiaries of those plans. Although Tanzania has many different ways of involving the people in development activities, there are still problems facing women towards full involvement in the development process. One of the areas in which women are not fully involved is participation in decision-making at various levels.

Participation in decision-making is a basic human right. Democratic participation play a positive role in ensuring that the views of the people are heard when various policies are discussed, made and implemented at all levels. One of the factors that can lead to effective participation in decision-making bodies is fair representation without gender discrimination.

Five case studies on workers participation conducted by the African Workers Participation Development Programme in Tanzania have shown that there are fewer women than men in decision-making bodies. Research done by Koda (1994) on women participation in decision-making bodies in the structures of the then Organisation of Tanzania Trade Unions (OTTU) showed that there were few women representatives.

This section, together with its sub-sections, explores further on women participation in decision-making bodies. The information is based on both the questionnaire surveys and one case study conducted by the Tanzania APADEP team aimed at investigating the participation of women in decision-making bodies within the trade union and workplace structures. The section also provides additional information on the following:

a) Why women are few or under-represented in the decision-making bodies;
b) Problems which give rise to under representation of women; and on
c) Ways of increasing women participation in decision-making bodies.

Women in Trade Union Leadership

The trade union movement, globally, has mainly been recruiting its members from the formal sector. Participation of women in the formal sector in Tanzania has been rather minimal compared to men. For instance, according to the 1988 Population Census some 12.2 million people above 15 years of age were categorised as economically active, 53 percent of them were women. However, only three percent of the women were employed in formal wage employment. Thus, there were more women than men in the labour force. But when it comes to trade union membership, it is obvious that women will be fewer in number than men given the fact that their number is small compared to the number of men in the formal sector.

Research done by the trade union has revealed that female membership in the trade union movement is low. In one of the studies conducted in 1988 by the Women Department of JUWATA, trade union membership in some of the regions in Tanzania was given as follows: Dar es Salaam (22.3 percent); Morogoro (21.1 percent); Kilimanjaro (38.5 percent); Mbeya (23.4 percent); Dodoma (33.4 percent); Mara (23.25 percent); Singida (23.5 percent); Kigoma (17.3 percent); Rukwa (26.3 percent); and Pemba (18.4 percent) (JUWATA, 1988). In addition, according to the same study by JUWATA, the representation of women in trade union leadership was much lower compared to their percentage in the trade union movement (Table 5.9).

Table 5.9: *Representation in Union Leadership by Gender*

Position	Male	% Male	Female	% Female	Total
General Council	240	87.9	33	12.1	273
Executive Committee	23	85.2	4	14.8	27
Heads of department	13	87.7	2	13.3	15
Regional Chairman	21	95.5	1	4.5	22
Regional Secretary	20	90.9	2	9.1	90
District Chairman	87	96.7	3	3.3	90
District Secretary	89	99	1	1.1	90
Total	493	91.5	46	8.5	539

Source: 1988 JUWATA Research.

Table 5.9 gives the general picture of the situation during the end of the 1980s. The question, however is, has the situation improved or has it worsened during the 1990s?

Throughout the 1990s, top positions of leadership in OTTU/TFTU were occupied by men. That is, the offices of Chairperson, Secretary General, and the two deputy Secretary Generals. The main bodies of the Federation were:

a) *The Executive Committee*: This consisted of all the top leadership of the elected leaders of the Federation, that is, Chairperson and Secretary General and the treasurer of TFTU; and all Chairpersons and General Secretaries of the 11 unions which were affiliated to TFTU. This was the executing body of TFTU, an important body. Yet it had no specific positions for women.

b) *The General Council*: This consisted of all members of the Executive Committee of TFTU and three members elected from each union affiliated to TFTU. The constitution provided for positions to female members to the General Council. Each union affiliated to TFTU elected one female representative to the Council.

c) *The Congress*: The Congress consisted of, among other members, one female representative elected from each union affiliated to TFTU.

From the above discussion, it is apparent that during the 1990s the trade union movement in a way tried its best to take into consideration female participation in trade union decision-making bodies. The TFTU constitution provided for a specific number of females to occupy positions in some TFTU bodies.

Departments in TFTU: All the directors of the three departments were women with good qualification and University education. They got these posts by being appointed, but the appointments had to be approved by all the relevant TFTU bodies.

GENDER AND LEADERSHIP IN THE UNIONS

The General Secretaries of 10 (out of 11) unions were men and only one union, CHODAWU, had a woman Chairperson - Ms. Maudlin Castiko. This situation tended to support the view that for a long time women have been marginalized in the trade union leadership. Being aware of this, the trade unions introduced, in their constitutions, positive discriminations measures with a purpose of increasing women participation in trade union leadership. At branch level this situation enabled trade union branches to have female representation. Taking the example of one of the unions, TUICO, section 7.3 of its constitution specified that at branch level members of the branch committee should be constituted as follows:

Number of Trade members	Number of Branch Committee members	Special Union women positions
10-50	5	1
51-100	10	3
101-500	15	5
501-1000	20	7
Above 1001	25	9

Due to the positive discrimination measures, there was an increase in women participation in the trade unions at branch level. However, the unions were not able to give us concrete up to date information on this issue. Even so, the fact still remains that there were few women compared to men holding trade union leadership positions, and thence, positive discrimination measures for women.

Women and TFTU's Youth Directorate

It is necessary here to provide elaborated information on the Women and Youth directorate of the TFTU since it created an enabling environment for the 11 Unions to take into consideration gender balance in their activities. In addition, it created awareness on the need of taking into consideration women participation in trade union activities. The roles of the directorate were:

* To mobilise women /union members of all trade unions (which were affiliated to TFTU) for greater involvement and participation in all affairs of their respective unions; and

◆   To provide education on trade unionism, labour relations and other related issues to women workers to enable them to participate fully in trade union activities and in employment generation/creation. Women's employment-related problems were dealt by this directorate including means or strategies to overcome them.

The various activities performed by the directorate which aim at improving working conditions of women workers included: trade union education; sensitisation programmes for women to be trade union members and aspire for leadership positions in the trade union; conducting research on various issues related to women workers so as to have deeper understanding of women problems at the work place; co-ordinating the implementation of women projects which aim at improving the working and living conditions of women workers (The projects included: Project on women workers and AIDS at work places, The MWEMA, 'Mradi wa Wanawake Mashambani', project which aim at integrating employment, income, and shelter needs of women in programmes and projects in the plantation sector. Another project was on Food Security and Technology which covered women workers in four sisal plantations of Tanga region); and promoting the formation of women committees at workplaces. All these efforts sought to enhance women participation in trade union activities since they created enabling environment for empowering women.

Reasons for Women Under-representation in the Leadership of the Trade Union Movement

At the decision-making levels of the unions there is chronic under-representation of women. Indeed, trade union leadership, since the inception of trade unions in the country, has been dominated by men. Although women membership in trade unions has been increasing over the years the involvement of women in leadership positions has proportionally remained low. Some of the reasons pointed out by members of the TFTU department of Women and Youth include: lack of confidence (and men take advantage of this by propagating the assertion that men are born leaders and women take only subordinate positions). Furthermore, a trade union leader is supposed to be able to talk with the management and present workers' demands without fear. As such there is a general feeling, especially on the part of the management, that trade union leaders are arrogant. Such attitude has scared women from contesting for trade union leadership.

Attitudes Towards Women Participation in Trade Union Leadership

Male trade union leaders are often reluctant to put issues that are of special concern to women workers and gender issues in general. This is simply because for many people, gender issues are mainly and wrongly associated with women and for them, women issues are better dealt by women themselves. Female participation at the leadership level can play an important role in making trade unions more sensitive to problems of women workers and gender issues in general.

There is a general view from the interviewees (particularly men) that women are now benefiting from being given opportunities to participate in various decision-making bodies in the trade union movement through a number of positions specifically set aside for women. Furthermore, women are given equal chances with men to contest for elections. In this way, their number in the participatory structures has increased.

Some of the people interviewed, however, pointed out that the issue is not only increasing the number of women but rather their effective participation. There is also the need to convince male representatives to support women issues. Some female trade union leaders had only been pushed to fill special seats set aside for women; as such they were still not prepared to take their positions as leaders in the trade union. They still lacked confidence. Even so, one can still argue that they can be trained or informed of their roles as trade union leaders while they already have a position in the trade union. Through experience, self-confidence can grow.

Potential Benefits of Women's Participation in Decision-making Bodies

The interviewees pointed out that women participation is beneficial to everybody. As such some of them praised TFTU for having female directors in the three departments of the Federation. But they believed that they got the post by mainly taking into account their qualifications and ability, and not their gender.

In the last five years trade union members have benefited from the move to involve women in trade union decision-making bodies by getting more education opportunities in the trade union through the Women and Youth Department. Various education programmes have been organised involving some trade union bodies like: National Women Technical Committee; Executive Committee of OTTU; Trade Union Leaders from TUICO, TUGHE, and RAAWU; District, Regional Secretaries and Trade Union leaders at the Head office; and Leaders from Women Committees from workplaces in the Regions (see OTTU, 1995). In addition to this, other education projects in the trade union like APADEP have a deliberate policy of having at least 25 per cent of participants being women in its activities. The APADED education manuals cover the issues of women participation in decision-making bodies at all levels. There are also other education manuals/booklets prepared by the trade union that covered the following:

+ Situation on Women and employment;
+ Women Workers and the law;
+ Women and Culture;
+ Essential services for women;

- Women Participation in the Trade union; and
- Sexual Harassment at Workplaces.

Problems Faced by Women Aspiring to Contest for Trade Union Positions

Many of the interviewees were of the opinion that during the election process you need to have a lot of courage. This is because, potentially, there is a lot of harassment a contestant is bound to face. All sorts of allegations can be thrown to him/her. Many women fear to face this challenge. There is also the problem of lack of solidarity among the women. There is a tendency for women to side with men contestants rather than giving support to fellow woman contestants. One of those we interviewed supported this by presenting her experience during the election of the chairperson of CHODAWU. Though the elected chairperson was a woman, there was clear evidence of lack of solidarity during the campaign because women were not united to support the female contestant. The same feeling was also pointed out during the OTTU Congress in Dodoma. Women were not united for the purpose of having a female leader. The main reason is that many women lack self-confidence in themselves and have little confidence/faith in fellow females as leaders.

Ways of Ensuring Effective Participation of Women in Trade Union Leadership

Education and Training

Availing more education and training opportunities to women to increase their abilities. All the unions should take a lead on this. Encourage the use of educational manuals, study tour, and promotion of trade union libraries. The trade union offices have a lot of reading materials that are scattered in offices. Each Union should establish a library and encourage its members, especially women to learn more through reading.

Participation in Decision-making

It is important to ensure equitable gender representation in all executive and management bodies. This should be specified in the constitutions of all the unions. Encouragement of employment of women in formal and informal sectors is also beneficial. Currently, union membership is mainly from the formal sector. If women employment in these sectors is promoted and trade union membership extended to the informal sector, then trade union membership for women can be increased hence increasing the possibilities of having more women in leadership positions. Encourage women participation at international levels. Through it they will get to know what other organisations are doing to promote women participation.

WOMEN REPRESENTATION: THE QUESTIONNAIRE SURVEY

Participation by women is an important issue, particularly in Tanzania where fewer women than men work in the formal sector and as a result there are very few women in trade union and participation structures. To what extent do our questionnaire survey findings validate this observation? Four variables were utilised to find the number of women in representative structures:

a) The percentage of women in trade union branch committees;
b) Positions/offices held by women in trade union branch committees;
c) Percentage of female representation in Workers' Councils;
d) Positions held by women in Workers' Councils.

The percentage of women's representation in trade union and participation structures was calculated by using the information given by the respondents on the following categories:

* Number of people in the trade union branch committee and in the workers' council;
* Number of men in the respective trade union branch committee and in the respective workers' council; and
* Number of women in the same trade union branch committee and workers' council.

The number of women in trade union branch committees varied from zero to 28 with a mean of 2.67 and a standard deviation of 2.56. Their number in workers' councils ranged from zero to 74 with a mean of 3.41 and a standard deviation of 5.08 (Table 5.11).

Table 5.11: *Number of Women in Trade Union Committees and Workers' Councils*

	Mean	Std. Dev.	Minimum	Maximum
TU Committee	2.67	2.56	.00	64.00
Workers' Council	3.41	5.08	.00	74.00

The percentage of women in these two organs ranged from zero (mentioned by 7 percent and 12 percent of the respondents) to more than 80 percent in trade union branch committees and workers' councils respectively (Table 5.12).

The median class in both structures was from 21 to 40 percent. That is 56 and 71 percent of the respondents (i.e. the 595 and 590 valid observations) indicated that the percentage of women in trade union branch committees and in workers' councils ranged from zero (no women) to 40 percent respectively. These results tend to indicate that on the average, there are fewer women than men both in the workers' councils and in trade union branch committees. But the problem of women under-representation cannot be established by these figures simply because we lack the necessary information to do so, i.e., the actual proportion of women in the enterprise. Even so, the figures do indicate that the problem of women under-representation is not as serious as we previously thought. Indeed, if we recall that the percentage of women in formal employment in the country was only three percent in 1988, the figures show that there has been great improvement in women participation. This improvement is perhaps due to the positive discrimination measures by trade unions as we pointed out earlier on in this chapter.

Table 5.12: *The Percentage of Women in TU Branch Committees and WCs*

	TU Committee			Workers' Council		
	Freq.	%	Cum.%	Freq.	%	Cum.%
No women	40	7	7	68	12	12
Less than 20 percent	119	20	27	196	33	45
From 21 to 40 percent	175	29	56	155	26	71
From 41 to 60 percent	83	14	70	74	12	83
From 61 to 80 percent	114	19	89	52	9	92
More than 81 percent	64	11	100	45	8	100
Total	595	100		590	100	

Notes: i) TU stands for Trade Union
       ii) WCs stands for Workers' Councils
       iii) Table excludes those answering: I don't know, No TU branch/WCs.

Positions Held by Women in Trade Union Branch Committees and in Workers' Councils

Another issue closely related to women participation in trade union activities and in participation organs is offices or positions women occupy in these structures. Table 5.13 provides such information based on the questionnaire survey.

Table 5.13: *Position of Women in Trade Union Branch Committees/Workers' Councils*

Multiple responses, exclusive non responses	Union branch committee		Workers' Council	
	N	%	N	%
No women	165	19	97	12
Member, Discipline committee	160	18	--	--
Member, Social Welfare committee	155	18	--	--
Secretary	153	18	135	17
Member, Education Committee	123	14	--	--
Chairperson	59	7	39	5

Table 5.13: *Continued...*

Multiple responses, exclusive non responses	Union branch committee N	%	Workers' Council N	%
Member, Defence/Security Committee	51	6	--	--
Member, Political Committee	33	4	--	--
Other position	200	23	52	6
Ordinary member	--	--	598	74
BASE DE %	868	100	810	100

12 and 19 percent of the respondents indicated that there were no women in their workplace workers' councils and trade union branch committees respectively; 74 percent indicated that women were ordinary members of the workers' council at their work place; 18 and 17 percent indicated that women occupied the position of Secretary at their trade union branch committees and workers' councils at workplace respectively. Only seven and five percent of the respondents reported that women occupied the office of chairperson in their trade union branch committees and workplace workers' councils respectively (Table 5.13). The picture that emerges from these figures is that women appeared to have been more fairly represented in leadership positions in trade union branch committees than in workplace workers' councils. However, even in trade union branch committees, women were still under-represented. According to the respondents, the main reasons behind under-representation of women in various organs ranged from (a) lack of confidence (b) less exposure to trade union activities (c) lack of interest in public office (d) men don't want to be represented by women to (e) over burdened by other commitments (Table 5.14).

Table 5.14: *Reasons for Women's Under-representation in Various Organs*

Multiple responses, exclusive non responses	TU branch committee (%)	Workers' Councils (%)	Other Rep Organs (%)*
Lack of confidence	57	50	53
Less exposed to trade union activities	24	15	13
Not interested in public office	10	17	17
Men don't want to elect women	10	14	14
Overburdened by other commitments	11	9	16
Traditional norms and values	8	7	9
Discouragement from husbands	2	3	9
Women don't want to elect fellow women	2	2	2
Other reasons	7	9	8
I do not know	5	6	4
	N=1060	N=1063	N=1075

* Other representative organs in the country.

The one single reason mentioned by at least 50 percent of the respondents (57 percent in the case of trade union branch committees, 50 percent for workers' councils and 53 percent in the case of other representative bodies in the country), was 'lack of confidence' on the part of women. This was also the number one reason pointed by TFTU leaders.

How to Increase Women's Participation

The respondents were also asked to give their opinion on what can be done to increase the number of women in trade union branch committees, workers' councils and other representative organs. Each respondent was allowed to suggest up to three ways of increasing the representation of women. The three most popular means suggested were the following (see Table 5.15):

a) Educate women to take up trade union roles (64 percent)
b) Provide positive discrimination to women during elections to office (26 percent); and
c) Educate/make society in general more aware of women's potential (21 percent).

Table 5.15: *Means of Increasing the Number of Women in Trade Union Branch Committees and Other Participation Organs*

Multiple responses, exclusive of non responses	N	%
Educate women to take up trade union roles	692	64
Positive discrimination in elections	284	26
Make society more aware of women's potential	222	21
Provide child care facilities	14	1
Change of meeting time to day time	12	1
Others	136	13
I do not know	45	4
Base De %	1074	100

Thus, according to the respondents, education and positive discrimination were seen as the major means of increasing the number of females in various representative bodies. These means of increasing the number of women in union branch committees and other participatory organs were also suggested by trade union officials during case studies.

Roles in Household Activities and Family Life

The questionnaire survey also sought information, from the respondents, that provides an indicative picture of roles played by women in household activities and in family life. Ten indicators were used to define household activities. These were money earning, food preparation, taking care of children, washing dishes, shopping, washing clothes, craftwork, farm work, cattle herding, and hawking/street-vending/trading.

For each indicator, respondents were asked whether the activity represented by the indicator was mainly done by men, women or both. This information is deemed necessary in shedding more light on the nature of household division of labour by gender as well as the extent to which women are overburdened in such arrangements.

Activities that are mainly performed by women are preparation of food, washing dishes, and laundry while the other remaining household activities are mainly performed by both men and women. According to the respondents there was not a single activity that was/is mainly performed by men (see Table 5.13). This shows that women are overburdened in so far as household division of labour is concerned.

As for roles in family life, this was targeted on information of the degree of integration of male and female members of a household in decision-making. The results were as follows:

+ Men and women always make household decisions together (33percent);
+ Men and women often make household decisions together (45percent);
+ Only male members make household decisions (18percent); and
+ Only female members make household decisions (4percent).

Table 5.16: *Role Assignment in Household Division of Labour* (%) N=1116

Indicator/Activity	NA	Men	Women	Both	Total
Money earning	0	24	5	71	100
Food preparation	0	4	86	9	100
Taking care of children	0	2	46	52	100
Dish washing	0	1	89	10	100
Shopping	0	14	24	63	100
Laundry/washing clothes	0	2	62	36	100
Craft work	40	20	12	27	100
Farm work	15	7	9	70	100
Cattle herding	33	13	6	48	100
Hawking/street-vending/trading	52	10	14	23	100

These results tend to indicate that the degree of integration of male and female members of a household was/is very high for one third of the respondents in the sample. It was high for nine out of every 20 of the respondents and was very low for 22 percent of all the respondents. On average, one can say that there was/is a high degree of integration for male and female members of a household for over three quarters of the respondents in our sample.

What emerges from our discussion so far is that although there is, to some extent, a fair degree of integration among male and female members of a household, the division of labour is still such that women tend to be overburdened.

CONCLUSION

Several issues have been presented and discussed in this chapter. These included: trade union structure and conditions in which unions operated during the 1990s; trade union election procedures, activities and resources at branch level; education/training organized and/or funded by trade unions; and gender, employment and participation.

On trade union structure from 1995 to 30th June 2000, we pointed out that there were 11 industrial unions and one trade union federation, OTTU/TFTU. All the 11 unions were affiliated to OTTU/TFTU. The 11 unions had organizational structures that closely resembled each other. The link between the unions and the federation was through legislation (all had to be affiliated to OTTU by law), payment of affiliation charges and representation in different organs or bodies. Initially (from 1991-95), OTTU had five departments but when the process of forming industrial unions was completed and it changed its name to TFTU, it remained only with three departments. Both OTTU/TFTU and the unions had two positions for deputy Secretary General/General Secretary, one for Mainland Tanzania and the other for Zanzibar. The new Trade Union Act that became operational from 1st July 2000 has rendered the second office for deputy Secretary General or General Secretary redundant simply because labour matters are no longer a union issue. Thus, the new unions and their federation/s will/or cater for only one part of the URT, i.e. Mainland Tanzania or Zanzibar.

Regarding trade union election procedures at branch level, questionnaire survey data revealed that majority of the worker representatives (90 percent) who were office bearers were elected to their positions (63 percent through secret ballot and 27 percent through open ballot). Furthermore, over 50 percent of the respondents indicated that procedures were in place for both controlling and recalling office bearers. Thus, one may conclude that the trade union branches were democratically run. Activities performed by a trade union member, in this case worker representatives, were many, ranging from engagement in grievance handling to collection of union dues. The data also tend to indicate that most of the unions at branch level were poor in terms of resources. For instance, one-third of all the respondents revealed that their respective trade union branches had none of the following four resources: a room for office, means of transport, a budget and other resources. Only 3 percent of the respondents said that their branches had all four of the resources.

As for provision of education/training to their members and workers in general, there was an indication that few unions provided education/training to their members. Indeed, for 37 percent of the respondents the APADEP seminar in which the questionnaire survey was integrated were their first education/ training organized by trade unions. Lack of education/training by unions translated into high levels of ignorance of the country's labour laws amongst the representatives.

Throughout the period under review, the trade union in Tanzania operated under difficulty conditions of economic hardships, reduction in union membership and implementation of SAPs that are known to be hostile to unions. Partly because of this, its success in influencing policies that promote the interests of workers was not impressive.

On gender, employment and participation in leadership positions, the trade union situation was not different from that of the country as a whole. There were fewer women than men as union members as well as in trade union leadership at all levels, especially in decision-making organs. Under-representation of women (in terms of numbers) is mainly due to factors associated both with low levels of education and traditional norms and values. Even so, the worker representatives singled out 'lack of confidence' amongst women as the main constraint to women's participation in trade union branch committees, worker's councils and other participation organs in the country. Both OTTU/TFTU and the unions formulated a number of programmes, both short and long-term, geared at instilling/raising confidence amongst women employees. It is our hope that the new unions and their federation/s will adopt and continue to implement them so as to increase women's confidence and participation in decision-making bodies at all levels of the trade union movement in the country.

6

DEMOCRATIC PARTICIPATION

INTRODUCTION

The main pre-occupation in this chapter is twofold: first, workers' participation values and attitudes; and secondly, workers participation structures. The main sources of data are questionnaire surveys. Regarding the first concern, our focus is on how participation is perceived by worker representatives (the respondents). That is, according to the respondents, what is meant by participation? How did they perceive it? And what is their general attitude towards workers' participation: do they favour it or not? As for workers' participation structures, this chapter is mainly concerned with the various participatory structures or forms of participation that exist in work places and with describing their function. Achievements and limitations of workers' participation in Tanzania are also discussed.

WORKERS' PARTICIPATION: VALUES AND ATTITUDES

In an attempt to get some insight into how participation is perceived by the respondents, the questionnaire survey included a number of variables responding to the following questions: What is workers' participation according to respondents? How do they perceive participation? Do they favour it or not? The variables to answer these questions were grouped in three areas: valuation of workers' participation, attitudes to workers' participation, and perceived workers' participation capacity.

Table 6.1: *Meaning of Workers' Participation*

Multiple responses, exclusive non responses	N	%
Involvement in decision-making	802	74
Improvement of workers condition	123	11
Contribution to productivity	110	10
Cooperation between workers/mgt/TU	78	7
Involvement of workers in development	68	6
Freedom of expression	67	6
I don't know	59	5
Having a share in the profits	46	4
Others	42	4
Greater responsibility to workers	25	2
BASE DE %	1086	100

Regarding evaluation of workers' participation, two variables were used to asses how respondents define workers' participation (open-ended questions) and priority values in workers' participation. For the majority of the respondents (74 percent), workers' participation meant 'involving workers in decision-making;' for 11 percent it meant 'improvement in the conditions of workers;' for 10 percent it meant 'contribution to productivity;' for seven percent 'cooperation between workers, management and trade union;' for six percent, participation meant 'freedom of expression' (Table 6.1). These results imply that for 80 percent of all the respondents, participation meant 'democracy,' i.e. freedom of expression and involvement in decision-making.

Respondents were also asked to choose three things they appreciated most in workers' participation from a total of eight indicators distributed evenly between four values of participation:

Values	Indicators
1. Humanisation	a. Getting more respect as a worker
	b. Better relations between workers and managers
2. Democratisation	c. Having more say on important matters
	d. Giving more power to the working class
3. More economic equity	e. Getting a fair wage/salary
	f. Better distribution of jobs
4. Better use of human resources	g. Working better and harder
	h. Contributing to the country's development

The three mostappreciated things by the respondents (worker representatives) in participation were: better human relations (72 percent); getting a fair wage/ salary (59 percent); and being better respected as a worker (54 percent). The fourth was working better and harder (40 percent) followed by having more say on important matters - 35 percent (Table 6.2).

Better human relations, getting a fair wage and being better respected as a worker scored higher than others (over 50 percent) perhaps reflecting the particular importance that Tanzania had for three decades since 1967 placed on *Ujamaa* (brotherhood).

Regarding attitudes to workers' participation, these help to confirm the respondent's perception of what workers' participation should be. Are they in favour of it? To what degree do they think they should be informed and consulted on important decisions in the enterprise? To what degree do they think they should be involved with the right to vote on important enterprise decisions? And to what degree they think they should share in profits and ownership of an enterprise?

The responses to the question: "Are you in favour of workers' participation? were as follows. Out of 1,105 who answered the question, 1091 (99 percent) said 'Yes;' 11 (1percent) answered 'No;' and 3(almost 0 percent) indicated that they did not know whether they favoured participation or not. It is obvious from these results that almost all the representatives were in favour of participation. The implication is that participation is considered too valuable to be thrown away not withstanding the social, economic and political changes that have taken place since the late 1980s. As a matter of fact, for the majority of the respondents, participation meant democracy and this is what most regimes in Africa, including Tanzania, now identify with.

Table 6.2: *Things Appreciated in Workers' Participation*

	N	%
Better worker/manager relations	801	72
Getting a fair salary/wage	649	59
More respected as a worker	595	54
Working better and harder	538	40
Having more say	392	35
Contribute to country development	168	15
More power to workers	110	10
Better/fair work distribution	33	3
BASE DE %	1108	100

However, a good number of the representatives were also on their guard in that whereas 55 percent of them were ready to accept participation unconditionally, 42 percent stated that they accept it provided that the conditions for its success are met.

The attitudes to workers' participation were also captured through the following five questions, do you think that workers should:

• Be informed on important decisions in enterprise?
• Be consulted on important decisions of enterprise?
• Be involved with right to vote on important decisions of enterprise?
• Share in profits of enterprise?
• Share in ownership of enterprise?

To each of the above five questions, workers' representatives were asked to choose only one of the following responses: 'No'; 'that would be a privilege;' and 'that is a right of the workers.' Over two thirds of the respondents claimed "that is a right to the workers" for all the above modalities of participation (Table 6.3). These results indicate that not only were the majority (55 percent) of the respondents prepared to opt for workers' participation unconditionally, but also they adopted a militancy policy to achieve it. The majority of them thought that workers have an absolute entitlement to be informed (93 percent) and consulted (89 percent), to be involved in decision-making (84 percent), and to share in profits (80 percent) and in ownership (69 percent) (Table 6.3). However, when asked if they thought that workers had the capacity to participate in enterprise decision-making, Eleven percent of them answered 'no', 30 percent said 'it depends' and 59 percent answered 'definitely.' This confidence in participation increased with age at 2 percent level of significance, Chi-square = 15.1 and p. = 0.0197 (Table 6.4). This means that the thirsty for participation increases with age.

Table 6.3: *General Attitudes To Workers' Participation* (in %, N = 1116)

Should workers:	No	Privilege	Right	Total
1. Be informed on important decisions?	3	4	93	100
2. Be consulted on important decisions?	4	7	89	100
3. Be involved on important decisions?	9	7	84	100
4. Share in profits of enterprise?	8	12	80	100
5. Share in ownership of enterprise?	15	16	69	100

A major issue in labour relations in general, and workers' participation in particular is the so-called managerial prerogatives. That is "rights which management assert to be exclusively theirs and hence not subject to collective bargaining with trade unions, nor to joint regulation with unions or employees" (Marsh and Evans, 1973: 195). We classified decision-making prerogatives into six variables and for each variable three indicators were chosen.

Table 6.4: *Workers Have Capacity to Participate in Decision-Making by Age*

Count Row Pct Col Pct	Age in Years				Row Total
	Below 25	25 - 34	35 - 44	45 and above	
Definitely	11	207	319	112	649
	1.7	31.9	49.2	17.3	59.1
	45.8	54.6	60.9	65.5	
Depends	6	127	149	45	327
	1.8	38.8	45.6	13.8	29.8
	25.0	33.5	28.4	26.3	
No	7	45	56	14	122
	5.7	36.9	45.9	11.5	11.1
	29.2	11.9	10.7	8.2	
Column Total	24	379	524	171	1098
	2.2	34.5	47.7	15.6	100.0

a. Decision-making on major business decisions (indicators or represented by decision-making on): investment; profit allocation; and enterprise expansion

b. Decision-making on personnel matters (indicators or represented by decisions on): disciplinary procedures; dismissals; and grading/promotions.

c. Decision-making on questions of production (i.e. decisions on): maintenance; new technology; and purchase of new equipment/machinery.

d. Decision-making on questions of organisation of work, (i.e. decisions on): working hours; breaks and shifts; appointment of supervisors; and work organisation.

e. Decision-making on terms of employment contract, i.e. decision-making on: transport facilities; wages; and provident fund/pension schemes.

f. Decision-making on welfare matters, i.e. decision-making on: availability of clean drinking water; safety and health; and canteen/toilet facilities.

Table 6.5: *Decision Making Prerogatives (in %, N=1108)*

Who should decide on:	managers alone	Inform workers	Consult workers	right to vote	right to veto
Investment	5	18	46	25	6
Profit allocation	7	17	44	25	7
Enterprise expansion	11	22	50	13	4
Grading/promotions	18	32	32	14	4

Table 6.5: *Continued....*

Who should decide on:	managers alone	Inform workers	Consult workers	right to vote	right to veto
Dismissals	10	25	40	18	7
Disciplinary procedures	6	22	44	23	5
Maintenance of equipment	9	18	50	16	6
New production technique	9	17	55	14	5
Purchase of new equipment	13	24	47	12	4
Working hours, breaks, shifts	11	26	40	18	4
Appointment of supervisors	20	25	32	19	4
Work organisation	19	27	40	11	3
Transport facilities	12	21	43	18	7
Wages	15	21	44	15	5
Provident /pension schemes	13	22	47	13	6
Safety and health issues	11	15	49	18	7
Canteen and toilets	13	13	56	14	6
Clean drinking water	10	12	53	16	9

Note: Sometimes percentages add to 99 or 101 due to rounding.

In total there were 18 indicators/questions that appeared twice in the questionnaire in the perspective of decision-making prerogatives. The first compared managerial prerogative to different degrees of participation: (a) managers should decide alone; (b) workers should be informed; (c) workers should be consulted; (d) workers should have the right to vote; and (e) workers should have the right to veto (Table 6.5). The second compared managerial prerogative to the negotiation/participation option. The values were: (a) better leave these decisions to management; (b) better negotiate independently through trade unions; (c) better to have workers' participation on this; and (d) better to have negotiation and participation (Table 6.6).

In all 18 issues, the most popular view was that 'workers should be consulted' (32-56 percent) followed by 'workers should be informed' (12-32 percent). This was followed by 'workers should have the right to vote' (11-25 percent). The most unpopular opinion was 'workers should have the right to veto over such decisions' (3-9 percent) followed by 'managers should decide alone' (5-20percent) (Table 6.5).

If we drop the most unpopular opinion 'right to veto' in table 6.5, we notice that views were somehow evenly spread on the following issues which had a comparatively large proportion of respondents with the opinion that managers should decide alone: appointment of supervisors (20 percent); work organisation (19 percent); and grading/promotions (18 percent).

Turning to the negotiation or participation option, the objective here was to know from the respondents, which decisions are considered a subject for independent negotiation, or for workers' participation, or both. But an option was given to the respondents to answer whether or not he/she thinks that the decision remains an exclusive managerial prerogative for validity reasons and control of reliability. There is also need to point out that we were interested in the respondents point of view regardless of the extent to which workers are represented in the participation organ and the level at which participation takes place (e.g. workers'/works council, board of directors, etc.).

Table 6.6: *Negotiation or Participation Over Various Decisions (%, N=1108)*

Who should decide on:	leave to managementt	negotiate through TU	better to have WP	better to negotiate & WP
Investment	5	16	50	28
Profit allocation	4	16	47	32
Enterprise expansion	20	12	46	23
Grading/promotions	23	20	36	22
Dismissals	8	35	34	24
Disciplinary procedures	6	28	43	24
Maintenance of equipment	21	10	48	21
New production technique	8	13	51	28
Purchase of new equipment	23	11	43	22
Working hours, breaks, shifts	14	18	46	22
Appointment of supervisors	35	14	32	19
Work organisation	19	16	41	24
Transport facilities	8	18	43	31
Wages/salaries	12	23	33	32
Prov. funds/pension schemes	20	20	32	28
Safety and health issues	7	21	45	28
Canteen and toilets	8	20	46	27
Clean drinking water	8	19	48	25

Note: Sometimes percentages add to 99 or 101 due to rounding off.

If we combine the last two columns in Table 6.6, we find that the most popular opinion in all the decisions was a demand for workers' participation: an average of 61 percent for organisation of work and personnel matters; 66 percent for employment contract; 71 percent for production decisions; 73 percent for welfare matters; and 75 percent for major business or economic decisions. Actually, if we compare the percentage of respondents who answered 'negotiate through trade union' to those who preferred to 'have workers' participation' it is apparent that for all types of decisions except one, the majority answered 'better to have workers' participation.' This means that the representatives had more faith in participation than in trade union negotiation. The only type of decisions in which they had more faith in trade union negotiation (35 percent) than in participation (34 percent) was on dismissals. On disciplinary procedures, 28 percent of all the respondents preferred 'better negotiate independently through trade unions.' Other types of decisions in which one-fifth to one-quarter of the respondents had the same opinion were: wages/salaries (23 percent), safety and health issues (21 percent), and 20 percent for grading/promotions, provident fund/pension schemes, and canteen and toilets (Table 6.6). The message and challenge to trade unions in Tanzania is clear: Worker representatives are yearning for participation, they have a lot of faith in it and they also want their unions to do more in promoting and defending workers' interests.

On the appointment of supervisors, the majority of the respondents (35 percent) were of the view that such decisions were exclusive management prerogatives. The opinions on issues related to 'grading/promotions' and 'provident funds/pension schemes' were somehow more evenly distributed over the four possible answers (Table 6.6) suggesting less discontent with them.

WORKERS' PARTICIPATION AT WORKPLACE

As already pointed out, workers' participation is essentially a process whereby workers or their representatives take part (i.e. are involved) in one way or another in the decision-making process of their enterprise. Differences do exist as to the manner and form this involvement takes. The forms and structures may differ from one enterprise to another even within the same country. Furthermore, participation can be formal or informal. Informal participation occurs when management consults/involves workers before taking decisions on various issues but without a laid down structure within the enterprise for such consultations or involvement. 'Participatory management style' and even general assemblies of all members of an enterprise, constitute forms of informal workers' participation.

Workers' participation becomes formal once procedures, rights and duties are laid down in some form of rules and/or regulations. The most common forms are the suggestion box, various forms of workers' committees (including such committees as safety, health and other committees in which workers are included), representation on the Board of Directors of enterprises, profit and/or ownership sharing. Furthermore, participation in general can be regarded not only as an act of democracy but also both as an essential and necessary link between democracy and sustainable development. It is therefore a necessary condition for the success of the SAPs now being implemented in the country since the mid 1980s. A brief description of the different forms of workers' participation at enterprise level, the problems or limitations as well as achievements as revealed by APADEP research (Questionnaire Surveys) in Tanzania is in order.

Forms of Workplace Workers' Participation in Tanzania

APADEP's comprehensive research sought answers to the following questions: What forms of workers' participation exist at the enterprise level in Tanzania and to what extent have these participatory structures been effective and meaningful?

However, the research did not seek to establish any correlation between workers' participation and enterprise productivity in those that have one form of workers' participation or another. Indeed, case study data indicates clearly that productivity (and financial performance) of enterprises was affected by many factors external to these enterprises. These included the liberalisation policies (unfair competition), and shortage of hard currency, power, raw materials, and spare parts.

Research studies in a number of enterprises (public and private) in the country confirmed however the existence of several forms of informal and formal workers' participation.

Informal Workers' Participation

In the questionnaire surveys, five questions were asked to assess the extent of informal participation and/or its effectiveness; that is, frequency of management consultation of workers; management receptivity to (listening to) workers' suggestions; management preparedness to implement workers suggestions; and management (supervisors and managers) respect for workers. The results are as shown in Table 6.7.

The majority of the respondents indicated that enterprise management sometimes consult the workers (57 percent); listen to workers (60 percent); and implement suggestions given by the workers (60 percent). A good number of them indicated that management often did consult (20 percent), listen (23 percent) and implemented (19 percent) suggestions made by the workers while others (16 - 23 percent) indicated that enterprise management never do those things.

Table 6.7: *Forms and Frequency of Use of Informal Participation (in %, N=1116)*

	Always/often	Sometimes	Never
Does management consult workers	20	57	23
Does management listen to workers	23	60	17
Does mgt. implement suggestions	19	65	16
Do supervisors respect workers	51	42	7
Do managers respect workers	42	48	10

These results show the existence of these informal forms of workers' participation although management did not make use of them very often. They have also been somehow effective since management were prepared to implement or carry out some of the suggestions from the workers. As for management respect for workers, the majority (51 & 42 percent) responded 'always/often,' followed by 'sometimes' (48 & 42 percent) for supervisors and managers respectively (Table 6.7). These results tend to indicate the existence of good relations between workers and management, especially with supervisors.

If however, we recode the values 'always/often' to mean 'yes' (i.e. existence of this form of participation) and make a count of 'yes' we get the result that only seven percent of the respondents indicated the existence of all the above five forms of informal participation.

Regarding the relationship between informal participation and size of the enterprise, the questionnaire survey results were as follows:

+ There was no significant relationship (at 5 percent level) between the various forms of informal participation with both size and ownership of the enterprise;

+ There was significant association between size of enterprise with only one type of informal participation: Managers' respect for workers, at 5 percent level of significance - with the proportion of those saying 'yes' (i.e. 'always/ often') increasing with decreasing size of enterprise. When the five forms are taken together it is found that contrary to our expectation, questionnaire survey results indicated no significant relationship or association between informal participation and size of enterprise;

+ As for type of ownership and informal participation, there was significant association with several types of participation as follows: management consulting workers before taking decisions; management preparedness to listen to workers suggestions; and management preparedness to implement those decisions with a high percentage of respondents from public owned firms more often saying hardly or never (at 1 percent level of significance).

+ There was no significant relationship (at 5 percent level) between managers respecting workers and type of ownership.

From the discussion so far, it is evident that in so far as informal workers' participation is concerned, what matters most is not the size of the enterprise but the type of ownership.

Over and above the abovementioned forms of participation, case study data also indicate the existence of other informal (benevolent) forms of workers' participation. Examples include the departmental general meetings and general assemblies (*barazas*). These general meetings are held besides the other formal participatory structures in the public and private enterprises. Normally, the management as well as the local trade union organise these general assemblies/ meetings. If the local trade union organises them, then it has to obtain the approval of the management. These meetings are normally arranged on a flexible basis when the need arises. Enterprise management usually arrange these meetings at least once a year, when the results of operations and problems of the company are discussed. Usually, the chief executive or general manager of the company chairs the meetings.

Once the meeting is open, then heads of departments present the results of their operations verbally followed by discussions from the floor. The head of department responds and takes note of the views and opinions from the floor. Proposals from the meeting are then passed to a higher level for final approval. The importance of general assemblies/meetings cannot be over-emphasised here. Suffice it to point out the following:

One, they provide a forum for workers to air their views and grievances. Through them, management get to know of impending conflict/labour disputes and in efforts to avoid it they usually take measures beneficial to the workers. In addition to this, informal participation can have some comparative advantages vis-à-vis the other formal participatory structures. First and foremost, informal participation is much more direct and democratic and it allows participation for all. Many rank-and-file feel very happy to be given the chance to talk to management face-to-face. This is particularly true in the large enterprises, where there can easily occur a communication breakdown between the workers' representatives and the mass of workers at the grassroots level. Moreover, general assemblies also seem to be easily organised and managed at lower administrative costs. Although it is normally large companies that organise general meetings, it is certain that this form of workers' participation can be more effective in the small and medium-sized enterprises which are, by their very nature, conducive to informal communication and participation.

Secondly, sometimes the workers or their unions use such forums to prepare for industrial action. In Tanzania, where it is very difficult to organise legal strikes, workers sometimes resorted to what they term 'extended Baraza' - a euphimism for a strike or soldiering. This was common during the early 1990s. All in all, such forms of informal participation are valuable in that they are democratic, direct and in principle they allow the participation of all. Even so, further studies are needed to establish their strong points and limitations.

Forms of Formal Participation

The questionnaire surveys employed six variables to indicate six forms of formal workers' participation. These were the existence of: suggestion boxes; workplace trade union branch committees; workers' councils; workers' representation in the board of directors; worker profit sharing schemes; and the possibility of workers buying enterprise shares or worker share-holding scheme.

The existence of each of the different types of formal workers' participation was looked at and the proportion of respondents indicating its existence recorded. But the response category 'I do not know' was also included. We thought that it could be possible that a good number of the respondents might not know whether a certain form existed or not. Our fears were justified (Table 6.8).

As in the case of informal participation, a count of those saying 'yes' to the existence of each of the six types mentioned was made. Only one percent of all the respondents indicated the existence of all the six types of participation that were asked; five percent (five types); 14 percent (four types); 28 percent (three types); 30 percent (two types); 14 percent (one type) and eight percent indicated zero existence of any one type.

Further analysis of data indicates that there is a weak association between type of ownership and the number of various types of formal workers' participation. That is, the type of ownership seems to matter as to how many different types of formal participation are in place in an enterprise.

Table 6.8: *Forms and Frequency of Formal Workers' Participation (in %, N=1116)*

Existence of	Yes	No	Don't know
Suggestion box	28	72	0
Workers' (TU) committee	89	10	1
Workers' Council	72	27	1
Worker reps. in the Board	33	63	4
Profit sharing scheme	17	78	5
Share ownership scheme	10	78	12

As for size of enterprise and the various types of formal participation, there was no association between them. In other words, size of an enterprise was independent of the number of various types of formal workers participation to be found in Tanzanian enterprises. Again, just like in the case of informal participation what seem to matter in so far as participation is concerned is the type of ownership and not the size (in terms of number of employees) of the enterprise. Below we briefly discuss the existence of each form separately.

Suggestion Boxes

Suggestion boxes are used by many institutions, especially those that offer services (commercial or otherwise) to people. Through these boxes the institutions concerned get to learn/know a lot from those they serve: e.g. what people say about their services/product, problems, suggestions for improvement, etc. at no cost except for somebody to open the boxes read/take note of the contents. It is a form of suggestion where both employees and non-employees of the institution concerned participate. In our opinion it is also one of the simplest and cheapest form of participation to administer. Yet only about three out of ten (28 percent) of the respondents indicated the existence of suggestion boxes at their workplaces (Table 6.8). This indicates that this type of participation (one of the cheapest and simplest) was not common and has been ignored by management of most enterprises. This finding might appear a bit strange since 51 percent of our respondents were from the service sector (see Table 1.1). Actually most of the respondents who indicated the existence of suggestion boxes at their workplace were from the service sector. What ever the case, it is an oversight on the part of enterprise management not to put in place this form of participation given the many and potential benefits which can be derived from it at almost zero cost.

In computations seeking to find out if there is any relationship between a particular type of formal participation with both size and type of ownership, the response category "I Don't Know" was dropped and the level of significant adopted at 1 percent and 5 percent level of confidence. There is a strong relationship (at 1 percent level) between size of enterprise and existence of a suggestion box. The bigger the size of an enterprise, the larger the percentage of respondents indicating the existence of a suggestion boxes. As for ownership and this type of participation the results seem inconclusive.

Trade Union Branch Committee

From Table 6.8, it is evident that workers' participation through trade union branch committees is the most widely spread form of participation in Tanzania, 89 percent of all respondents indicated the existence of such committees at their work places. These committees discuss a wide range of issues related to production, finance, personnel, workers' problems, communication between workers and managers/workers and workers, social welfare, etc. (Table 6.9). However, all issues discussed in these committees are sent to the workers' council for further discussion and/or approval.

Further analysis of data reveals a strong association between existence of workers' committee and size of enterprise. The percentage of respondents indicating the existence of such a form of participation increases with the size of enterprise. Furthermore, there is also a strong relationship between existence such committees and ownership. There is also a significant association between existence of a workers committee and ownership with higher percentage of respondents in publicly owned enterprises indicating its existence.

Table 6.9: *Important Issues Discussed at Workplace Trade Union Committees*

	N	%
Raise productivity, efficiency	425	42
Grievance handling, discipline	381	38
Wages, salaries, overtime	347	34
Annual bonus, allowances	231	23
Health, medical care, hygiene and safety	214	21
Communication	154	15
No trade union	140	14
Social welfare	131	13

Table 6.9: *Continued....*

Victimisation, harassment by management	54	5
Do not know	52	5
Others	341	34
BASE DE %	1004	100

It is important to point out that before the re-introduction of multiparty politics in Tanzania, these trade union branch committees were also organically entrenched within the ruling Chama cha Mapinduzi (CCM) party because the then workers union (JUWATA) was a mass organisation of CCM (from 1977 to 1991). From 1992 to 1995 these committees were known as OTTU branch committees following the formation of OTTU in 1991, which was independent of any political party. Furthermore, with the formation of industrial or sector-based trade unions from 1992 to 1995, these trade union branch committees took the name of the particular trade union operating in the enterprise concerned.

Workers' Councils

The second widespread form of participation in the country is through workers' councils, which was mentioned by 72 percent of the respondents (Table 6.8). In Tanzania, the workers' councils are the main form of workers' participation as per the provisions of the Presidential Directive of 1970. In most cases workers' council meetings are held twice a year to discuss enterprise/company plans and results of operations. Meetings of the councils are, in most cases, chaired by company's general managers or a senior official of a particular company or enterprise. They also usually discuss a wide range of issues including performance review, setting production targets, how to raise productivity, workers' education, etc. (Table 6.10). A close look at Tables 6.9 and 6.10 reveals that trade union branch committees tend to discuss issues that are much more relevant to workers (grievance handling; wages, salaries and overtime; allowances and annual bonuses; health, medical care, hygiene and safety; etc.) than workplace workers' councils. Furthermore, the issues that are brought for discussion in the councils are usually too technical for workers' representatives to digest and offer a convincing alternative. The implication of this is that for most of these matters, management has already decided and the matters are only raised in the workers' council for rubber stamping. The decisions made in these councils are mostly not binding to the enterprise's Board. But one good thing about them is that they are worker-dominated in terms of numbers.

There is a strong association between the existence of workers' councils and enterprise size. In other words, the percentage of respondents saying that they had workers' councils at their workplaces increased with increasing size of enterprise.

Table 6.10: *Important Issues Discussed at Workplace Workers' Councils*

	N	%
Others	434	44
How to raise productivity	315	32
Annual budget	308	31
There is no workers' council	244	25
Performance review	210	21
Setting production targets	143	14
Workers' education	107	11
Efficiency in distribution of work	86	9
Don't Know	81	8
BASE DE %	991	100

There is also a strong relationship between the existence of workers' councils and type of ownership. This is in line with the fact that in Tanzania, workers' councils were established trough a Presidential directive that covered only the parastatal sector. Perhaps what is worthwhile noting here is that in spite of the Presidential directive that confined the establishment of workers' councils in the public sector the private sector also did establish such participatory structures. Indeed, 45 percent of all the private sector respondents indicated the existence of workers' councils at their work places.

Workers' Representation in Board

Direct workers' representation in the enterprise Boards is almost non-existent in Tanzania, although 33 percent of the respondents (see Table 6.8) indicated that they had workers' representatives in their Boards. At best, workers are represented in the Board by at most three worker directors (trade unionists) - appointed by the trade union from outside the enterprise. This is in accordance with the 1970 Presidential circular on workers' participation. The chances are that such worker directors know very little of the workers' problems and interests at the enterprise and the task of informing workers on the deliberations of the Board is left to the management. Thus, the important question of workers sitting in the Board of their enterprises appears to be a distant dream.

This form of participation appears to be independent of the size of enterprise. As for the type of ownership, there is a strong association with this form of participation. That is, a correspondingly bigger percentage of respondents within the public/parastatal sector indicated that they had workers' representatives in the Boards of their enterprises. This finding is in line with the Presidential Directive of 1970 on workers' participation.

Profit Sharing Schemes

This is one of the new forms of participation and only 17 percent of the respondents reported its existence (Table 6.8). Officially, companies can give bonuses - a form of profit-sharing. To this effect, the planned production and financial targets of a company should be registered with a government body. Once these targets are surpassed, then workers are entitled to some form of bonus. Practically, however, our data suggests that many companies do not go for this heavily regulated arrangement. Besides, many companies find it difficult to meet/surpass targets and make profits, because of the bottlenecks and factors beyond their control including the direct and indirect effects of structural adjustment policies. But where these incentives exist, they are welcome by workers.

There is no significant association between this form of participation and size of enterprise. However, there is a strong association between the presence of profit sharing schemes and the type of enterprise ownership. The relationship is such that a correspondingly higher percentage of respondents within the parastatal enterprises indicated the presence of this form of participation. One may conclude that profit sharing schemes on the part of workers are more likely to be in place in those enterprises with mixed (public and private) ownership.

Shares Holding

This is a new forms of workers' participation whose benefits on the part of workers is still being debated. Nevertheless only 10percent of the respondents reported its existence (Table 6.8). The relationship between this type of participation with size of enterprise is not conclusive. However, there is a strong relationship (at 1percent level) between it and type of ownership. That is, a comparatively higher proportion of respondents from the parastatal/mixed ownership enterprises indicated its existence. Thus, the possibility of having share-holding schemes is largely dependent on the type of ownership of the enterprise.

From the discussion on formal workers' participation thus far, it follows that the existence of the various forms of it is more a function of the type of ownership than enterprise size. Furthermore, public and mixed ownership or joint ventures between the Government and private entrepreneurs appears to be much more amenable to various form of workers' participation than solely private owned ones. Since participation is at the heart/centre of democracy, it follows therefore that if democracy is to be promoted under the on going reform policies, then the selling of publicly owned enterprises should take the form of mixed/joint ownership. Otherwise, for the sake of promoting democracy and sustainable development (for which participation is a necessary condition), urgent legislation is needed to extend at least one of the main workers' participation structures through representation (i.e. works or workers council) to cover both the public and the private sector .

ACHIEVEMENTS, OBSTACLES AND SUPPORT NEEDS

This section takes stock of the achievements and problems of workers' participation at the workplace from the point of view of the workers and management. It concludes with the support needed to enhance effective and meaningful workers' participation. We shall confine our discussion to the structures of participation as stipulated in the 1970 Presidential Circular on workers' participation. Unless stated otherwise, the information contained in this section relies exclusively on the qualitative analysis of the case study data.

Workers' participation can be beneficial to both workers and management/owners. But it is also possible for workers' participation structures to exist and function while at the same time participation remains ineffective and meaningless especially on the part of workers. The following internal components of workers' participation are necessary for effective and meaningful participation:

a) Participation in decision-making, whether direct or by elected representatives;
b) Frequent feedback of economic results to all employees in the form of money, not just information;
c) Full sharing with employees of management level information;
d) Guaranteed individual rights (legal protection);
e) An independent board of appeal in case of disputes;
f) A particular set of attitudes and values on workers' participation.

Achievements

On the positive side of workers' participation, three achievements will be emphasised namely, access to information, consultation and material benefits.

Access to Information

Workers' representatives have had access to a variety of information which has enabled them to discuss a wide range of issues. Indeed, at times, they may get too much information to digest. In one public enterprise, for instance, the workers' representatives in the workers' council receive all the production and financial information prepared in the company, including the sales plan, the production plan, the purchase plan, the capital expenditure plan, the manpower plan and the annual financial statements (i.e. the income statement and the balance sheet). Despite the problems of interpreting this information, the mere receipt of information is quite an achievement for workers. Otherwise, this information would have been the sole property of management kept strictly confidential in a typical non-participatory enterprise. Access to this information has been beneficial to the workers as well as their enterprise in many ways. On the one hand, this information helps workers to make informed decisions and demands. On the other hand, the information helps the workers to make proposals to improve the financial and production performance in those instances when their companies are financially distressed. As such one can say that some of the achievements of workers' participation in Tanzania include 'solving some problems facing workers and the enterprise (Chambua, 1997: 303).

Consultation

Another achievement of workers' participation is having the opportunity to be consulted on a wide range of issues of immediate concern to workers as well as management (Tables 4.9 and 4.10). It is true that workers' councils can be described as being more consultative than participatory (Bavu, *et. al.* 1985); but they provide a forum for workers to air their views and grievances. This, in turn, contributes not only in promoting good industrial relations (stability and harmony), but also helps management to make sound decisions (Chambua, 1997: 303). Given the traditional model of the non-participatory approach where almost all these decisions are considered to be managerial prerogatives, it is not difficult to conclude that consultation is a step in the right direction and can be considered as an achievement.

Material Benefits

Workers' participation does not only give the workers' representatives the platform to talk to management, but through workers' participation the worker representatives can also manage to secure (for fellow workers) a wide range of material benefits. These include salary increases and payment of wages/salaries on time; improvement in the quality of drinking water; loans; catering for workers' welfare on sickness and terminal benefits, medical facilities and minimisation of victimisation by management. Furthermore, management also benefits. Sometimes management organise *barazas* to solicit workers' opinions on how to tackle the production and financial problems of the enterprise. Workers' participation is, therefore, not just a talking shop: every party is benefiting: workers as well as management.

Limitations

It would be erroneous, however, to conclude that workers are entirely satisfied with the way workers' participation functions in their workplaces. While aware of the achievements they have made, workers have made it clear that they are more than aware of the obstacles and problems that negatively affect effective participation, some of which are:

Lack of legal backing

Workers' participation, through workers' councils was originally imposed from above by the political elite to, *inter alia*, mobilise workers' support. As such, workers' participation lacks any binding legal legislation. The functions, organisation and composition of participatory structures (WCECs, and workers representation in Board) are part of a presidential directive or guidelines. To add to this problem, these directives or guidelines are only applicable to the shrinking public sector.

Questionnaire survey data also indicates another problem: some of the meetings of the workers' councils do not take place as regularly as they were supposed to. The responses to the question, 'when was the last meeting of the workers' council? by respondents who reported to have workers' council at their work place were as follows: last six months (68 percent); six months to one year (19 percent); and one to two years (18 percent). The meetings of trade union branch committees are more regular than those of the workers' councils. Replies to the question concerning the last meeting of these committees for those respondents who indicated their existence at their enterprises were as follows: last month (42 percent), two to three months (30 percent), and over three months (28 percent).

Victimisation

Because of the lack of legal backing, and despite management's assurances that workers are free to air their opinions, some workers have expressed fears of dismissal if they speak out in the participatory process. Indeed, the presence of workers' representatives and their heads of departments and/or sections at the same meeting makes it difficult for the former to air their views freely. This is particularly so if and when they are called upon to give their opinions or criticisms related to the running of departments or sections. Consequently, the workers' representatives have developed their own tactics to avoid victimisation. In one private company, some workers' representatives believe that they "have to keep quiet." Thus, one can say that there is lack of effective participation in workers' council discussions by elected worker representatives. Those from management dominate the discussions in these meetings (Chambua, 1997: 304).

Advisory Status of the Participatory Structures

Case study data, as well as questionnaire survey, clearly indicate that workers' participation never amounted to co-decision making. Almost all the formal participatory structures have an advisory status and refer their decisions to top management hierarchies for final approval. To make things worse, worker,s representatives never seat on decision-making bodies of the enterprises, such as boards. Further more, the representatives have no obligation to consult with their constituencies or report to them. In all the enterprises studied, the minutes of the workers' council meetings are confidential as were those of the boards.

Poor Communication of Information

Some worker representatives have also complained of the poor communication channels. In most cases, for instance, information is disseminated to them to prepare for meetings in English rather than in Kiswahili and the majority of worker representatives are not able to express themselves fluently in English. This is yet another reason why management dominates the discussions in those situations where the meetings are conducted in English. Sometimes the representatives get the information rather late. Some information still remains undisclosed because of confidentiality. Moreover, case study data show communication breakdown of another type: this time between the workers' representatives and the rank and file. As mention earlier, workers at the grassroots level are left in the dark on the deliberations of the participatory structures.

Poor Education on Workers' Participation

All the case studies suggest that one problem common to all enterprises studied is lack of training/education on workers' participation. This is mainly due to the supposed lack of resources. The problem is aggravated by low education levels of most of the workers' representatives. The gravity of the problem is well captured in the survey questionnaires. Answers to the question: 'apart from this seminar, have you ever attended any other seminar or trade union education/training at the following levels? The results are as shown in Table 6.11.

Table 6.11: *Frequency of Trade Union Education/Training (N=1116)*

TU training at:	No (%)	Yes, once (%)	More than once (%)
Workplace	37	29	34
District level	64	20	16
Regional level	77	13	10
National level	88	6	6
Abroad - Africa	95	3	2
Abroad - Outside Africa	97	2	1

It is clear from Table 6.11 that the frequency of trade union education and training at all levels is very low. Even at the workplace level, about four out of ten of the representatives, the APADEP seminar was their first trade union education/ training to attend. Clearly something has to be done to address this problem, lack of resources not withstanding. Both employers and trade unions should, if necessary by law, include in their budget funds for workers' education and training and strike a gender balance in such activities.

Manipulation of Workers' Participation Structures

The analysis of the case studies indicates that most managers of public and private enterprises are in favour of workers' participation, yet experience suggests that management can hijack it to promote more the interests of owners/ management than those of workers. No wonder the title of one of the case studies we conducted was, "Workers' Participation Hijacked? A Case Study of a Tanzanian Public Enterprise." In some privately owned enterprises, management used the participatory structures as a platform to restrain demand for pay increases and focus on the company problems and the need to improve productivity. Of course, for employers their main interest in participation is its contribution to efficiency and productivity. But this can only happen if participation is free of manipulation and there is a balance between workers' interests and those of employers.

Women Under-representation

Another common problem is the under-representation of women in the participatory structures. This is due to three reasons: (a) there are fewer women than men in the formal sector; (b) lack of confidence among some women to represent fellow workers; and (c) too much work at home. These issues are not new, suffice it to point out that democratic participation should entail equal representation and participation for all, men and women.

What emerges from our discussion so far is that workers' participation in Tanzania has been meaningful but not very effective. Yet, despite the limitations mentioned above, there is still hope and yearning for it in that:

• Both workers and members of management interviewed while conducting case studies were in favour of it;
• Nearly all (99%) of the workers' representatives (respondents to the questionnaire survey) were also in favour of it; and, what is more, they were also in favour of introducing a new legislation that would enforce workers' participation in both the private and public sectors; and,
• On many enterprises' issues or decisions, the representatives had more faith in participation than in trade union negotiations.

The only people who are sceptical about it are some government officials and some members from the employer associations who, erroneously, associate rather closely workers' participation only with socialist/communist regimes. Otherwise, the yearning for democratic workers' participation is still great in the country and need to be supported.

Support Needed

Workers as well as managers, have shown enthusiasm for workers' participation. All are in favour of capitalising on its achievements and avoiding the obstacles.

No one on either side has called for the dismantling of these participatory structures. Indeed, managers and workers are clear to point out the necessary support needed to strengthen workers' participation and make it more effective and meaningful. The following are some of their proposals.

Legalisation

Almost all workers and managers were in favour of legalising workers' participation by introducing necessary laws to up-date the current guidelines and directives, to extend participation to the private sector, and to give a legal backing to participation. This is deemed necessary to give enough protection against any managerial victimisation. Moreover, because of the current wave of privatisation, most workers and managers maintain that these laws should be extended to the private sector as well. The Tanzanian government, as pointed above, has since 1998/99 been discussing the enactment of such a law.

Workers' Participation in Decision-making

So far, workers' participation in Tanzania, has only amounted to consultation. Though this is a step in the right direction, workers believe it is not enough. Thus, many workers are calling for the representation of workers in the decision-making structures of the enterprise, notably enterprise boards and for the workers' councils to be given final decision-making powers on some issues, especially those which do not need the approval of enterprise boards.

Education and Training

Workers' representatives, as well as managers agree that continuous education and training on workers' participation is a prerequisite for effective and meaningful workers' participation. Thus, trade unions and employers should both set aside resources for workers' education and training.

Gender

Workers and managers, male and female, are calling for more women representation in the trade unions and participatory structures through reserving quotas for women and more education for women on their rights.

DEVELOPMENT PRIORITIES AND TRADE UNION POLICY

DEVELOPMENT PRIORITIES AND TRADE UNION POLICY

W orkers in general, and trade unionists in particular, are interested in the social economic development of their country. This is because experience has shown that workers and trade unions are able to strike better terms of service when the economy is performing well. The study on which this book is based was done at the time when the country was implementing the IMF/World Bank sponsored SAPs, which were conceived without the involvement of neither the workers nor their unions. The purpose of this chapter is, therefore, to highlight on three kinds of information:

- Information on development problems that are considered by the worker representatives as priority problems of the area (region and district) where they live as well as priority problems of workers specifically;
- Respondents suggestions on how to solve the problems in the regions and districts to which they belong; and
- Desired trade union policy in general and trade union education policy in particular.

Perceived Development Priorities/Problems

There are many developmental problems confronting each and every district in the country. Most of them are, however, common to all districts. Respondents to the questionnaire survey were asked to list down five major problems confronting the development of their respective districts. This was an open-ended question and we had to provide codes for 15 different types of problems common in many districts. According to the representatives (see Table 7.1), the five major problems in district development were:

* Poor transport (mentioned 75 percent of the respondents);
* Inadequate health facilities (44 percent);
* Inadequate sources of water and/or inadequate water supply (42percent);
* Inadequate education facilities (34 percent); and
* Poor agriculture (21 percent).

Poor Transport

Poor transport was seen by the worker' representatives as the number one problem both in district development and the problems facing workers in the districts. Under it we included poor/bad roads, inadequate transportation vehicles for both people and goods, and badly maintained transportation facilities. It is indeed a big problem in Tanzania, especially in rural areas.

Table 7.1:   Major Problems in District Development

Multiple responses	N	%
Poor transport	812	75
Inadequate health facilities	478	44
Inadequate water supply	459	42
Inadequate education facilities	368	34
Poor agriculture	224	21
No electricity	172	16
Poor communications	166	15
Inappropriate development plans	140	13
High cost of living	115	11
Poor housing	111	10
Inadequate material resources	110	10
High unemployment	83	8
Low wages/salaries	83	8
Poor working conditions	54	5
Security of employment	11	1
Others	263	24
Don't know	7	1
BASE DE %	1088	100

Transportation plays a crucial role in promoting economic development. Improved and quicker transport network leads to the following:

a) Reduction of transportation costs thereby lowering of marketing costs. These transportation costs may fall by 15 to 60 percent as a result of improved transport infrastructure (Mabele, 1995: 69);

b) Minimising the losses suffered by agricultural producers due to inadequate infrastructure. In Tanzania in 19988, for example, "about 50 percent of the cotton in three regions, eight percent of the rice in another region, and 50 percent of all seeds and fertilisers and other chemicals in another area were lost due to impassable rural roads" (Mabelle, *ibid* 70);

c) Integrating the country thereby making political governance much easier and cheaper; and

d) Widening of the market which, in turn, induces increased agricultural produce and other economic activities.

The current state of the transport sector (especially roads and railways) cost the economy dearly through higher vehicle operating costs, delays in moving goods and damage both to the vehicles and goods being moved. The World Bank has estimated that higher vehicle operating costs alone cost the economy about 33 percent of the country's annual foreign exchange earnings. The Bank concluded that if "the current transport problems are taken into consideration, it would be impossible to see how Tanzanian goods could be competitive in the world market, or how the cost of living could be held down" (World Bank, 1990: 3).

The point being made here is that the current state of the transport sector is indeed a major developmental problem in Tanzania and as such the representatives have to be commended for singling out 'poor transport' as a number one problem in district development and as a problems facing workers in districts. The state of the transport sector leads to not only problems in transporting workers (to and from workplace) and goods, but also to accidents that may lead to destruction of life (deaths) and property.

Inadequate Health Facilities

Health services in Tanzania are provided directly by the government and indirectly through parastatal organisations, voluntary agencies and private institutions. The Government of Tanzania emphasises equity in the provision of health services and views access to such services as a basic human right.

The country's health policy evolved in early 1970s with the aim of providing comprehensive health services to all citizens equitably. It placed special emphasis on rural health, on preventive and promotion services, and on building small health units rather than hospitals. Consequently, large numbers of mid-level health workers were trained and in most categories, the targets set in the policy were surpassed. Furthermore, a number of preventive programmes like Maternal and Child Health and Family Planning (MCH/FP), Expanded Programme on Immunisation (EPI), TB/Leprosy, etc. were launched. Implementation of the policy led to an extensive health infrastructure (Table 7.2) that, in turn, tremendously increased access to health services. By 1980 about 72 percent of the population was living within five kilometres from a health unit.

Table 7.2: *Health Facilities in Mainland Tanzania, 1998*

	Government	Parastatal	R/Vol inst.	Private	Other	Total
Special hospitals	6	0	2	1	0	9
Regional hospitals	15	0	0	0	0	15
District hospitals	39	1	10	0	0	50
Other hospitals	4	3	50	33	0	90
Health Centres	211	9	38	11	0	269
Dispensaries	2019	110	543	396	10	3078
Other	8	3	2	4	1474	1491
Total	2302	126	645	445	1484	5002

Source: Economic Survey (1998: 217)
Notes: R/Vol inst. = Religious and Voluntary institutions.

Existing statistics (Table 7.2) show that in 1998 there were a total of 5002 heath facilities in Tanzania (Mainland) as follows: 164 hospitals, 269 health centres, 3078 dispensaries and 1491 other health facilities. Overall, the Government owned 46 percent of all the health facilities: 39 percent of all the hospitals, 78 percent of all the health centres and 66 percent of all the dispensaries.

This extensive health infrastructure not withstanding, the representatives identified inadequate health facilities as one of the major (ranked second) problems in district development. This is not surprising given the fact that the provision of health services has been facing mounting operational problems due to reduced resource allocation and economic difficulties facing the country. In addition, the quality of services has been deteriorating because of shortage of essential supplies and equipment as well as the poor physical state of health units, especially health centres and dispensaries.

The situation has been compounded by a shift of donor support in the mid-1980s from social sectors to productive sectors in line with the government's implementation of the IMF/World Bank sponsored SAPs (since 1986). The implementation of SAPs has negatively affected the provision of social services, especially health and education. "This view has found support, and may even originate, from the government itself" (Semboja, 1995: 149). However, towards the end of the 1990s, both the Government and donors developed renewed interest in the improvement of the social sector. A social sector strategy has already been developed incorporating a Health Sector Reform Action Plan, 1996-1999.

The Action Plan is an attempt to arrest the deteriorating quality of health services that began at the end of the 1970s and accelerated in the mid 1980s. Under the plan, cost sharing will be extended from hospitals to health centres and dispensaries. Ccommunities are expected to take full responsibility for financing their health services through formal and informal risk policy mechanisms such as a community health fund. Major consultant as well as district designated hospitals will be granted autonomy, and the private sector given a greater role in health provision. No wonder therefore that inadequate health services was the third most frequently mentioned problem facing the workers.

Water Scarcity

Tanzania is a well-watered country with moderate to good rainfall and with many rivers and lakes. This broad statement, however, hides the problem in that in most areas of the country, rainfall is seasonal and water is not readily available especially during the dry season. Thus, for many people in both rural and urban areas, water for drinking, washing, and other daily uses, is in short supply. This has led to frequent incidences of water related diseases such as diarrhoea, cholera, typhoid and dysentery. The water supply situation in the country in the 1990s was as follows:

◆   In 1992, only 47 percent and 69 percent of the total rural and urban population respectively had access to clean and safe drinking water (see Economic Survey, 1997: 193);

◆   In 1998, only 48percent and 68percent of the total rural and urban population respectively had access to clean and safe drinking water (see Economic Survey, 1998: 190).

Apart from domestic consumption, water is also important for socio-economic development. Both productive activities and delivery of social services need water. Actually, water is needed for crop cultivation, livestock development, generation of electricity, industrial production, etc. Thus, we concur with the representatives that water scarcity is a major developmental problem.

This said, there is need to point out that soon after attainment of political independence, one of the Government's priority was universal water supply and preparation of water master plans. A target to provide portable water to all to within 400 metres by 1991 was set. But by 1991 only 42 percent of the rural population and 50 percent of the urban population were served with water. Thus, the target was not met due to, *inter alia*, financial constraints and has now been shifted to the year 2002.

Inadequate Education Facilities

From independence up to the late 1970s the Tanzanian Government set aside more-or-less adequate resources to education and training. This enabled the expansion of primary, secondary and technical education, the opening of the University of Dar-es-Salaam and additions of faculties thereof including the Faculty of Engineering (in early 1970s) and that of Commerce in late 1970s, increasing the number and size of vocational training schools, and the provision of such education/training free of charge.

In mid-1970s there was the adoption of Universal Primary Education (UPE) policy. As a result of this, primary school gross enrolment reached 90 percent in 1980. However, due to the serious economic crisis from the late 1970s to 1980s, there has been a decline in primary school enrolment as well as worsening quality of educational services. Thus, gross primary school enrolment had dropped to 78 percent by 1998. The introduction of cost sharing as a result of the implementation of SAP measures has also aggravated the situation. The privatisation of education and the redirection of the financing of education towards parents and end-users has negatively affected the development of education. This is because most of the communities that have to bear the burden are poor and it is estimated that about 50 percent of the people in Tanzania live in abject poverty with incomes less than US $1 per day. According to the Government (see *Economic Survey,* 1998: 183-189), the education and training sector is faced with, inter alia:

a) Low teacher-student ratios at all levels of education;
b) Over crowding of students in classrooms especially in urban areas;
c) Shortage of qualified teachers for teaching science subjects;
d) Severe shortage of quality housing especially in the rural areas;
e) Shortage of education materials and equipment; and
f) Expansion of primary and community day secondary education institutions without considering the national capacity to finance and equip them with necessary basic education materials.

Under, these circumstances, the respondents were justified to view inadequate educational facilities as a major developmental problem in their respective districts.

Poor Agriculture

Poor agriculture is closely associated with the poverty of the people and has been aggravated by SAP measures of removing government subsidies on agricultural implements and inputs. The agricultural sector contributes about 50percent of Tanzania's GDP, and it accounts for more than 55 percent of foreign exchange earnings. The sector also provides employment to more than 80 percent of the population. Thus, and for a long time now, agriculture is the predominant economic activity. Yet, it is mainly dominated by rain-fed low technology. This means that production of agricultural crops is, to a large extent, affected by changes in weather and the outbreak of pests.

Droughts, late arrival of rain and out break of crop-destroying pests have been common since the early 1970s to-date. These factors coupled with low technology (use of hand implements, poor extension services, low use of modern inputs such as fertilisers, etc.) have been the major contributors to poor agriculture and thence, occasional declines in the production both of food and export crops. Since the country economy is mainly dependent on agriculture, poor performance of this sector implies also poor economic performance. That is why the respondents have identified poor agriculture as one of the major problems in district development.

Other problems mentioned with their ranks in brackets were the following: No electricity (6) mentioned by 16 percent of the respondents; Poor communications (7) mentioned by 15 percent of the respondents; Inappropriate development plans (8) by 13 percent; High cost of living (9) which was mentioned by 11 percent; Poor housing (10) by 10 percent; Inadequate material resources (11) by 10 percent; High unemployment (12) by 8 percent; Low wages/salaries (13) mentioned by 8 percent of all the respondents; etc (see Table 7.1).

Problems Facing the Workers

The respondents were also asked the following open-ended question: "What are the five major problems facing workers in your district? The responses to this question were as follows (listing the five most frequently mentioned problems): (a) poor transport (71 percent); (b) low wages/salaries (48 percent); (c) inadequate health services (28 percent); (d) poor housing (27 percent); and (e) inadequate education facilities (19 percent)(Table 7.3).

Table 7.3: *Problems Faced by Workers in Districts*

Multiple responses	N	%
Poor transport	767	71
Low wages/salaries	518	48
Inadequate health services	305	28
Poor housing	296	27
Inadequate education facilities	208	19
Inadequate material resources	177	16
High cost of living	172	16
Inadequate water supply	141	13
Poor working conditions	114	11
Inappropriate development plans	86	8

Table 7.3: *Continued...*

Multiple responses	N	%
Poor communications	74	7
Poor agriculture	73	7
High unemployment	53	5
Security of employment	40	4
No electricity	39	4
Others	231	21
Don't know	12	1
BASE DE %	1079	100

These are the same problems as those mentioned as major problems in Table 7.1 above in district development, except for minor variations in their ranking. For instance, poor transport ranked as a number one problem in both cases, i.e. in district development and in problems facing workers in the districts while inadequate health and education facilities raked second and fourth in the latter case. Low wages/salaries and poor housing were not amongst the five major problems in district development, they ranked 13 and 10 respectively. The implication of this is that although workers are faced with the problems of low wages and poor housing, they nevertheless did not consider these as being major developmental problems.

Solutions to Workers Problems

The respondents were also asked to list down what they considered to be solutions to workers problems. The responses to this question are as follows:

♦ Creating a strong participation in decision-making process (mentioned by 39 percent of the respondents);
♦ Through improvement in transport (25 percent);
♦ Through more workers' education (17 percent);
♦ More investments to create more jobs (15percent);
♦ Through improvement in housing (10 percent); and
♦ Other solutions mentioned by less than ten percent of the respondents were creating a strong trade union, change of attitude of managers and top management, and the government should change labour legislation.

It is interesting to note that the respondents had a lot of faith in participation and they see it as a solution to the problems of workers. The second solution suggested was improvement in transport followed by more workers' education. The fourth solution suggested by the workers' representatives was more investments to create more jobs. The fifth solution was improvement in housing.

It is obvious from the above results that respondents have a high level of awareness about development problems in their respective districts/regions and are willing to participate in finding solutions to those problems. Indeed, the solutions they suggested are realistic and in their opinion the single most important means of solving them is through stronger participation in the decision-making process.

Desired Trade Union Policy

Apart from seeking information on desired development policy, there were also other questions that sought to obtain various suggestions on both general trade union policy (i.e. what trade unions should do, what means can help strengthen the trade union movement and increase its membership) and on priorities for trade union education policy. Four variables were used to capture this information, namely:

* Priorities for trade union action;
* Suggestions on how to strengthen trade unions;
* Suggestions on how to increase trade union membership; and
* Priorities for trade union education.

The results, as discussed below, indicate that the respondents had apple suggestions on what ought to be the main priorities for trade union action and how to strengthen them.

Trade Union Priority Actions

Respondents were asked to list down six most important activities that s/he thinks or would like the trade union undertake them in the coming years. The six most important activities, according to the respondents, are:

* Defending wages and salaries (suggested by 52 percent of the respondents);
* Improving workers' participation (49 percent);
* Workers' education (37 percent);
* Security of employment (19 percent);
* Collective bargaining (13 percent); and
* Change of labour legislation (suggested by 5 percent of the respondent).

Only four percent of the respondents indicated that they did not know what were the important activities to be undertaken by their unions in the coming years. Given the socio-economic changes taking place in the country, it is not surprising that defending wages and salaries ranked number one, followed by improving workers' participation and provision of workers' education ranked third. Trade unions actions in the future should also be directed to security of employment and collective bargaining. Although change of labour legislation was suggested by only five percent of the respondents, there is need to point out that this is a very important suggestion. Indeed, the other activities could be carried out in the interests of workers if there is change in labour legislation especially in the areas of dispute settlement as well as enacting a new law that gives workers' participation a legal basis and extend it to the bourgeoning private sector.

Strengthening Trade Unions

Regarding suggestions on how to strengthen the trade unions, opinions were many and varied although each respondent was required to provide only three suggestions. If however we disregard those suggestions mentioned by less than 10 percent of the respondents, the opinions on this issue are:

a) Find/allocate more resources to the trade unions to enable them perform their functions (33 percent);
b) Hold frequent meetings and seminars (33 percent);
c) Have better communication and information (22 percent);
d) Workers should unite to form a strong union (17 percent); and
e) Trade unions should have strong and committed leadership (15 percent).

Other opinions ranged from "representation in parliament' (2 percent) to "government should assist in the change of labour legislation' (6 percent). From these suggested means of strengthening unions, it appears that the unions lack adequate resources to perform their functions properly; meetings and seminars are not as frequent as the respondents would have liked; there are no good means of communication and information sharing; (some unions) lack strong and committed leadership; and there is also the problem of workers' unity/ solidarity. In our opinion, these are genuine problems/suggestions and the unions would benefit a lot if the leadership doubled its effort to address them.

Increase Trade Union Membership

Opinions on how to increase unionised members were also many and varied. These included measures to:

♦ Provide more education and training to workers (62 percent of the respondents);
♦ Trade unions should be seen to be defending workers' rights (23 percent);
♦ Unions must hold regular meetings (18 percent); and
♦ Trade union leaders should communicate with branch committees (8 percent).

Other opinions ranged from trade union branches should receive some percentage of their member's collections (2 percent) to unions should be successful in collective bargaining (4 percent).

The single most popular opinion mentioned by 62 percent of all the respondents is provision of more education and training to workers. That is, according to the respondents, one way of attracting more workers to join the trade union movement is for the unions to be seen and actually providing education and training to its members. If the unions are seen to be defending workers' rights as well as being more democratic (holding regular meetings) this would also attract more workers to join the unions.

Asked specifically about what policy trade unions should adopt in order to effectively defend or claim workers' rights/interests, the responses were as follows:

◆ 67 percent of the respondents opted for 'participation in decision-making, accepting responsibility for the decisions;
◆ 20 percent answered 'participation in decision-making, without accepting responsibility for the decisions; while
◆ 13 percent were of the view that the best policy is 'making demands, totally independent of management.

Thus, of the two main forms of claiming workers' rights (i.e. negotiation or participation), the majority of the respondents (87 percent) were of the view that the best policy that their unions should adopt in order to effectively defend workers' interests/rights is participation in decision-making. This shows that the respondents still had a lot of faith in participation in spite of its limitations as discussed in the Chapter 6.

Regarding participation aspirations, a question was included to assess whether a respondent felt that s/he participated enough in enterprise decision-making or would like to participate more and for those who wanted to participate more, the level of participation they desired. The results are that:

◆ 55 percent of the respondents claimed that they had no enough say in decisions made at their workplaces;
◆ 7 percent said that they 'would like to have more say only in decisions that directly concern work and working conditions;
◆ 10 percent replied that they 'would like to have more say in decisions concerning the enterprise/company as a whole; and
◆ 28 percent answered that they 'would like to have more say both in decisions concerning their work and the company as a whole.

The above results indicate that over half of the respondents (55percent) were not involved in decision-making in their workplaces. Of the 45 percent who had some say in enterprise decisions, would like to participate more in decision-making at their respective workplaces.

At this juncture, there is need to recall that the respondents suggested that holding frequent/regular meetings as one of the ways of both strengthening the unions and increasing union membership. This further indicates that they are not only eager to participate in enterprise decision-making but also in union decision-making organs. What then were their views on how to improve democracy in formal participation structures? Their views on this issue were captured by asking them what, in their opinion, was the best procedure for constituting the following participation organs: trade union branch committee, workers' council and trade union executive committee. The majority of the respondents opted for one person/member one vote (42 percent for workers' council; 46 percent for trade union branch committee; and 60 percent for trade union executive committee).

Appointment by both the trade union and management was the second most favoured election procedure for members of both the workers' councils (38 percent) and of the trade union branch committees (31 percent). The third most favoured method for selecting members to participation organs was appointment by the unions (mentioned by 33 percent of the respondents for trade union executive committees; by 15 percent for workers' councils; and by 19 percent for trade union branch committee) (see Table 7.4). What is to be noted from the results in Table 7.4 is that apart from one person one vote, the respondents had much faith in 'joint appointment by the trade unions and management than by trade unions alone even for trade union branch committee members. This is yet another challenge to the trade union movement in Tanzania.

Table 7.4: *Best Ways of Constituting Formal Participation Structures*

	TU Branch Committee	Workers' Council	TU Executive Committee
One person, one vote	46	42	60
Appointment by TU	19	15	33
Appointment, management	1	1	NA
Appointment, TU & Mgt.	31	38	NA
Other	3	3	7
Total (percent%)	100	99	100

Note: TU stands for Trade Union.

Desired Support for Participation

Suggestions were also sought from the respondents about how support can be given to participation organs, specifically workers' councils. As to what support could be given to make workers' councils more effective, the three most popular opinions were: workers' council should have the power to make decisions (48 percent); put more emphasis on meetings of workers' councils; and have specific law protecting workers' councils at workplaces (Table 7.5). These suggestions can also be viewed as constituting the limitations of workers' councils in the country.

As to who should extend support for the better functioning of workers participation structures, specifically the workers' councils, the opinions were as follows (see Table 7.6):

a) Management (60 percent of the respondents);
b) The workers at each workplace (59 percent);
c) The Trade Unions (56 percent);
d) The Government together with trade unions (42 percent); and
e) The Government (11percent).

Table 7.5: *What Support to Workers' Councils is Required to Make Them More Effective?*

Multiple responses, exclusive non responses	N	%
WCs should have power to make decisions	517	48
Put more emphasis on WC meetings	298	28
Have a specific law to protect WCs at work	188	18
Changing the chairperson	12	1
Others	579	54
I do not know	86	8
BASE DE %	1071	100

Note: WCs stands for workers' councils.

Table 7.6: *Who Should Assist Workers' Councils to Enable Them Perform Better*

	N	%%
Management	667	60
Workers at their workplace	656	59
The Trade Unions	615	56
Government together with trade unions	459	42
The Government	120	11
Others	6	1
BASE DE %	1103	100

Priorities in Trade Union Education

Provision of more education and training was the most popular opinion as on how to increase union membership while "workers' education' ranked number three in priorities for trade union action. Thus, the respondents have a big faith in education. What then, according to them, should be the priorities in trade union education? Suggestions on this included the following subjects or areas:

a) Labour laws (mentioned by 46 percent of the respondents);
b) Workers' participation (36 percent);
c) Economics (28 percent);
d) Trade unionism (23 percent);
e) Workers and the work environment (22 percent); and
f) Industrial relations (16 percent).

Other suggestions ranged from 'role of women in trade unions (2 percent) to 'collective bargaining' (5 percent) while eight percent of the worker representatives said they 'did not know.'

From these results it is apparent that the respondents would like trade union education to be directed to the fields of labour legislation, workers' participation, economics, trade unionism and workers and the work environment.

RECAPITULATION

In this chapter, we have presented and discussed the views and opinions of the respondents on various issues related to economic development, strengthening of trade unions, and trade union policy. According to the respondents, the major developmental problems in their regions/districts include poor transport; inadequate health facilities; water scarcity; inadequate education facilities; and poor agriculture. These, according to our analysis are indeed the major problems facing many districts in the country.

On workers problems, the worker representatives identified the following as being the major problems: poor transport; low wages/salaries; inadequate health services; poor housing; and inadequate education facilities. Again, these are genuine problems facing most of the workers in Tanzania even today. Regarding solutions to these problems, the most popular opinion was the creation of strong participation in decision-making process, followed by improvement in transport, and then by provision of more workers' education. This shows that the respondents had a lot o faith in participation; ranking it number one in their solutions to workers' problems.

As for ways and means of strengthening trade unions, the most popular suggestion is for he trade unions to be more vigilant in defending wages and salaries followed by enhancing and promoting workers' participation. Once again, promoting participation is considered to be one of the ways of making the unions strong. This is not surprising given the fact that for the majority of the respondents (80 percent), participation for them means democracy. A democratic procedure (one person one vote) is also ranked number, one of the best means of constituting participatory organs.

The respondents also had a lot of faith in education, in that provision of more education and training is the most popular opinion while "workers' education' ranked number three in priorities for trade union action. As for what should be the priorities of trade union education/training, labour laws and workers' participation were ranked number one and two respectively.

From our discussion so far, it is obvious that the respondents are aware of the problems facing district development and workers and are eager to participate in finding solutions to those problems. Furthermore, they have a lot of faith in participation (democracy) and education in solving problems.

8

TOWARDS EFFECTIVE AND MORE MEANINGFUL PARTICIPATION IN TANZANIA

THE LIMITS OF THE CURRENT PARTICIPATION PRACTICE

It may be recalled that the official adoption of workers' participation in Tanzania took place in 1970 through a Presidential directive. The directive spelled out the objectives of workers' participation and directed the creation of participatory organs in all public enterprises with at least ten employees. The stated objectives, powers and functions of the participatory organs were and still are such that they serve more the interests of management and owners than those of workers. This is not surprising given the fact that at that time the country was under one political party rule and the major means of production were under state control. The main limitations of workers' participation (as discussed in Chapter Six of this book) include lack of legal facilitation, advisory status accorded to the main organs of participation (the workers' councils), preparation of the agenda for workers' council meetings by management, and failure on the part of worker's representatives to participate effectively during meetings due to low levels of education and the use of English language.

The lack of a legal basis made it easier for management to manipulate the participatory organs as they saw it fit. The only participatory organs that had a legal baking were workers' committees. From 1964 to 1975 workers' committees were outside the union structure and therefore independent of the ruling political party. Because of this it was not easy to manipulate them. In 1975, however, workers' committees were banned, again through legislation, and their functions transferred to trade union branch committees which were indirectly under the control of the ruling political party since the then trade union, NUTA, was affiliated to the ruling party - then TANU.

Ideally, workers' participation ought to be beneficial to both workers and management/owners. But it is also possible for structures of workers' participation to exist and function while at the same time participation remains ineffective and meaningless especially on the part of workers. It is also possible to have a middle course position like what has taken, and is currently taking, place in Tanzania, i.e. participation being meaningful but not effective. The following internal components of workers' participation are necessary for effective and meaningful participation:

a) Participation in decision-making, whether direct or by elected representatives.
b) Frequent feedback of economic results to all employees in the form of money, not just information.
c) Full sharing with employees of management level information.
d) Guaranteed individual rights (legal protection).
e) An independent board of appeal in case of disputes.
f) A particular set of attitudes and values on workers' participation.

It should also be recalled that due to economic and political reforms from the mid 1980s, the trade union movement was freed of direct political party control in 1991. This was achieved through an Act of Parliament, the OTTU Act, which dissolved JUWATA and established OTTU. In spite of these changes, workers' participation in the country continued to be guided by the (out dated) Presidential circular of 1970. The economic reforms have been accompanied by retrenchment of public employees and privatisation of public enterprises. Consequently, the public sector has considerably shrunk while the private sector is expanding. Since the Presidential circular on workers' participation did not include the private sector, this constitutes yet another limitation of workers' participation in Tanzania today. The above limitations not withstanding, there is still a great yearning for participation as evidenced from questionnaire survey data. Almost all (99 percent) respondents were in favour of participation, had a lot of faith in it, wanted participation to be extended to the private sector as well and they also wanted enactment of a law to give workers' participation legal protection (see chapter six). One may say that participation in Tanzania has been meaningful though not effective. What the respondents fear is that unless participation is extended to the private sector and given a legal authority there is every danger that it is going to die given the increasing dominance of the private sector. Of course, the type of participation we are referring to here is representative participation through the institution of works or workers' councils.

This is not to imply that other forms of participation are not important. Rather, that these other forms can and should be promoted without abandoning works/ workers' councils. As pointed out by Kester and Adu-Amankwah (1999: 59),

> Participation, like democracy, is a dynamic process which has to be constantly proposed and learned, achievements need to be defended and new challenges have to be tackled. Any shortcomings in the short-term are not proof of participation's failure. Rather, they are lessons - part of the learning process.

For workers' participation to be sustainable, effective and more meaningful to workers, a legal culture of rights and duties must underpin it. In turn this will make democracy itself sustainable,

CREATING AN ENABLING ENVIRONMENT

Workers' participation becomes effective and more meaningful to workers when:

a) Workers or their representatives have the ability to, and actually, influence management decisions in an enterprise; and

b) Participation itself is democratic. But in order for them to take part effectively in enterprise decision-making, they have to have the ability to participate competently. In other words, they must be able to:

+ Read, analyse and interpret information concerning the enterprise including financial and production performance;
+ Have a responsible and mature attitude that promotes good relations between people;
+ Communicate with management and their unions; and
+ Listen to what people are saying and take into consideration their point of view.

For workers' participation to be democratic it must involve all the workers (female and males) from all levels of the enterprise and both workers or their representatives and management have to communicate with each other on a regular and equal basis. Involvement of all the workers should be interpreted to mean worker representatives are chosen through an agreed democratic procedure, can be held accountable to the employees and report their activities to fellow workers regularly (Reardon, 1997).

In addition to the necessary internal components of participation mentioned above, there are other necessary conditions for participation to be effective and more meaningful to workers. These additional conditions have to be created and enhanced where they do not exist. These include having free and autonomous trade unions, political and legal support and clarity on what participation is intended to achieve, i.e. the objectives of participation, on the part of both workers and their unions on one side and employers/management including the government on the other side.

Free and Autonomous Trade Unions

In order to have free and autonomous trade unions, the laws of a country should allow for the freedom of association and the unions to engage in defence of workers' interests without fear of intimidation, or fear of legal and/or political reprisals. Furthermore, dispute handling procedures should be simple as opposed to being complex and the right to strike should have minimum legal qualifications.

From 1964 up to the early 1990s, the trade union movement in Tanzania was neither free nor autonomous. The establishment of OTTU in 1991 was one of the steps taken towards the creation of free unions. But the unions that were established under the 1991 OTTU Act were forced, by the same Act, to be affiliated to OTTU. Thus, the unions lacked the freedom of association. As discussed in chapter two of this book, the dispute handling procedures are still complex, lengthy and that makes the execution of a legal strike virtually impossible. No wonder therefore that in spite of the poor working conditions that has prevailed in the country, OTTU organised and executed only one strike (an illegal strike) throughout its existence. In that sense, OTTU and its affiliates were neither free nor autonomous organisations. True, they were free from direct state and ruling political party control. But the government retained the powers to dissolve them and this is what happened when the 1998 trade union Act came into force on 1st July 2000 as discussed in Chapter Two. The Act, it may be recalled, unlike the previous enactments did not establish any trade unions or a trade union centre. Its provisions, however, provide for freedom of association and both workers and employers are free to organise and establish trade unions of their own choice. Thus, the newly established Trade Union Congress of Tanzania (TUCTA) and the industrial unions have more freedom and autonomy than their predecessors (OTTU and its affiliates). Even so the government, through the Register of Trade Unions and the Minister for Labour still have a lot of control over the unions that have been or are going to be established (after 1st July 2000). The implication of this is that the trade union movement in Tanzania has to struggle for more freedom and autonomy. It must wage a struggle for review of the 1998 Trade Union Act as well as the dispute handling procedures to give the trade union movement more freedom and autonomy in defending the interests of workers.

If one were to compare the trade union situation with the health of a person, then from 1964 to 1991 the trade union movement in Tanzania was in an intensive care unit; the OTTU Act moved the patient out of the intensive care unit but not out of the hospital; and now (as a result of the new 1998 Trade Union ACT) the patient is continuing with medication outside the hospital.

Political and Legal Support

Another condition necessary for effective and more meaningful workers' participation is political support and legal facilitation. Since all political parties in Tanzania including the government are in favour of democracy and the rule of law, then the unions have to convince all political leaders of the links between democracy and workers' participation. In addition to this, participation can also be defended on the grounds that it is a human right. Seen in this light, all political parties and other stake holders have to be engaged in advocacy for political support for effective workers' participation for employees in the public and private sector.

Once a political decision in favour of participation is made by the government, then legal facilitation is important to make it sustainable. In other words, what is needed for participation to be effective and meaningful are clear regulations founded in law dealing with constitutional and procedural requirements, rights and duties for the parties involved. This entails clarity about what participation is intended to achieve on the part of workers and their unions, employers/management and the government.

OBJECTIVES OF WORKERS' PARTICIPATION

For participation to be effective and meaningful a clear and shared understanding of what participation is intended to achieve by all parties involved is mandatory. In Chapter Six four values of participation were identified: humanisation, democratisation, more economic equity and better use of human resources. From these values the main objective of workers' participation, i.e. democratic involvement of workers in enterprise decision-making, ought to be: To make work and work relations more humane. This entails the following:

- Workplaces to be characterised by freedom of expression without fear of victimisation on the part of workers as well as by mutual respect for all - employees and management. This we have argued increases the motivation of workers to work hard and efficiently thereby increasing labour productivity;
- Providing, on the part of management, the necessary information to workers' representatives well ahead of time before meetings are held;
- Offering special training to workers and their representatives to have and/or increase their ability to participate competently;
- Gradually increasing the range of decisions over which workers' representatives exercise influence;
- Increasing and/or enhancing the social services provided for workers and other benefits including bonuses and profit sharing.
- Ensuring better use of human resources through provision of adequate and

better working tools and equipment, workers' education/training aimed at skills development for the benefit of both employees and their enterprises, and taping the knowledge and experience of many persons as opposed to only that of management personnel in running enterprises.

At this juncture, there is also need to point out what workers and trade unions should avoid in their struggle for effective and meaningful participation. First, they should avoid having only one form of participation. That is several forms of participation should be encouraged at any work place. These different forms should be complementary.

Second, no scheme of workers' participation should be seen as a substitute of collective bargaining. Participation and collective bargaining should be conceived as tools strengthening each other. Experience shows that where issues previously dealt with through collective bargaining are handled through participation alone, the influence of workers on management decreases. "Except in the cases where workers have a right to co-decision, the influence exerted by the workers on the decision-making process is weaker than in collective bargaining" (ILO, 1994: 35).

Third, effective and meaningful participation should not be allowed to undermine trade unions or their power and influence. As a matter of fact, there is no better power and defence of workers than the organised strength of workers in free trade unions.

Fourth, all enterprise decisions cannot be subjected to democratic control at once. The experience in other countries, notably Western Europe, has been that a high degree of participation, i.e. co-decision-making, on questions that determine the policy of the workplace on crucial matters for workers was obtained after a long struggle as compared to those related to the workers' immediate work environment such as welfare and transport.

THE TASK AHEAD

Tanzania, like many other African countries, was confronted with an unprecedented economic crisis from the 1980s. In its efforts to deal with the crisis, the government was compelled to adopt and implement the IMF/ World Bank sponsored SAPs from the mid-1980s. The measures taken included price decontrol, trade liberalization, devaluation of the Tanzanian shilling, government budget cuts especially to social services, privatisation and retrenchment of civil servants. The SAP reforms were vigorously applied, especially from 1993 to 1999.

Implementation of SAPs and other measures managed to restore economic growth and stability and inflation has been brought down from over 35 percent in 1990 to 6 percent in 2000. But at the same time there has been growing unemployment and income differentials. For instance, absolute poverty levels increased during the period 1991/92 - 2000 from 48 percent of the population (earning less than 1 US $ per day) to well over 50 percent. Working conditions did not improve significantly during the period under review. Wage/salaries have remained very low and workers have been forced to engage in other income supplementing/generation activities. In spite of this engagement, sufficiency of household income to meet expenses of basic needs is very low, ranging from 5 percent (income sufficient for paying for children's education) to 18 percent (income sufficient for paying house rent and purchasing firewood/charcoal/ kerosene respectively). This means that it is the workers and the peasants who are paying dearly for the economic reforms.

Workers and their trade unions were not consulted before the introduction of SAPs. Had they been consulted, the reforms would have been carried out in such a way that they are more beneficial to them and to the development of their country in general. Workers and their unions have a lot to offer (in terms of ideas and otherwise) for the development of their country. Chapter seven of this book contains views and opinions of the respondents on various issues including economic development. From the data presented in chapter seven it is obvious that the respondents (workers' representatives) are aware of the problems facing district development and workers and are eager to participate in finding solutions to those problems. Furthermore, they have a lot of faith in participation (democracy) and education in solving problems. The task ahead is therefore to ensure that participation is also developed and promoted beyond the workplace. In other words, workers and their unions (and indeed the civil society in general) should be involved and participate in considering, planning and implementation of development plans or programmes. Without the participation and hence support of the people any development programme is bound to fail. As a matter of fact, if the living conditions of the majority do not improve even the current economic growth will not be sustainable. The reason is simple, if the purchasing power of the majority of the people continues to be low, the domestic market will remain small and demand will not be sufficient for the growing supply. This in turn will act as a brake on economic development since neither foreign nor local investors will be attracted to invest in the country. The consequence will ultimately be economic stagnation.

Economic policies under SAPs and/or globalisation are increasingly being dominated by market liberalism and this is increasingly leading to deregulated capital markets. Nearly all developing countries are competing for the favours of owners of financial capital and are compelled to adopt more or less identical financial policies irrespective of the political colour of the governments. The main aim is to keep inflation rates low because this gives a better return to the owners of finance capital. The implication is that governments are competing with each other to reduce public expenditure through reducing taxes, cutting back social welfare and weakening of employee rights. Such developments are not conducive to effective and more meaningful participation for workers. Ultimately they are not also conducive to democracy and sustainable development.

Furthermore, these developments brought about by globalisation, politically imply a tremendous shift of power away from popularly elected representatives to owners of international capital. It seems that the only power that is capable of challenging the players in the capital markets is the organised strength of the people in their free and autonomous organisations, especially in trade unions. Thus, we need to have strong unions with committed, enlightened and competent leadership capable of defending and promoting both the interests of workers and of their respective countries. In this task, unity among all stakeholders: unions, intellectuals and other civil society organisations is absolutely vital.

BIBLIOGRAPHY

Abendroth, W (1972)
A Short History of European Working Class, New York: Monthly Review Press.

Adams G. R and D. Schvanevelt (1985)
Understanding Research Methods, Longman: New York.

Adu-Amankwah, K and Kester, G (eds.), (1999)
How to Make Democratic Participation A Success? An African Trade Union Challenge, Rotterdam: APADEP publication.

Anstey, M (1997)
"Trends in Employee Participation: A Comparative Overview," in M. Anstey (ed.), *Employee Participation and Workplace Forums*. South Africa: Juta & Co. Ltd.

Bavu, I.K., et al, (1981)
"Tanzanian National Report," in ICPE, Workers' Self-Management and Participation, National Reports vol. II: Algeria, Guyana, India, Tanzania, Ljubljana: International Centre for Public Enterprises in Developing Countries (ICPE).

Bayat, A (1991)
Work, Politics and Power: An International Perspective on Workers' Control and Self-management, London: Zed Books Ltd.

Bernstein, P. (1976)
Workplace Democratization: Its Internal Dynamics, Kent State University, USA.

Besha, M (1982)
"Workers Participation in Tanzania," Unpublished M.Sc Dissertation, Institute of Social Studies, The Hague, The Netherlands.

Bigou-Lare, N and G. Kester (1997)
Book V: The Operationalisation of an APADEP Questionnaire, The Hague: APADEP Publication.

Blinder, A. S (ed.), (1990)
Paying for Productivity: A Look at the Evidence, Washington, D.C: The Brookings Institution.

Blumberg, P (1968)
Industrial Democracy: The Sociology of Participation, London: Constable.

Blunt, P. and M.L. Jones (1992)
Managing Organizations in Africa, Berlin: De Gruyter & Co.

Centre for Development Research (1995)
Structural Adjustment in Africa: A Survey of the Experience, Copenhagen: Ministry of Foreign Affairs.

Chambua, S. E (1995)
"Workers' Participation in Tanzania: The Case of Kilombero Sugar Company and Mtibwa Sugar Estates," Dar es Salaam: IDS, University of Dar es Salaam.

Chambua, S.E and H..H. Semkiwa (1995)
"Undemocratic Workers' Participation in Tanzanian Public Enterprises: The Case of Morogoro Canvas Mills Ltd," IDS Dar es Salaam: APADEP Research Report.

Chambua, S.E and Naimani, G.M (1996)
"Effectiveness of Trade Union Movement on Education/Training at the National and Enterprise Levels," APADEP Research Report.

Chambua S.E. and Naimani G.M. (1996a)
"The Worker's Strike of 1st to 3rd March 1994 in Tanzania: OTTU's strike or Strike Against OTTU," IDS Dar es Salaam: APADEP Research Report

Cole, D. H. (1975)
"Collectivism, Syndicalism and Guilds," in Vanek, J (ed.), *Self-Management*, London: Penguin.
Cooley, M. (1987)
Architect or Bee? The Human Price of Technology, London: Hogarth Press.
Hansen, K. (1997)
"Mozambique: Organise or Disappear," in Kester and Sidibe (eds.) *Trade Unions and Sustainable Democracy in Africa*, Aldershot: Ashgate Publishing Ltd.
Hazlewood, A (1989)
Education, Pay and Work in East Africa, Oxford: Clarendon Press.
ILO (1986)
Collective Bargaining: A Workers' Education Manual, Geneva: International Labour Organisation.
ILO (1994)
"Political Transformation, Structural Adjustment and Industrial Relations in Africa - English Speaking Countries," Geneva: International Labour Office, *Labour-Management Relations Series* No.78
IMF/IDA (2000)
" Tanzania: Decision Point Document Under the Enhanced Heavily Indebted Poor Countries (HIPC) Initiative," (Mimeo): Dar es Salaam.
International Center for Public Enterprises in Developing Countries (ICPE) (1986)
Workers' Self-Management and Participation in Practice, Vol. 1: Case Studies from Bolivia, Malta, India, Sri Lanka, Tanzania and Zambia, Ljubljana Yugoslavia: ICPE.
ICPE (1981)
Workers' Self-Management and Participation, National Reports, Vol II: Algeria, Guyana, India, Tanzania, Ljubljana Yugoslavia: ICPE.
Jackson, D (1979)
"The Disappearance of Strikes in Tanzania: Incomes Policy and Industrial Democracy," *Journal of Modern African Studies*, 17, 2 (219 - 51).
Jones, J and D. Seabrook (1969)
"Industrial Democracy," in Coates, K (et al), *Trade Union Register*, London: Merlin Press.
JUWATA (1990)
"Waraka Kuhusu Mageuzi Katika Umoja wa Wafanyakazi Tanzania" - Toleo la Awali, Dar es Salaam.
Kagarlitsky, B. (1990)
The Dialectic of Change, London: Verso.
Kalombo, J. F. (et al 1985)
"Zambia: ROP (1975) Limited, Ndola", in A. Vahcic and V. Smole-Grobovsek (eds.), *Workers' Self-Management and Participation in Practice* Vol. 1: Case Studies from Bolivia, Sri Lanka, Malta, Tanzania India and Zambia, Ljubljana Yugoslavia: ICPE
Kamaliza, M (1965)
"Labour Policy," in P. Bomani (ed.), *Forward Tanzania*, Dar es Salaam: Tanzania Publishing House.
Kapinga, W. B. L (1985)
"State Control of the Working Class Through Labour Legislation," in I. G. Shivji (ed.), *The State and the Working People in Tanzania*, Darker: Codesria.
Kasilati, T. M (1994)
"The Role of Political Parties in Democratic Society," in ESAURP (1994), *The Cost of Peace: Views of Political Parties on the Transition to Multiparty Democracy*, Dar es Salaam: Tanzania Publishing House.

Kester and Sidibe (eds. 1997)
Trade Unions and Sustainable Democracy in Africa, Aldershot: Ashgate Publishing Ltd.

Kester, G and F. Schiphorst (1987)
Workers' Participation and Development: Manual for Workers' Education, The Hague: Institute for Social Studies.

Kester, G and Pinaud, H (1996)
"Introduction - Democratic Participation: A Challenge for Democracy," in G. Kester and H. Pinaud (eds.), *Trade Unions and Democratic Participation in Europe: A Scenario for the 21st Century,* Aldershot: Ashgate Publishing Ltd.

Kester, G., (1996)
"Guiding Principles for a Strategy for Democratic Participation" in Kester and Pinaud (eds.), *Trade Unions and Democratic Participation in Europe.* A Scenario for the 21st Century, Aldershot: Ashgate Publishing Ltd.

Levine, D. I and L. D. Tyson., (1990)
"Participation, Productivity and the Firm's Environment," in A. S. Blinder., (ed.), *Paying for Productivity,* Washington D.C.

Lusinde, J (1976)
"Workers' Participation in Industrial Management in Tanzania," in Mapolu, H (ed), *Workers and Management.* Dar es Salaam: Tanzania Publishing House.

Mabele, R. B., (1995)
"Transport and Agricultural Development Under Structural Adjustment in Tanzania: Successes, Failures and Future Perspectives," in L. A. Msambichaka, A. A. Kilindo and G. D. Mjema (eds.), *Beyond Structural Adjustment Programmes in Tanzania,* Dar es Salaam: Economic Research Bureau.

Mapolu, H (1976)
"Workers' Participation in Tanzania," in Mapolu, H (ed.), *Workers and Management,* Dar es Salaam: Tanzania Publishing House.

Mapolu, H (1976)
'The Organisation and Participation of Workers in Tanzania," in Mapolu, H (ed.), *Workers and Management,* Dar es Salaam, Tanzania Publishing House.

Maseko, I. J (1976)
"Workers' Participation at TANESCO and Friendship Textile Mill", in H. Mapolu (ed.), Workers and Management, Dar es Salaam: Tanzania Publishing House.

McConnell, C.R and Brue, S.L (1998)
Contemporary Labour Economics, New York: McGraw-Hill Book Company.

Mjema, G.D (1999)
"Gender and Employment in Tanzania: Some Reflections From the Formal and Informal Sectors," *Tanzania Journal of Population Studies and Development,* Vol. 6 Nos. 1&2 (79-90).

Mihyo, P (et al) (1986)
"The National Bank of Commerce and Urafiki (Friendship) Textile Mill Limited" in ICPE, *Workers' Self-Management and Participation in Practice,* Vol. 1, Ljubljana Yugoslavia: ICPE.

Mihyo, P., Masanja, P and I.K. Bavu (1981)
"Workers' Self-Management and Participation in Decision-making as a Factor of Social Change and Economic Progress in Developing Countries" in Avendano, J., Ghezali, M., Grozdanic, S. and K.C. Sethi (eds.): *Workers' Self-Management and Participation, National Reports,* Vol II: Algeria, Guyana, India, Tanzania, Ljubljana Yugoslavia: ICPE (290?291). (265-304).

Mihyo, P.B (1983)
Industrial Conflict and Change in Tanzania, Dar es Salaam: Tanzania Publishing House.
Mlimuka, A. K. L. J and Kabudi, P. J. A. M (1985)
"The State and the Party", in I. G. Shivji (ed.), *The State and the Working People in Tanzania*, Darker: Codesria.
Musa, E.A (1992)
"Workers' Participation Hijacked? The Case of a Tanzanian Public Enterprise," IDS, University of Dar es Salaam.
Musa, E.A (1997)
"Sudan: What Future?" In Kester, G., and O.O. Sidibé (eds.), *Trade Unions and Sustainable Democracy*, Aldershot: Ashgate Publishing Limited (273-285.
Musa, EA (et al) (1994)
"Workers' Participation Under Structural Adjustment: For Whose Interest? The Case of a Tanzanian Private Enterprise," The Hague: APADEP, Institute of Social Studies.
O.A.U., (1990)
"The African Charter for Popular Participation in Development and Transformation" International Conference on Popular Participation in the Recovery and Development Process in Africa, Arusha - Tanzania, 12-16 February 1990.
OTTU (1994)
"Taarifa ya Mgomo wa Tarehe 1-3 Machi 1994," Dar es Salaam.
OTTU (1995)
"Taarifa ya Shuhuli za OTTU 1991-1995," (mimeo), Dar es Salaam.
Palloix, C (1976)
"The Labour Process: From Fordism to neo-Fordism", in *Conference of Labour Economics* (CSE), The Labour Process and Class Strategies, London: CSE.
Pelikan, J. (1973)
"Workers' Councils in Czechoslovakia," *Critique*, Vol. 1, No. 1.
Pinaud, H., (1996)
"The Role of Social Actors During Recent Developments in Worker Participation in Ten Countries of Western Europe", in G. Kester and H. Pinaud (eds.), *Trade Unions and Democratic Participation in Europe: A Scenario for the 21st Century*, Aldershot: Ashgate Publishing Ltd.
Poole, M (1986)
Towards a New Industrial Democracy: Workers Participation in Industry, London & New York: Routledge and Kegan Paul.
Pratt, C (1976)
The Critical Phase in Tanzania 1945 - 1968: Nyerere and the Emergence of a Socialist Strategy, London: Cambridge University Press.
Reardon, G (1997)
Participation in Practice: A Study Circle Handbook for Use by Workers' Representatives, The Hague: APADEP Publication.
Rutinwa, B (1995)
"Legal Regulation of Industrial Relations in Tanzania: Past Experience and Future Prospects," Labour Law Unit - University of Cape Town: Southern Africa Labour Monographs, 1/95.
Schophorst, F (1997a)
"Apex Case Study, Harare and Gweru," APADEP Case Study Report, ISS - The Hague (January 1997).

Schophorst, F (1997b)
"Dunlop Case Study: Bulawayo," APADEP Case Study Report, ISS - The Hague (February 1997).

Semboja, J (1995)
"State Financing of Basic Social Services During the Structural Adjustment Period in Tanzania", in L. A. Msambichaka, A. A. Kilindo and G. D. Mjema (eds.), *Beyond Structural Adjustment Programmes in Tanzania*, Dar es Salaam: Economic Research Bureau.

Smith, S. A (1983)
Red Petrograd, Cambridge: Cambridge University Press.

Stephens, E.H. (1980)
The Politics of Workers' Participation, New York: Academic Press.

Tandau, A (1965)
Historia ya Kuundwa Kwa TFL 1955 - 1962 na Kuanzishwa kwa NUTA 1964, Dar es Salaam: Mwananchi Publishing Company.

URT (2000a)
Poverty Reduction Strategy Paper (PRSP), Dar es Salaam: Government Printer.

URT (2000)
"Tanzania Assistance Strategy (TAS): A Medium Term Framework for Promoting Local Ownership and Development Partnerships," Dar es Salaam.

URT (1991)
"Tanzania: The Informal Sector Survey," Dar es Salaam: Planning Commission and the Ministry of Labour and Youth Development.

URT (1998)
"The Trade Union Act No.10"

URT (1993)
"The Labour Force Survey, 1990/91," Dar es Salaam: Bureau of Statistics (Planning Commission) and Labour Department (Ministry of Labour and Youth Development).

URT (Various Years)
The Economic Survey, Dar es Salaam: The Government Printer.

World Bank (1990)
"Integrated Roads Project in Tanzania, Staff Appraisal Report (mimeo).